SOVIET NATIONALITY PROBLEMS

SOVIET
NATIONALITY
PROBLEMS

AUTHORS: *Edward Allworth, Alexandre Bennigsen,*
Zbigniew Brzezinski, John N. Hazard,
Hans Kohn, Václav Lamser, Robert A. Lewis,
Marc Raeff, and Paula G. Rubel

EDITOR: *Edward Allworth*

1971
COLUMBIA UNIVERSITY PRESS · NEW YORK & LONDON

Copyright © 1971 Columbia University Press
Library of Congress Catalog Card Number: 77–166211
ISBN: 0–231–03493–8
Printed in the United States of America

ABOUT THE AUTHORS

Edward Allworth is Professor of Turco-Soviet Studies and Director of the Program on Soviet Nationality Problems at Columbia University. He has traveled in four major nationality areas of the Soviet Union and has written, as have all the authors in this book, about Russia and the USSR. A selection of the extensive writings relating to the Soviet Union and its nationality problems by him and the other authors is included in the "Suggested Readings" at the end of this volume.

Alexandre Bennigsen is Director d'Études, École Pratique des Hautes Études, Paris. He lectured about nationality problems at Columbia University in Spring, 1970. His special field of research is devoted to the former Muslim people of Czarist Russia and the USSR, with particular attention given to the Volga Tatars. He has traveled and worked in Turkey and Afghanistan, sometimes among groups of emigrants from the Soviet East.

Zbigniew Brzezinski is Professor of Government and Director of the Research Institute on Communist Affairs, Columbia University. He has served as a member of the Policy Planning Council, U.S. Department of State, and has made a very important contribution toward focusing American attention upon the significance of Soviet nationality affairs. He has lectured extensively on the subject of Soviet and international politics and has traveled in the Soviet Union several times in recent years.

John N. Hazard is Professor of Public Law, Columbia University. His research has been concentrated upon Soviet political and legal institutions. He has made frequent trips to the Soviet Union and received the Certificate of the Moscow Juridical Institute in 1937 after three and one half years study in the USSR.

Hans Kohn, Professor of History Emeritus, City College of the City University of New York, died shortly after completion and final checking of his contribution to this volume. Throughout a long and distinguished career he wrote extensively, and was widely known for his work on nationalism and nationality problems in the Soviet Union and other areas. He spent substantial periods of time in the USSR during World War I and in 1931.

Václav Lamser was visiting Professor of Sociology at Columbia University, 1969–70, and presently is Professor of Sociology, University of Bielefeld, West Germany. He formerly was Chairman, Department of Sociology, Institute of Sociology, Prague, Czechoslovakia. During the 1960s he traveled and conducted research in the Soviet Union repeatedly, giving attention to urban and rural population problems.

Robert A. Lewis is Associate Professor of Geography, Columbia University. Russian and Soviet population, migrations, urbanization, and nationality problems comprise his special fields of interest. He has traveled to many of the nationality areas of the Soviet Union recently.

Marc Raeff is Professor of History, Columbia University. His principal research focuses upon the history of Russia before 1900. Touching the general area of nationality problems, he has written, in addition to the essay appearing here, upon earlier developments in Siberia.

Paula G. Rubel is Associate Professor of Anthropology, Barnard College. Concentrating upon social anthropology, she has completed research upon the Kalmyks, both those of the Soviet Union and the emigrant colonies of the West. She has visited Soviet Central Asia and Siberia and carried out research in Moscow and Leningrad.

PREFACE AND ACKNOWLEDGMENTS

Nationality problems among "socialist nations" are strictly a communist family matter, Soviet Communist Party Secretary Leonid Brezhnev said during the Czechoslovak affair (*Pravda,* September 26, 1968, p. 4). His interpretation of the Russian intervention in East Central Europe probably constitutes Brezhnev's principal theoretical contribution to Soviet theory about the nationality question to date. In addition to projecting Soviet nationality policy militarily into an independent neighboring state, Russian leadership has also persistently spread the notion farther afield that its own earlier solution to domestic nationality problems in the USSR (administrative division of the country according to the nationality principle) has proved superior to other formulas. Now Moscow pushes hard for the assimilation of all Soviet nationalities with the Russians, and for eventually erasing internal nationality boundary lines. The leaders at the same time promote the contrary idea abroad—especially in states with a mixture of nationalities in their population—of the need for separation or segregation into nationality units. (For example, see *Land Without Nationality Rights* [*Strana natsional'nogo bespraviia,* Moscow: Politizdat, 1966], about the United States.)

These factors seem to have urged Western observers to a much greater awareness of nationality problems concerning the Soviet Union and their importance to the rest of the world than had been the case before summer, 1968. Perhaps not entirely by coincidence, though unconsciously, the research Seminar on Soviet Nationality Problems originated in Columbia University at the beginning of the academic year 1968–1969. Its goals, realized to a rewarding degree within these first two years of activity, have been, first, to supply a multidisciplinary forum, open to the learned community in the greater metropolitan area of New York, devoted to the chosen subject. Equally significant, it was felt, has been the aim of drawing together both graduate students and faculty on a par, so far as formalities were concerned to discuss the presentations of specialists. Finally, the Seminar was meant to attract other persons with qualifications and interest in Soviet nationality problems to Columbia for exchange of ideas, periodically, within the widest range of social science and humanities disciplines and of problems discussed.

Seminar sessions exposed our ignorance as well as our interest in the field, and demonstrated the need for further work along these lines as well as the development of suitable studies, research aids, bibliographies, and the like for the advancement of research. For these reasons and others, this volume includes not only contributions regarding a series of problems but also deliberately adds a substantial bibliographical offering to serve scholars and other readers. The papers published here constitute only a selection of the total given before the Seminar. These ten were developed wholly or in part out of presentations and discussion sessions held by the research Seminar.

Treatment of the Soviet Union's many different nationalities as individual groups has been purposely avoided, except where they serve as examples for the authors in discussions about problems in history, politics, sociology, and other disciplines. For an up-to-date understanding of population trends in general, salient portions of the 1970 Soviet census, preliminary report, have been reproduced (see end sheets and appendix), and two separate essays devote particular attention to such developments and their import for the nationalities.

Aside from that offered in the historical sections, there is a lack of humanistic study, much needed with respect to Soviet nationality problems, in the present volume. It is hoped that this deficiency can be rectified in future efforts undertaken by the Seminar. A distinction has been maintained throughout the text between "the nationalities," on one hand, and the Russians, on the other. Use of this convention serves as helpful shorthand in writing and in many situations to clarify the realities of relations in the USSR. There is a possibility that retaining the distinction will continue to be a convenience in the future. Whether the Russians slip once more into minority status, numerically, in the USSR—which many have predicted will be shown in the future—and this will mean an alteration in the polarity between "the nationalities" and the Russians—remains to be seen.

It will be obvious to attentive readers that the scholars represented in this volume, some of whom assert no special claim to the nationality field, disagree upon a number of fundamental issues. The politically oriented may feel that economics holds the key to the future of the nationalities; an anthropologist regards politics as the determinant. There is a doubt that language will remain the hallmark of nationality in the USSR. Clearly, "problems" have been raised but not solved. Future research should go in the direction of true interdisciplinary (not multidisciplinary) effort, and that should help bring together divergent views and conflicting attitudes. Whether such a method will reconcile these contradictions, or should try to, cannot yet be predicted.

In one sense this book wrote itself. The need for serious consideration of the subject, widely felt, compelled the scholars involved to record their observations as a basis for further thought and discussion. Encouragement for putting the volume together came also from varied, specific origins. At Columbia University Professors Marshall D. Shulman and John S. Badeau, Directors of the Russian and Middle East Institutes respectively, repeatedly offered both moral and material support in this pursuit.

John Hanselman, graduate student in political science at Columbia University and a participant in the research Seminar on Soviet Nationality Problems, gave intelligent, energetic assistance to the research Seminar's activity, and especially helped in completing the bibliographic research basic to the concept of this volume as a building stone for further Soviet nationality studies in Columbia University and elsewhere. Richard Rowland, also a participant in the research Seminar and graduate student in geography at Columbia (now teaching at Rutgers University), executed the cartography for the six excellent maps, printed here, under the supervision of Professor Robert A. Lewis, and assisted in preparing statistics used in the essay concerning demography of the USSR. Aman B. Murat and Lauri Hanneman also materially advanced the Seminar's efforts during the 1968–1969 sessions.

The editor acknowledges gratefully the kindness of Professors Immanuel Wallerstein, Paula G. Rubel, Theodore C. Hines, and Dr. George Lowy and Dr. Ervand Abrahamian of Columbia or Barnard College in giving thought to the content of the book as well as theoretical and practical questions of bibliography for this particular enterprise. The transliteration system employed for titles of publications in Soviet languages comes from Edward Allworth, *Nationalities of the Soviet East. Publications and Writing Systems* (1971).

Map 1, appearing in the fourth essay, has been reproduced here, with considerable modification, by permission of the *Annals* of the Association of American Geographers, Vol. 59, 1969. Professor Lewis acknowledges, with gratitude, support for his research provided by the International Institute for the Study of Human Reproduction, Columbia University, and good counsel given by Abram J. Jaffe, Senior Research Associate, Bureau of Applied Social Research.

The research Seminar received important financial support from the U.S. Department of Health, Education and Welfare for carrying out the first two years of its scholarly activities. A considerable part of the program reflected in the substance and organization of this publication was performed pursuant to a contract with the Department of HEW, Office of Education, under the provision of Public Law 85-864, Title VI, Section 601, as amended by Public Law 88-665 and PL 89-698, and PL 85-864, Title VI, Section 602.

Thanks at last to Janet Allworth and Mildred O'Brien, who gamely persevered with the transcribing and typing to the eleventh hour and thus made the timely appearance of the book possible.

E.A.

New York
July 31, 1970

CONTENTS

MAPS, CHARTS, AND TABLES

Maps

Chart

Tables

SOVIET NATIONALITY PROBLEMS

Kilometers

0   500   1000

Boundaries

—·—·—·—	USSR	
————————	SSR	(1–15)
————————	ASSR	(16–35)
—·—·—·—	AO	(36–43)
··············	NO	(44–53)

1 Armeni
2 Azerbai
3 Belorus
4 Estonia
5 Georgia
6 Kazakh
7 Kirgiz
8 Latvian
9 Lithuan
10 Moldav

11 Russian SFSR	21 Chuvash	31 Severo-Ossetin	41 Nagorno-Karabakh	51 Taimyr
12 Tajik	22 Dagestan	32 Tatar	42 Evrei	52 Ust Orda
13 Turkmen	23 Kabardin-Balkar	33 Tuvin	43 Iugo-Ossetin	53 Yamalo-Nenets
14 Ukrainian	24 Kalmyk	34 Udmurt	44 Aga Buryat	
15 Uzbek	25 Karakalpak	35 Yakut	45 Chukchi	
16 Abkhaz	26 Karelian	36 Adyge	46 Evenki	
17 Adzhar	27 Komi	37 Gorno-Altay	47 Khanty-Mansi	
18 Bashkir	28 Mari	38 Gorno-Badakhshan	48 Komi-Permyak	
19 Buryat	29 Mordvin	39 Karachay-Cherkess	49 Koryak	
20 Chechen-Ingush	30 Nakhichevan	40 Khakass	50 Nenets	

EDWARD ALLWORTH

RESTATING THE SOVIET NATIONALITY QUESTION

Altering the routine followed by most westerners studying the Kremlin during the two previous decades, the American nationality-watcher today commonly scrutinizes words and deeds of leaders in republic capitals Union-wide. He observes more closely than before the stance Moscow takes toward areas like Lithuania, Armenia, or Uzbekistan, individually and collectively. This attentive vigil for nationality signals proceeds, ordinarily, according to a Soviet chronology. It is synchronized carefully with the issuance of the latest Party congress resolution or anniversary speech but is still attuned to the policy statements originating from the center.

To find out what "they" are up to and what can be learned from, more than about, the nationality phenomenon is the usual purpose of that American research. Its products largely comprise the preliminaries for the move of our scholarship concerning this field into the 1970s.

My brief inquiry here will take a different course. Now seems an appropriate time to find out what "we" are doing; to turn about and watch the watchers in order to learn what adherence to the Soviet schedule and initiative is doing to us; and to reconsider our understanding of some homonymic terms common to East and West in the controversy over nationality development (*natsional'noe stroitel'stvo*) in the USSR. Above all, we must consider other ways of looking at the Soviet nationality question, ones which may provide an alternative to our long preoccupation with Party calendars, enumeration, and prepared political statements.

A central argument raised by the pursuit of those new aims
concerns the efficacy of assigning a subjective value to the term
"problems," or of choosing between a negative or a positive approach in our academic study of the Soviet nationality question.
Consideration of the research and writing carried out in the past
upon the subject will show just how important this decision may
be for both substance and methodology. And even before suggesting what sort of question the nationality question is, or what
meaning should be attached to the term "Soviet nationality question," it will be useful to consider the significance given to that
expression by either Western or Eastern authors.

An American awareness of the subject began to grow generally in the early 1940s. Considering the progress made in the
field since then, it is startling to admit that our innocence about
the nationality question of the USSR lingered beyond World
War II. To the United States, starting after the 1930s, the War
had finally brought an inkling that the Soviet Union was composed of dynamic, varied nationality groups. Before that a few
lonely missionaries like Walter Batsell, Samuel Harper, Hans
Kohn and Avrahm Yarmolinsky had spread the word about that
nationality question. In addition, Marxists and partisans of the
USSR in this country also made the subject more familiar by
disseminating publications and giving lectures about their view
of the question. Certainly the wartime alliance with "Russia"
and establishment of the United Nations headquarters in New
York stimulated wonder over the lists of different Soviet people,
their numbers and noticeable characteristics. Interpretive study
of the basic nationality question, though seldom published in
America at that time, reflected strong ideological disagreements,[1]
but it explicitly defined "the question" not at all.

Today hardly any doubt remains that during and after that
War emigrants from the USSR—activists, journalists, publishers,
and scholars—laid the groundwork for the expansion of the
Soviet nationality study in the United States which soon became
so evident. Without their dedication to the subject and tireless
persistence in explaining the basis for the nationality dilemma
of the USSR, the American scholarly community might have

delayed much longer in reaching even its present imperfect competence in an intricate set of problems.

It cannot have been fortuitous that the growth in American interest regarding the subject coincided to a considerable extent with a time when the Soviet situation finally developed free of Stalin's direct control. When the advance came it was fueled also by the depth of feeling brought to classrooms and publications by the informed teacher and writer of Soviet nationality extraction and by the rising "know your enemy" psychology invading the campuses as well as the public consciousness as a product of the cold war. Though some sensed the nationality question as a weak spot in the Soviet fabric, few, if any, authoritative American scholars would then have called the nationality question the most critical or neglected area of Soviet studies in American educational institutions. Not everything favored the development of this field. Our Russian specialists, in whatever disciplines, were then often impatient, as they are today, with this new concern for non-Russians in the USSR. The government of the United States remained virtually blind to the existence of race or nationality, anywhere. These factors may have deterred prompt development of studies in this area. Nevertheless, scholarly interest regarding both Soviet policy in connection with the non-Russian people and the situation of populous groups like the Ukrainians and the Turkic nationalities, for example, enlarged and flourished. All in all, this curiosity exhibited a defensive coloring.

A sudden upsurge of serious interest in the nationality field appeared among advanced graduate students around the United States and Canada in the 1950s. Was there a paradox in this rise in American scholars' more general recognition of the Soviet nationality question at a time when that broad subject seemed to have declined greatly in prominence inside the USSR, compared with the peaks reached there in the 1920s and 1930s? If so, the American academic lag was occasioned by the slow increase in awareness described just now and the shortage of instructors prepared to supervise this sphere of Soviet studies.

Despite the handicaps, the development continued, and several

indicators verify the timing of this growth in academic commitment to the field. New dissertations were the harbingers. They,
plus periodic bibliographies registering scholarship about the
USSR completed in this country and general listings of works
published in the humanities and social sciences, in addition to
Soviet critiques, have told the story.[2] Under the classification
"Soviet Nationality Policy and Nationalism" some fourteen
American, Canadian, and British Ph.D dissertations were completed in the 1950s, and numbers of others from the same period
closely related to the question could be added to that list. In the
next four years only two or three resembled those of the fifties,
and between 1965 and 1969 the annual output averaged around
three, though the graduate student population in the field apparently had not greatly enlarged. The students of the 1950s
concerned themselves mainly with policy, or the experience of a
particular nationality on its way to Soviet republic status, to the
exclusion of most other problems making up the complex subject.

American progress in this research work has received recognition of another sort in Soviet reviews and publications. The recent acceleration of our activity in certain sectors of the nationality field has been received uneasily by a few Soviet critics.
Their lists of Western publications on this subject remind us, as
no previous compilation of our own, how fertile this scholarly
ground has recently become.[3]

When Western authors produced articles and books between
the 1920s and 1950s respecting the Soviet nationality question,
they first concentrated largely upon its operative side. As they
saw "the question," it posed a danger to the Czarist empire and
Soviet Russia from the fragmentation brought about through a
process of rampant secession likely to be set off by exercise of
self-determination among the non-Russians. Thus regarded, the
question was clearly a political matter. It was necessarily linked,
too, with other factors, having no separate, constant life of its
own but changing with the political weather.

For those partial to the official Soviet view regarding nationality problems, "the question" had been resolved by the time
World War II was over. Dissenters from this position called the

question a differentiation between nationalities, even an amalgam of distinctions, which still had to be contended with. Or, a few decided that the tensions between nationalities seemingly made up the question. A basis for these anxieties, thought writers in the early 1950s, lay in the persistent national sentiments or feelings of the nationalities.

Many formulations indicated that "the question" consisted of active Russian ethnocentrism in its drive to sweep away smaller identities and implant Russia's image everywhere in the USSR. Others held the principle of nationality itself to be the culprit. But an occasional voice was heard to wonder if "the question," once political, had not already become de-politicized. Most writings agreed in regarding the question as an obstacle to the achievement of total control by the Russians.

Following the lead of the Soviet dialecticians themselves, perhaps, the nationality-watchers of the West by the late 1950s were generally seeing "the question" merely as an increment in larger issues confronting the Soviet Union. This made the question something more acted upon than acting. At different times the status of nationalities became an equivalent for the question itself. Since the XXII Congress of the CPSU (Communist Party of the Soviet Union) in 1961 once again placed strong emphasis upon the nationality question, there has been a tendency among us to feel that resolving the question has become a matter of attaining a uniform level of development among the many nationalities of the USSR. From 1964, around Khrushchev's ouster from political preeminence, we have concentrated upon a doctrinaire presentation describing "the question" as a dialectic between accelerated assimilation and prolonged separate existence of nationalities. Political writers seemed to regard nationality relations as the crux of the matter, the gauge of such relations being simply the rapidity of the unification process, whether via assimilation or drawing together.

Although the knowledge of American scholars regarding the Soviet Union constantly grew, as late as 1967–1968 the nationality question continued to be characterized as a matter of harmony or frustration between nationality groups, with the Rus-

sians often counted as one such group. An urge to national self-
assertion was also somehow considered to be innately democratic,
and losing or retaining ethnic identity was pointed out as the
embodiment of the nationality question. The question was in at
least one instance turned back into a concept of diversity and
away from preoccupations with the Union's potential homogeneity. This time there were said to be many questions tied individually and selectively to the different people ranged throughout
the numerous nationality areas of the USSR. Elsewhere, the fact
that certain people exercised a choice to remain among their
own tribal or nationality group, rather than to mix with others,
was felt to evidence, in an old way, the seed of the basic question.
The comfort of "minorities" with their status, or of the central
authorities with the status of the minorities, some think, constitutes the question. By extension, the question represents in itself
the self-interest of the different nationalities in preserving or re-
linquishing their special identities, as balanced with the desire of
the authorities to persuade them to abdicate the social or political
content of those identities in the interest of the centralized government and state.[4]

The burden of these many commentaries and interpretations
may be summarized as follows: (1) The Soviet nationality question is a matter of sustaining or dismantling the state structure;
(2) "The question" consists of inter-group relations; (3) It tran-
scends individual nationality group interests or internal developments; (4) It is embodied in the waxing or waning of separate
group identity and feelings about identity. Although such writings deal predominantly with nationality policy, none of our
résumé has deviated intentionally from the broader nationality
question in general to the subordinate problem of nationality
policy as such, or to the settling of the question or solving of
nationality problems. We are mainly concerned here with the
way American and Western scholars generally see "the question,"
but even more with an understanding of the basis for redefining
it and thus drawing attention to the need for a fresh approach to
the matter through academic research or informed reading. Before these inquiries can be properly completed, therefore, we

must also comprehend the Russian perception of this same, if it is the same, nationality question (*natsional'nyi vopros*).

In early Soviet days, when the nationality policy of the USSR had not yet become the monopoly of one man, opinions about this policy diverged or collided. Leon Trotskii at one point seemed to brush off the idea of divisions into nationality as a non-question. G. I. Broido described "the question" in essence as the solving of problems relating particularly and exclusively to Party and multinationality in state development. Stalin, long before he became dictator or the top leader of the Party, treated the question in a way hardly clear to most: From an early assertion that the mobilization of the sentiments of nationalities, individually, along with what he called their natural right to decide their destiny, constituted the question, he moved, in about a decade to formulating the question in terms of oppression, even backwardness, of the nationalities under certain conditions, internal or external to a particular state. With slight variations, this presentation survived Stalin himself. It was reiterated later on as an equation between, on one side, oppression or inequality and, on the other, "the question," and was subordinated to the class struggle while being linked inseparably with what was called the more general question of the dictatorship of the proletariat. The Stalinist version persisted at least until his desacralization in 1956.

Not astonishingly, the most outspoken remark uttered by a recent Soviet leader about his domestic nationality question came from Nikita Khrushchev. He delivered it at the XXII Congress of the CPSU. The question had been, he said, a matter of the interrelations between nationalities, and, though the Party had already settled this most complex of questions for the USSR, the subject had agitated mankind for ages and continued to plague the capitalist countries. Though Khrushchev relegated "the question" in the USSR to the past, his meaning was clear, and relevant enough to the present. Leonid Brezhnev subsequently echoed this interpretation.

Striking, among the many recent commentaries intended to show that the nationality question has been settled in the USSR,

is a theme which characterizes the question as a matter of freedom (*svoboda*). The exercise of this freedom is said to produce
free nations through Soviet-style self-determination and voluntary unification of nationalities. "In multinational Russia the
nationality question—one of the most critical *social* [ital. added]
problems—was settled. Under Soviet government conditions all
nations (*natsii*), nationalities (*natsional'nosti*), and subnationalities (*narodnosti*) found genuine freedom (*svoboda*)." So
wrote authors of a work from the publishing house for "Juridical
Writings" in 1968.[5]

Among the multitude of others who had much to say about
nationality policy and other problems, few added much to our
understanding of "the question" itself, though they have sometimes clarified current attitudes toward it. Proof that active interest continues to flourish among the informed Soviet circle in
all phases of nationality problems can be found very easily in
the bibliography of Soviet writings about them for 1967–1969
located at the end of this volume. A Soviet statistical report has
claimed also that for the decade before 1967 more than three
hundred books, pamphlets, and articles pertaining to but one
problem, nationality formation, came out in the USSR.[6]

In 1970 there could be no doubt that Soviet leaders still regarded the nationality question with gravity. Just as the themes
officially proclaimed for the 50th anniversary of the CPSU in
1967 manifest this, so theses later advanced by the Party in honor
of Lenin's Centenary, observed in April, 1970, make that clear.
Within each of the four major sections of the Centenary declaration, "the question" emphatically arises. Thus, at the start of the
new decade, whether the governing group speaks in retrospect
of Lenin the founder of the new proletarian political party, or of
the present and future route to Communism, they cannot ignore
"the question." Furthermore, though several American scholars
cited above have called harmony and equality the essence of that
question, on the occasion of Lenin's 100th birthday celebration
Soviet ideologists repeated that settling the nationality question
constitutes the prerequisite for achievement of social equality
and unity within the Soviet population. In this Russian view, our

question acquires the aspect of an unruly, but apparently tamable, force, one which perhaps exists in the realm of attitudes or passions rather than cool calculation or political arrangements.

That interpretation is given some credence by the persistence with which the current Soviet press describes the question as "age-old," and as a question settled through measures which can only serve to outline their target (the nationality question) for us as stubborn individualism. For it seems that every effort taken to settle this question, according to Soviet writers, has aimed toward *bringing together* political-administrative units, toward *unifying* economic and political organizations, making ideas and cultural life *uniform,* adopting a *unified* ideology. Finally, the nationality question is delineated in the Centenary theses by a concluding emphasis upon the necessity to eradicate "by consistent struggle" (surely evidence of *consistent,* balky individualism) every expression of uniqueness, called variously national egotism, nationalism, exclusiveness, isolation, narrow-mindedness, chauvinism, superiority, *mestnichestvo,* and the like.[7]

Indications that an ageless question continues to exist do not, of course, define it precisely or directly, yet the constellation of official attitudes reveals a profile silhouetted as plainly as if it had been traced out in black and white: the villain is group (nationality) self-interest, or more basically, nationality survival, certainly an elemental drive in a viable society, culture, or body politic.

The great amount of attention focused upon the Soviet nationality question by political writers on both sides of the world has not failed, as we have noticed, to reveal fundamental dissimilarities in their interpretation of particular topics. Such basic disagreement could logically be anticipated, but it may seem less obvious that the differences of opinion lie mainly in opposing views of consequences stemming from the question or of the influence exerted by it upon political decisions within the USSR. In fact, fair accord seems to exist between those who have spoken out, on the two sides of the world, upon the idea that "the question" is a matter of reconciling Moscow's centralism with active and passive nationality desires for separatism among the non-

Russians. About the question itself, throughout Western and Soviet discussions, runs a common refrain: In both East and West, among most nationality-watchers, the question is heard as a tone of discord, its major effect as negative. Probably one reason is because political writers normally listen for order, regularity and pattern rather than improvisation—Beethoven, not Dizzy Gillespie or Bob Dylan.

That may explain why, in a basically political framework, the troublesome "question" so frequently becomes transformed into "problem," with its not always unspoken attributes "difficult," "serious," or "dangerous." Khrushchev himself formulated the nationality question exactly in that manner during the 1961 CPSU Congress. No wonder authors sharing this attitude toward "problems" generally tend to think of nationality, *per se*, as a destructive force, rather than a creative one. The impact of such views goes beyond semantics to the very cognition of the question and the choice of scholarly treatment accorded it.

As a result, to see that "problem" and "question" are regarded as something other than synonyms for hindrance or obstacle will probably be the hardest thing to accomplish in reordering attitudes toward the Soviet nationality question. From the outset such "difficulty" invests nationality problems with negative value. Because political writing about this subject has led the scholarly field so far, it is especially important now to re-examine the political approach. The usual version of "the question" has been stated in terms of an adversary relationship which invariably pits the Muscovites against all others—nationalities vs. Russians, Russian influence upon . . . ; periphery vs. center; ruler against ruled; and so forth.

The lack of substantial conceptual or theoretical progress needed for studying Soviet nationality problems effectively as a whole in America or the USSR may even be in part caused by the prevalent (negative) view toward such problems. If this is not the case, there can be a strong presumption that a purely political approach to "the question" may never bring us closer to the understanding we seek. Our experience to date in this field of investigation obviously suggests that either the nationality question of the USSR is not fundamentally a political matter, or is not of a traditional political kind susceptible to traditional analyses, though it sometimes patently carries important political implications (see Zbigniew Brzezinski, this volume).

Thus, we say the Soviet nationality question is not entirely or necessarily political, it may not always entail a relationship between nationalities and the Russians, and the question need not be approached through one particular scholarly discipline. The old dichotomy—Russia vs. non-Russia—governing our view of this question for so long probably is over simple in the 1970s, and should be replaced or at least augmented by concentration upon oppositions between nationalities or regions, relationships often more telling in connection with the Transcaucasus and Central Asia, for example, than those habitually examined. Nationality groups vary, as humans vary. "The question" has in part to do with these variations as well as with similarities. One reason that the Stalinist model of nationality departs so greatly from the reality presented by many Soviet nationalities today is that this old Marxist theory cannot accommodate adequately to diversity. Like the outdated Soviet theory of nationality, our essentially political view of the nationality question cannot adjust to the needs of the present scholarship. The fact that this subject is germane to a number of other disciplines can be conceded. That we require new approaches to the question is the suggestion now to be offered.

Three important qualities missing from much of our present work about the question might usefully be brought to it in the future. One has to do with the mood surrounding and insinuating itself into perception of the Soviet nationality question; the second with the disciplinary dimension or scale of the scholarly method employed in the approach to it; while the last relates to modernity or the lack of it in our conception of the research problem. The question, to begin with, requires at some stage affirmatively neutral treatment. With suitable objective skepticism, it needs to be viewed at least at the outset as an opportunity, a matter composed perhaps of positive as well as negative value, even a possible virtue under certain circumstances or a potential force for goodness. Some students of the subject may complain that nothing can be found in its pattern to occasion optimism in the scholar. The rebuttal to that follows: there are many potential and actual pluses as well as minuses which may be sought, but that is only part of the response. In truth, nationality as a human group's expression can be a productive, creative force, not merely a disruption of law and order (centralized control). Despair or revulsion aroused through observation of outrageous political or social abuse of those vital (nationality) forces may understandably drive some authors to articulate this unhappiness on paper, but the result will probably not constitute a detached presentation of research so much as an editorial commitment.

There is a value in subordinating our perhaps too quantified representation of this fascinating question to a greater concern with genuine human factors, if the approach is to realize its greatest potential. Giving attention to expressions of behavior, identity, and attitude, not always on a mass scale, will deepen and humanize the question and will move the scholar much farther toward discovering the residence of nationality itself (not as a romantic abstraction, but as living energy). To find out what actually originates, raises, and sustains "the question" in the Soviet context will bring an intellectual breakthrough worth the price of the effort.

For this purpose, the nationality question requires either rephrasing, in terms common to the various academic disciplines, or no less than drastic reinterpretation without obligatory concern for previously held convictions. Our definition has been delayed until this stage in the discussion because in one sense it is the goal of this effort. It was held in abeyance also in order to permit the others cited above to speak their minds first and, learning from them, to arrive at a formulation more nearly suitable for the aims of the present debate and the proposals immediately to be advanced. Defining this question in a manner which will clarify its scope and therefore its accessibility to scholars from various disciplines will similarly open the way for freer, wider recognition of problems which call for research and whose investigation, it is to be hoped, will lead to fuller comprehension of the broad question at hand. The Soviet nationality question may be usefully seen, then, as a composite of the many general problems necessarily connected with nationality (the strongly felt, express desire of members for identity with their larger community or ethnic unit) in the USSR. Such problems may be raised by tradition, political inequality, particular genres of artistic expression, governmental policy, peculiar social organization, and the like. Though certain problems may arise for the first time, disappear, reappear, or change, the question as such—the disposition (arrangement) and satisfaction of ethnic nationalities culturally, socially, artistically, economically, and politically within the USSR—remains the same. In visual analogy, the question resembles the outer circle of the droshky wheel. The spokes reaching from the perimeter to the hub represent the problems, and the central axle around which everything turns is vital nationality itself. The necessarily neutral nationality question, put in an interrogative form for methodical examination, may ask: What role does (non-Russian) nationality play in the USSR (with such tributary queries as: What factors determine that role and the extent of it, and how, as well as with what effect, does nationality play its part)?

We should distinguish other kinds of subjects from the general "problems" attached to nationality. Whereas the Soviet nationality problems, collectively, describe the circumference or scope of the nationality question, never separate from the hub and axle of pure nationality, narrower individual subjects may be as detailed as local, particular issues can become. This use of the term "problem" denotes a topic of the sort normally spoken of in problem-oriented research where "topic" interchanges freely with "problem"; in other words, "problem" in an entirely neutral, constructive sense. Such might be some particular problem of language related to Kurds or to Russians, if either were treated as Soviet nationalities, for example, in a study. The more general problems are those which are common to several nationalities or have implications for them and support the axle through sustained contact at various points with the outer rim, that unbroken nationality question, the chief bearing surface upon reality (the ground—Russian-dominated, communist, multinationality Soviet territory).

Bringing a consideration of the basic nationality question back from exclusive concern with certain policy matters toward the center of the whole discussion will widen such study generally and augment the genres of political writing. An indispensable part of this broadening, for American scholarship at least, will involve the closer collaboration of several academic disciplines. Beginnings have already been made in this direction by a few social or political thinkers, not always specifically with reference to Soviet nationality problems but nevertheless with implications for them.[8] Isolated writings which have appeared outside the USSR in history and literature about particular nationalities help provide a basis for further work in most disciplines. Anthropology, linguistics (and language), literature, geography, history, and sociology at a minimum need to be drawn upon further in a drive for rounded understanding. The contributions of political science, because they nearly singlehandedly sustained and continue to predominate by far in the published research, may serve as a cornerstone for this wider attack upon the field of nationality problems.

Merely mixing the disciplines in this fashion may well improve our understanding of the Soviet situation. It seems likely that the new effort will need to go several steps beyond this formal reorganization if it is to elicit broadly significant insights concerning the nationality question. A hybrid scholar, possessed of extraordinary side vision, perhaps aptly described as a politicosociologist or a sociohumanist, for instance, will be required. In order to move past "nationality-watching" of the sort modeled after conventional Kremlinology, the new approach, freed from the constraints of the past, will be informed by a theoretical framework.

Significantly, since around the mid-1960s some Soviet scholars have been engaged in a similar reappraisal of the rationale behind their attack upon nationality problems. After long consideration of the Soviet approach in such scholarship, some have said that an empirical, rather than further theoretical discussion about such problems was now indicated. A nationality's distinctive language, we know, has been considered by Soviet Marxists the ineffaceable mark of the group's identity. Exactly in the analysis of language problems have these Soviet innovations been proposed. An interdisciplinary effort moved to bring philosophers, sociologists, and others together with linguists for joint research into nationality problems. What looked like the beginnings of such area studies had been made with establishment of a Union-wide commission for interdisciplinary (*kompleksnyi*) problems and research. It started work upon the elastic theme "Socialist Nations (*Natsii*) on the Road to Communism." Historians, economists, professors of law, linguists, literary scholars, and philosophers came together to organize the undertaking. In 1966 a Commission on Problems of Nationality Relations was created under the Section for Social Sciences, Presidium of the Academy of Sciences, USSR. Its task consisted of coordinating study into nationality problems in the USSR. In addition, Union-wide conferences concerning the history of the various nationalities and matters of "socialist internationalism" took place in 1968. Subsequently, because "the understanding of general laws of development of nations (*natsii*) demands a thoroughly rounded analysis . . . [in connection with] countries having differing social-political systems," a new Scientific Council on Nationality Problems (*Nauchnyi Sovet po Natsional'nym Problemam*) came into being in June, 1969. Its function is to unify work relating to nationality relations in the USSR as well as research upon nationality problems in foreign countries. Leaders of the new Council, feeling that effective study of these problems could be carried on only via the interdisciplinary route, brought together scholars from a variety of disciplines in the social sciences and humanities. If continued along these lines, such efforts could produce informative interpretations and findings for American as well as Soviet specialists and other readers.[9]

For Americans, a formidable bar to changing our approach is raised by the fact that we know relatively little about the Soviet nationalities or their general problems, particularly those matters which make up contemporary social, cultural, and political

life. Not only do we need to find new ways of approaching the
question, therefore, but new evidence and materials with which
to do it. This search is not hopeless. Aside from field research in
the area, presently out of our reach for the most part, there is a
huge reservoir of virtually untapped materials for academic
scrutiny available and waiting in the local-language press and
book publishing of the USSR. Greater exploitation of this source
might not only lead us beyond sterile rehearsals of old data often
designed for export, but could also open up a multitude of important possibilities for productive new research. Critics of this
suggestion will say that such local books and articles could not
possibly render a view of the nationality scene different from the
one we obtain via Moscow. That contention is uncertain on two
grounds. If we hardly know what the nationalities are saying in
what they print, we cannot yet pronounce certain judgment upon
the local press one way or other. Sampling of local writings suggests a great potential, however. Moreover, among vital nationality groups the local view of the nationality question is precisely
the one which counts, if the researcher wishes to ascertain what
it is that feeds and saves nationality in face of pressure of the
sort applied upon it in the USSR. Second, a number of the nationalities have long stood at a high level of sophistication in modern
Western as well as Eastern terms. Their future is as much at
stake as is the fate of the Union itself, because of them. If there
were no nationality problems today in the USSR, of course "we"
and "they" would not be writing so many articles, chapters, and
monographs about these subjects.

One of the shortcomings in our academic organization with
respect to Soviet nationality problems is that we have lacked a
hemispheric forum for bringing together and confronting our
ideas and queries, although the newly established (1970) Committee for the Study of Nationalities of the USSR and Eastern
Europe may supply the organization necessary for that purpose.
A genuinely appropriate journal for airing these problems broadly
is not being published in the West. An accessible center or series
of conferences with sufficient continuity and designed to accomplish the same purpose cannot yet be discovered. It is no mystery

that we often tend to write repetitively about the same things in isolation from each other, making too little progress beyond recording the change of faces or passage of events. Yet, we see that a hundred problems need serious, competitive examination. What is the inequality that Soviet and American political writers point to as the crux of the nationality question? Does equality mean homogeneity or conformity? Is there a necessary connection between economic equality and the nationality question? Does achievement of "equality" settle anything basic to that question? Is one single language essential to a nationality?

Inquiring into these and many other problems necessitates a thorough understanding of general Soviet developments, of course. Against that background, a fresh, objective approach via interdisciplinary methods can be built. The framework within which the problems selected will be examined will need redefinition, also. Clusters of nationalities, mixtures of nationalities, intersection of problems, migrations of themes, coincidence and juxtaposition of situations, vertical and horizontal mobility, regional concentration, geographical distributions, areal patterns, not of numbers alone but of variables meaningful to several disciplines—out of these reformulations may come the opportunity to solve problems which can give vitality to our work in the new decade. Acceleration in the emergence of Soviet nationality problems, as well as our keener perception of them, has surely paved the way for a remarkable advance in the period ahead. Given an imaginative response to these stimulating possibilities, nothing would be less surprising in Soviet studies in this country than to see this next ten years become the decade of the nationality question.

NOTES

1. Erich Hula, "National Self-Determination Reconsidered," *Social Research* Vol. X (Feb. 1943), pp. 1–22; Erich Hula, "The Nationalities Policy of the Soviet Union. Theory and Practice," *Social Research* Vol. XI, No. 2 (May 1944), pp. 168–201; Bernhard J.

Stern, "Soviet Policy on National Minorities," *American Sociological Review* (June 1944), pp. 229–35; Oscar I. Janowsky, *Nationalities and National Minorities (With Special Reference to East-Central Europe)* (New York: The Macmillan Company, 1945); Corliss Lamont, *The Peoples of the Soviet Union* (New York: Harcourt, Brace and Co., 1946).

2. Jesse J. Dossick, *Doctoral Research on Russia and the Soviet Union* (New York: New York University Press, 1960), and supplements to this book issued annually in *Slavic Review,* the December issue, beginning in 1964 and covering the years since 1960; *The American Bibliography of Slavic and East European Studies* (Bloomington: Indiana University Publications, 1957–1968) covering the years 1956–1965; *Social Sciences and Humanities Index* (New York: The H. W. Wilson Co., 1965–1969, first issued in 1916 as *Readers' Guide to Periodical Literature,* etc.); *International Bibliography of the Social Sciences* (Paris: UNESCO; Chicago: Aldine Publishing Co., 1952–   ), see under separate headings: *International Bibliography of (Sociology . . . Political Science . . . Economics . . . Social and Cultural Anthropology)*.

3. Examples are the books by R. A. Tuzmukhamedov, *Otvet klevetnikam. Samoopredelenie narodov Srednei Azii i mezhdunarodnoe pravo* (Moscow: Izdatel'stvo "Mezhdunarodnye Otnosheniia," 1969); E. A. Bagramov, *Natsional'nyi vopros i burzhuaznaia ideologiia. (Kritika noveishikh politiko-sotsiologicheskikh kontseptsii)* (Moscow: Izdatel'stvo "Mysl'," 1966).

4. Many scholars in addition to those cited here have contributed writings to this field, but the articles selected here and in note 1, above, seem to represent the train of thought about the Soviet nationality question, in general, over the span of years covered (listed in chronological order): I. Kurganov, "The Problem of Nationalities in the Soviet Union," *The Russian Review* (Oct. 1951), pp. 253–67; Julian Towster, "Soviet Policy on Nationalities," *The Antioch Review* Vol. XI (Dec. 1951), pp. 437–48; Frederick C. Barghoorn, "Nationality Doctrine in Soviet Political Strategy," *Review of Politics* Vol. XVI, No. 3 (July 1954), pp. 283–304; Hugh Seton-Watson, "Soviet Nationality Policy," *Russian Review* Vol. XV, No. 1 (Jan. 1956), pp. 3–13; Alexander G. Park, "The Pattern of Soviet Nationality Policy," *Bolshevism in Turkestan, 1917–1927* (New York: Columbia University Press, 1957), pp. 377–88; Richard Pipes, "The Nationalities," *The New Leader* No. 5 (April 1958), pp. 15–18; Alex Inkeles

and Raymond A. Bauer, "The Nationality Problem," *The Soviet Citizen. Daily Life in a Totalitarian Society* (Cambridge, Mass.: Harvard University Press, 1961, 2d ed.), pp. 338–73; "The Nationalities Policy of the Soviet Union: a New Phase," *Central Asian Review* Vol. X, No. 4 (1962), pp. 317–32; Alfred D. Low, "Soviet Nationality Policy and the New Program of the Communist Party of the Soviet Union," *The Russian Review* Vol. 22 (Jan. 1963), pp. 3–29; Geoffrey Wheeler, "Nationalities Policy: a New Phase?" *Survey* No. 57 (Oct. 1965), pp. 38–45; Oleh S. Fedyshyn, "Khrushchev's 'Leap Forward': National Assimilation in the USSR after Stalin," *The Southwestern Social Science Quarterly* (June 1967), pp. 34–43; Grey Hodnett, "What's in a Nation?" *Problems of Communism* Vol. XVI, No. 5 (Sept.–Oct. 1967), pp. 2–15; Peter Howard, "The Definition of a Nation: A Discussion in *Voprosy Istorii*," *Central Asian Review* No. 1 (1967), pp. 26–36; Richard Pipes, "Solving the Nationality Problem," *Problems of Communism* Vol. XVI, No. 5 (Sept.–Oct. 1967), pp. 125–31; Alex Inkeles, "Soviet Nationality Policy in Perspective," *Social Change in Soviet Russia* (Cambridge: Harvard University Press, 1968), pp. 244–63; Vernon Aspaturian, "The Non-Russian Nationalities," Allen Kassof, ed., *Prospects for Soviet Society* (New York: Frederick A. Praeger, 1968), pp. 143–98; John A. Armstrong, "The Ethnic Scene in the Soviet Union: The View of the Dictatorship," Erich Goldhagen, ed., *Ethnic Minorities in the Soviet Union* (New York: Frederick A. Praeger, 1968), pp. 3–49; Alec Nove, "History, Hierarchy and Nationalities: Some Observations on Soviet Social Structure," *Soviet Studies* Vol. 21, No. 1 (July 1969), pp. 83–89; V. Stanley Vardys, "Communism and Nationalities: Soviet Nation Building," paper read to The American Political Science Association (Sept. 1969), 22 pp.

5. John Reed, *Ten Days that Shook the World* (New York: Boni and Liveright, 1919), p. 52; I. Stalin, "K postanovke natsional'nogo voprosa," *Natsional'nyi vopros i sovetskaia Rossiia* Moscow: Gosudarstvennoe Izdatel'stvo, 1921), pp. 3–7; I. Stalin, "Ob ocherednykh zadachakh partii v natsional'nom voprose. Tezisy k X s"ezdu RKP(b), utverzhdennye TsK partii (1921 g.)," I. Stalin, *Marksizm i natsional'no-kolonial'nyi vopros. Sbornik izbrannykh statei i rechei* (Moscow: Partiinoe Izdatel'stvo, 1934), p. 70; I. Stalin, "Natsional'nyi vopros. Iz lektsii 'Ob osnovakh leninizma', chitannykh v nachale aprelia 1924 g. v Sverdlovskom universitete," *Ibid.*, pp. 144–47; *Desiatyi s"ezd RKP(b)* (Moscow: Partiinoe Izdatel'stvo, 1933),

p. 495; G. I. Broido, "Osnovnye voprosy natsional'noi politiki," *Zhizn' natsional'nostei* No. 3/4 (1923), p. 3; "Natsional'nyi vopros," *Bol'shaia sovetskaia entsiklopediia* vol. 29 (Moscow: Izdatel'stvo "Bol'shaia Sovetskaia Entsiklopediia," 1954, 2d ed.), pp. 296–99; N. S. Khrushchev, "O programme kommunisticheskoi partii Sovetskogo Soiuza," *XXII s"ezd kommunisticheskoi partii Sovetskogo Soiuza, 17–31 oktiabria 1961 goda. Stenograficheskii otchet* Part I (Moscow: Gosudarstvennoe Izdatel'stvo Politicheskoi Literatury, 1962), p. 153; L. I. Brezhnev, "Torzhestvo leninskoi natsional'noi politiki," *Izvestiia* (Dec. 30, 1962), p. 3; N. I. Matiushkin, "Razreshenie natsional'nogo voprosa v SSSR," *Voprosy istorii* No. 12 (1967), p. 3; *Natsional'naia gosudarstvennost' soiuznykh respublik* (Moscow: "Iuridicheskaia Literatura," 1968), p. 5.

6. V. Biche-ool, "K voprosu o predposylkakh formirovaniia tuvinskoi i iakutskoi sotsialisticheskikh natsii," *Iz istorii natsional'nogo stroitel'stva v SSSR* (Moscow: Izdatel'stvo "Mysl'," 1967), p. 45.

7. "K 100-letiiu so dnia rozhdeniia Vladimira Il'icha Lenina. Tezisy Tsentral'nogo Komiteta kommunisticheskoi Partii Sovetskogo Soiuza," *Pravda* (Dec. 23, 1969), pp. 1–4; "50 let velikoi oktiabr'skoi sotsialisticheskoi revoliutsii; tezisy Tsentral'nogo Komiteta KPSS," *Kommunist* No. 10 (July 1967), p. 26; *50 let velikoi oktiabr'skoi sotsialisticheskoi revoliutsii. Torzhestvennoe zasedanie Tsentral'nogo Komiteta KPSS, Verkhovnogo Soveta SSSR, Verkhovnogo Soveta RSFSR. 3–4 noiabria 1967 g. Stenograficheskii otchet* (Moscow: Izdatel'stvo Politicheskoi Literatury, 1967), pp. 27, 33.

8. Ralf Dahrendorf, "Towards a Theory of Social Conflict" in Amitai and Eva Etzioni, eds., *Social Change, Sources, Patterns, and Consequences* (New York: Basic Books, 1964), pp. 98–111; Karl W. Deutsch, *Nationalism and Social Communication: An Inquiry into the Foundations of Nationality* (Cambridge: M.I.T. Press, 1966, 2d ed.); S. Lipset and St. Rokkan, "Cleavage Structure; Party Systems, Voter Alignments: An Introduction," *Party Systems and Voter Alignments* (New York: Free Press, 1967), pp. 1–64; Max Weber, "The Nation" in C. Wright Mills and G. Gerth, eds., *From Max Weber* (Oxford: Oxford University Press, 1959), pp. 171–80; Clifford Geertz, "The Integrative Revolution. Primordial Sentiments and Civil Politics in the New States," Clifford Geertz (Ed.); *Old Societies and New States. The Quest for Modernity in Asia and Africa* (New York: The Free Press of Glencoe, The Macmillan Company, 1963), pp. 105–57, and other articles in the same volume.

9. M. S. Dzhunusov, M. I. Isaev, "Sotsiologicheskie voprosy razvitiia natsional'nykh iazykov (obzor literatury)," *Izvestiia Akademii Nauk SSSR,* Seriia literatury i iazyka, Vol. 24, No. 5 (Sept.–Oct. 1965), p. 433; L. M. Drobizheva, "Nauchnyi sovet po natsional'nym problemam," *Istoriia SSSR* No. 1 (1970), p. 222.

MARC RAEFF

PATTERNS OF RUSSIAN
IMPERIAL POLICY TOWARD
THE NATIONALITIES

Russia was a multinational empire. That seems obvious
to us now, but it was not always so apparent either to the imperial
government or to its subjects. Not until Peter the Great introduced it was the official adjective *rossiiskii* used by the government in referring to the "Russian" Empire. *Rossiiskii*, as distinguished from the traditional *russkii*, was derived from the Latin
and was supposed to point to the fact that the state fashioned by
Peter I was not exclusively Great Russian in composition.

We tend to view the "question of nationalities,"—the relationship of national minorities to the larger unit and its authorities
—in terms of our twentieth-century vantage point; that is,
through a mental set which is a legacy of what may be called the
revolution of national consciousness. We thus run great danger
of making an anachronistic analysis of the conditions and attitudes that antedated this revolution.

If the multinational character of the Russian Empire is to be
properly understood in its historical perspective,[1] several aspects
of the situation must be taken into consideration. These remarks
will concentrate upon the period during which basic attitudes and
policies toward the nationalities were formed—from about the
late sixteenth to the middle of the nineteenth centuries. After this,
there was still one more Russian expansion, into Central Asia,
but it came along with rapidly growing industrialization and

social modernization and partook rather of the Western style of new colonialism.

The first difficulty confronting a historian who wishes to analyze the evolution of attitudes and policies toward the nationalities in the Empire before the middle of the nineteenth century is the paucity of both historiography and published sources. Russian historiography is overwhelmingly "Great Russian" in orientation and barely takes into account the multinational character of the political entity with whose history it deals. Even one of Russia's foremost historians—V. O. Kliuchevskii—hardly acknowledged the fact that Russia comprised a multinational imperial polity. He did speak, it is true, of the early Slavic conquest and assimilation of Finnish tribes, but this is almost prehistory.[2] The historiographies of most nationalities are very recent, if we exclude medieval chronicles or epics, and have their obvious limitations in narrowness of focus. Understandably a product of the revolution of national consciousness we spoke of earlier, they often are so extremely chauvinistic as to be of little use. Finally, histories written in the Soviet period, although valuable for much factual detail, present historiographical and critical problems that are heightened by the ideological and political touchiness of the subject.[3] With respect to the publication of relevant sources, some progress has been made in recent decades; but there is still a shortage of documentation concerning political aspects of the problem.[4] Besides this, many recent source collections issued by the academies of sciences of the Soviet republics have been published only in the nationality languages.

A major factor in determining policies and attitudes of the officials toward nationalities is the time of the conquest or incorporation of non-Russian territory and the circumstances of the non-Russian populations. The imperial expansion of the Muscovite state began in the sixteenth century when one might have thought of differences both inside and outside it in religion, in family structure, in way of life, but not of nationalities. Neither Muscovites nor others were conscious of nationality in any sense that comes close to our modern usage. Moreover, the means of control available to the government of the czars were quite different from those of a modern state: conquest merely meant the extension of the sovereignty which the ruler exercised through his household or court (*dvor*). He depended on a small number of them to keep control over the new territory. For this reason he used existing institutions—particularly family structures—to exercise and maintain his authority, resorting to direct interference only in case of necessity. Conquest in the sixteenth century meant only the end of independent international status, but it did not necessarily entail a noticeable change in the social and economic organization of the conquered people. Unlike the lands that were forming the Habsburg Empire, for example, at approximately the same time, the territories conquered by Muscovy were little more than weak, loose political associations of traditional clans and families, bound merely by a common way of life. Moreover, in contrast to western Europe, there was no strong feudal tradition either in Muscovy or the newly acquired territories and, consequently, little respect for political autonomy, juridical separateness, and regionalism, those very elements so essential to the constitution of the monarchies and empires of the sixteenth and seventeenth centuries in the West. France, Spain, Burgundy, and Austria had expanded their boundaries by extending their monarch's suzerainty over principalities and lands that retained their own rulers, laws, and customs; this path was not available to Moscow. Even the absorption of the appanage principalities (*udely*) had been based on the tradition of common family authority and succession. This explains the almost immediate integration of the appanage lords into the retinue and household of the Grand Duke of Muscovy and the disappearance of the political distinctiveness of the principality.

There was also the quite obvious factor of geography. The beginnings of imperial expansion, meaning the bringing of non-Russian, even more of non-Slavic and non-Christian people, under the sway of Moscow, took place on a territory that was "open" and on which the sparse population had at all times been quite mobile. It was the stage of the perennial confrontation between the world of the nomadic cattle raiser and that of agricultural settlers. Many features of the conquest, as well as of the pattern of eventual absorption, have their roots in this basic geographic and social circumstance.

Conquest, for instance, was frequently only the continuing process of expanding settlement carried on by peasants or military colonists interested in acquiring more land and in securing their safety from raids launched by the nomads of the open steppe.[5] Undoubtedly there was a certain hypocritical sophistry in Prince Alexander M. Gorchakov's note of 1864, in which he explains why Russia had to push further into Central Asia: the settled communities of peasants have to be defended against the nomads; in so doing, control is imposed upon the neighboring nomadic tribe; but then one is confronted with the next nomadic people, who have to be subdued in order to provide security, and so on. This was obviously a poor justification for Russian colonial expansion into Central Asia. But it contained an important grain of truth if taken as describing the pattern of expansion accomplished in earlier periods.

Two major dimensions of the process of imperial expansion and of the incorporation of national minorities should be clearly kept in mind for purposes of analysis, even though they were frequently inextricably intertwined in reality: one is territorial and political, the other socioeconomic and cultural.

Beginning with the territorial and political dimension, it is evident at the start that the building of the empire was an almost unnoticed follow-up to the so-called gathering of Russian lands under the dominion of the Grand Duke of Moscow. In a sense, perhaps, the "gathering" itself may be described as a process of expansion, certainly so with respect to the northwestern territories such as Novgorod and Pskov. The line between the "gathering" in of lands that had once belonged together and were then dispersed and this "imperial expansion" is a rather thin one. The significant step beyond a "gathering of Russian lands" was made by the first czar, Ivan IV, with the conquest of the khanates of Kazan and Astrakhan, which secured the entire course of the Volga and allowed the czar to push beyond it. With Ivan's blessing and permission, the Stroganovs, salt and fur mer-

chants, hired mercenary cossacks to secure passage across the
Urals and begin the conquest of Siberia.

The push beyond the Volga found its natural conclusion when,
in the middle of the seventeenth century, the vastness of Siberia
had been crossed from the Ural Mountains to the Pacific Ocean.
At about the same time (1654) we witness the incorporation of
the Ukraine, first as a protectorate and then as a rapidly integrated entity in the Czardom of Muscovy. This was followed
by a more limited advance, albeit of great political and military
consequence, in the Baltic provinces during the reign of Peter
the Great, an advance that took place according to the prevailing
rules of military and diplomatic acquisition. A very sizeable extension of the empire's territory occurred in the late eighteenth
and early nineteenth centuries with the conquest of the shores of
the Black Sea and the Crimea, the partitions of Poland, the incorporation of Finland, and the beginning of a penetration into
the Caucasus. Finally, the colonial acquisition of Central Asia
took place in the second half of the nineteenth century.

Let us turn to the methods of acquisition and incorporation,
first leaving aside the modern military and diplomatic means
which were relevant only for the Baltic provinces, Finland, and
the partitions of Poland. The traditional way in which areas
were acquired and integrated seemed to be of prime importance
in setting the framework for the nationality problems in Imperial
Russia. In this process, conquest or acquisition was the first step,
incorporation the second, and assimilation the final goal. Traditional patterns developed in the early sixteenth century remained
operative throughout the succeeding centuries through the so-
called modernizing revolution of Peter the Great, and even into
the nineteenth century. For the first step—acquisition—the most
significant and characteristic of the several ways used may be
called that of social and political pressure (which did not exclude the use of military force, either directly or as a threat). Not
always quite consciously, sometimes at the invitation of one of the
parties concerned, Moscow would attempt to enroll the services
and loyalty of an influential segment of the non-Russian society.

This could be done by suggesting that they move away to new lands where they would be granted privileges and estates such as the "Czardom" of Kasimov; or individuals would be attracted into the service of Moscow by appropriate promises of rewards. Even after moving away, these people retained ties to their original society and could be of use in undermining it like a fifth column. In itself, their departure weakened their homeland, especially since they frequently constituted the more active, ambitious, and energetic military leadership. The eventual conquest of the territory then became a foregone conclusion. It may be noted that this pattern had been developed by Moscow in the course of its "gathering" of appanage lands. Such was largely the case of Kazan and Astrakhan, whose resistance had been undermined, not only by internal factional disputes, but also by the departure of military leaders and servitors in the reigns of Ivan III and Basil III, long before Ivan IV undertook the final conquest.[6] The practice of luring away military personnel prevailed in the sixteenth and seventeenth centuries, but it persisted into the post-Petrine period and was used to good advantage with respect to some Siberian groups and in Central Asia.[7] By then, of course, the power of Russia was so overwhelming that luring elites into its fold was not difficult, and it is hard to think of it as a repetition of the same method that had been employed in the early sixteenth century.

But military groups alone were not the object of such a lure. In the eighteenth and nineteenth centuries the Russian government's ability to persuade economically influential groups to move away from home undermined the local power of resistance and turned the take-over into a military promenade. This was the case of the Crimea in the 1780s. The government of Catherine II persuaded Greeks, Armenians, Georgians, and other Christians, who played a key role in Crimean trade and agriculture, to emigrate from the peninsula to the newly conquered shores of the Black Sea. This sapped the social as well as economic stability of the Crimean Tatar khanate that had been set up by the peace of Kuchuk Kainarji; the take-over followed automatically and easily.[8] In the Caucasus too, the government of St. Petersburg manipulated social groups that were in conflict with one another for religious as well as economic reasons and thereby softened any power of resistance to the conquest.[9]

Pressures of a political character, backing one contender to the throne against another, playing off one faction or clan against another, are commonly found in all forms of colonial conquests. The Russians used them whenever feasible, on their own initiative or at the request of one of the warring parties. Sometimes the initiative would come from political leadership trying to escape domination by another neighbor (one wonders how free such an initiative then was). This was why the Ukrainian cossacks turned to Moscow to save themselves from Poland. Protection might be asked, or offered, to assist a small Christian land against a threatening non-Christian neighbor, as it frequently was in the Caucasus. Finally, cultural pressures could take political form: appeal to religious solidarity—in the case of the Ukraine for protection against Polish Roman Catholicism, or in the Armenian lands against Persians and Turks. This act of selecting one means over the other, and taking advantage of one opportunity as against another, preconditioned the manner of the take-over and the initial relationship between the newly incorporated people and the imperial government.

But what was the purpose of expansion? An answer to this question, too, may offer a clue to the nature of the take-over and the resulting relationships. There was first the desire for more agricultural land. It led to peasant settlement beyond the state's borders, either with or without the consent of the government. At times the government moved reluctantly to protect Russian peasants who settled on or beyond the border; at other times the state's military initiative in securing a frontier led peasants to flock into the area. Because peasants do not leave records, and as this side of the Russian state's activity is poorly illuminated by our sources, it is difficult to know exactly when the peasants were used by the government and when, on the contrary, the farmers forced the officials' hand. It has been convincingly shown that both took place, at times almost simultaneously and inter-changeably.[10] This was certainly true of the territory between the Volga and Kama rivers and in the Urals, and frequently also in the south and in Siberia.

Obviously, considerations of security frequently motivated expansion. On the open steppe frontier, military security, by whatever means, was considered of paramount concern. It was at the origins of the expansion into the southern steppe and the Caucasus, and it played not an insignificant role in the advance into the steppes bordering on the Caspian Sea and on southern Siberia that paved the way to the conquest of Central Asia. Rarely, however, do we find the expectation of gain from commerce and the security of trade as a major factor in expanding the territorial boundaries of the Empire. Sometimes the lure of mineral wealth would lead to conquest, or at least penetration, as in the Urals and Siberia.

Much was written, especially in the nineteenth century, about the desire to protect or spread Russian Orthodoxy as a factor of imperial expansion. Naturally, this could also have its defensive side, too (in the Caucasus, for example), although to a modern ear the notion sounds rather hollow. There is practically no evi-dence of religious missionary zeal as the direct purpose of ex-pansion, although protection of Russian clergy did produce in-tervention in a few cases which in turn might lead to conquest, as in the Caucasus and Central Asia. There was no attempt be-fore conquest on the part of the Russian imperial government to spread Orthodoxy or to assist its missionary enterprises. This does not mean, of course, that religion was not used for purposes of diplomacy, but this is another story. The government was even reluctant to take advantage of opportunities offered by re-ligious affinity to expand the state's boundaries. Hence, the hesi-tations before extending protection to the Ukrainian cossacks or in responding to the appeals of Armenians and Georgians. But of course, the religious factor is not to be disregarded altogether, especially since it offered opportunities to local governors and commanders to extend their authority, notwithstanding the ab-

sence of direct instructions from St. Petersburg. Catherine II used
the argument of her duty to protect coreligionaries in creating
the conditions that led to the partitions of Poland.

What were the consequences deriving from these methods and
purposes of expansion? In the first place, there was little or no
awareness—especially in the earlier periods—of Russia's imperial extension. Because expansion had taken place gradually and
had largely been accompanied by the agricultural settlement of
Russian peasants, Russian society remained unaware of the
state's having become a multinational empire. The impression
was created that it had taken place elementally, naturally,
through people's movements and not through conscious policy
on the part of the government. Thus, the crucial period was not
that of conquest but that of incorporation, of absorption into
the fabric of Russia's policy. Having established their political
suzerainty, the Russians believed that this was not enough, that
the new territory had to become part and parcel of the Russian
land and that the new populations must live according to the
same social and economic pattern as did the Russian people. In
the absence of a strong tradition of localism and of administrative and political separateness or autonomy even for territories
inhabited by Russians (consider the brutal and rapid extinction
of the particularism of Tver and Novgorod in the fifteenth and
sixteenth centuries), there was a strong urge to impose administrative unity on the new territory. There was no tradition—as
there was in the West—of coalescing different historical units
and politico-juridical systems without destroying their particularism: the kind of feudal or protofeudal "federalism" that had
helped to create Burgundy, France, Spain, Austria. Once a territory was under effective control, the almost automatic reaction
of Russian administrators was to extend to it the social and administrative arrangements prevailing in the Russian provinces.
This was often done without any regard for the conditions which
might make such an extension undesirable or even feasible. For
example, when in 1775 Catherine II promulgated a new statute
for provincial administration which included the participation
of elective officials from among the local nobility, she automat-

ically extended it to Siberia (allowing a few years for transition) without reflecting that Siberia had no nobility. Clearly, one of the essential elements of the reform could not be implemented there.

The frequent coincidence of conquest and the expansion of Russian peasant settlement and administration resulted in a great deal of ethnic and administrative confusion. Indigenous groups mingled with the Russians that had moved in, and transfers of population resulted in linguistic and cultural mixtures within the same administrative unit. This applied primarily to conditions of expansion eastward to Kazan, Siberia, the Urals, and the southeastern steppes. There were some variations on this pattern which, however, did not change the picture too much. For instance, in the Ukraine the Cossack Host managed to preserve its autonomy and organization at least until 1709, and it even lingered on in a limited way until 1775. In 1709, as a consequence of Hetman Mazepa's siding with Charles XII at Poltava, the autonomy of the Dnieper Cossack Host was drastically curtailed. In 1775—following the Pugachev rebellion—Catherine II abolished the Zaporozhian *Sich* altogether. But here too, though slower, the process was similar, in that it aimed for and resulted in eventual absorption of the conquered people into and sociocultural integration with central Russia.[11]

In the Caucasus, linguistic and religious antagonisms had been part of the process of conquest, so that the government had to take them into account; and, in the first stages at least, the local population was allowed greater autonomy than those elsewhere in preserving its peculiarities. But this policy did not aim at preserving differences; rather, it acted merely as a political expedient to speed up the conquest and eventual incorporation by dealing first with the local non-Russian leadership on political terms. A similar pattern was to prevail in the conquest of Central Asia in the latter half of the nineteenth century.

Very different, of course, were the conquest and incorporation of the Baltic provinces, Finland, and Poland. Because the original acquisition had been accomplished through military conquest ratified by international treaty, the imperial government began by guaranteeing a special status to the newly conquered lands and by promising to respect the autonomy and privileges of the local ruling classes. This was the case in the Baltic provinces and in Finland.[12] The policy was less clear in Poland, where the occupation occurred in several stages. The first partition of Poland (1772) gave to Russia territories which were claimed to be "Russian," and which Moscow had been prevented from "gathering in" in the sixteenth century. Therefore, the Russian administration and juridical system were introduced here quite rapidly, allowing only for a very brief period of adjustment. But the Baltic and Finnish model were followed in the so-called Congress Kingdom of Poland, established under a personal royal union by the treaty of Vienna in 1815, until the revolts of 1830 and 1863 led to the abolition of all special statutes and privileges.

The acquisition of such totally alien territories under promise of respect toward traditional privileges and autonomies created a serious problem for the imperial government. It undermined the concept of the unitary nature of the Russian state and also raised questions as to the character of the sovereign, who, indeed, was a constitutional Grand Duke of Finland and King of Poland while remaining the autocratic Emperor of all Russia. The government, therefore, explicitly denied the existence of the problem, for to recognize it might have led to envisioning a federal structure for the empire. This, however, was anathema for historical as well as political reasons—and not only to the ruler and his officials, but also to a large part of Russian "public opinion,"—because the specter of a return to the appanage divisions seems to have been an ever-haunting theme. As if this were not complicated enough, the preservation of special statuses and privileges raised the question of identifying the genuine historical tradition of those lands that should be preserved. After all, here was a peasantry (Latvian, Estonian, Finnish) ruled by foreign nobilities, German in the Baltic provinces, Swedish in Finland. Preserving the privileges of these nobilities meant perpetuating the conquest of long-defeated or vanished powers and their descendants' subjection of the peasantry. Would it not be more advantageous for the Russian state to secure the loyalty of indigenous populations, who would benefit by being drawn into the orbit of often higher Russian culture and greater material prosperity at the expense of the privileges held by the foreign nobility dominating them? This is what the Russian government tried to accomplish in the second half of the nineteenth century, not without success in the Baltic provinces, but with little luck in Finland. But in acting in this manner and disregarding the "psychological" dimension of national consciousness while taking into consideration only legal forms, the imperial rulers unwittingly helped to promote nationalism among the non-Russian peasantry, adding to the explosiveness of the nationality question in the twentieth century.

While our sources permit the reconstruction of the steps by which the empire was created and territories integrated into the Russian administrative framework, it is not so easy to trace the process of cultural and social integration. Available documentation is spotty, and many of the sources simply do not provide the answers to the kind of questions we are interested in. Yet, an attempt must be made, even if only a few general remarks on the dynamics of the process may be hazarded at this point.

The imperial expansion of Russia started in the middle of the sixteenth century and first moved east and southward. From its beginnings it involved the conquest of non-Christian, nomadic societies and people who were socially and economically less complex than contemporary Russia, less developed not only in terms of a western European standard but also in terms of contemporary Muscovy. The difference, to be sure, was rather slight in some cases. Thus, it has been suggested that, with respect to the khanates of Kazan and Astrakhan, Muscovy was only continuing the tradition and practices of the "political system of the steppe" as one of the successor states of the Golden Horde.[13] Of course, some of the people or societies conquered by Muscovy may, like Central Asia in the Middle Ages, have had a very high and brilliant culture in the remote past. What is at issue here is their condition at the time of conquest. Therefore, feelings of religious and cultural superiority on the part of the Russians were unmistakable, and quite strong as early as the sixteenth and seventeenth centuries. This sense of superiority, giving rise to self-righteous justifications of the conquest, though historical, legal, and religious arguments were advanced too, was reinforced by what often seemed a supine acquiescence on the part of people who were absorbed. Such passivity also made it possible to take advantage of the split between the upper and lower classes within the alien populations. The upper classes, heads of clans, families, former military leaders of the khans, were wooed by the Russians and converted into instruments of Moscow's administrative and judicial control. This happened in Kazan, Siberia, and the Caucasus. It is also fair to say that these indigenous leaders were attracted by the superior wealth of the czar, as well as by the opportunities that incorporation into the Russian ruling class might offer. The example of those of their compatriots who had been lured away before the conquest also served as an incentive.

The Russian social and political system made it possible to translate that wooing and attraction into concrete material and social, as well as political, benefits in favor of the wooed. The Russian nobility constituted a service class whose ranks were relatively open to newcomers. Anyone from the upper levels of the conquered societies, by taking up service, could acquire the rank (*chin*) which would put him on a footing of equality, or at least provide this opportunity for his children, with his Russian counterpart within the framework of the dominant "Establishment." This might be accomplished by merely carrying on the traditional leadership role within the clan or tribe, but only as an agent of the Russian administration. Social and cultural Russification provided an additional avenue for acquiring a status of equality with the Russian service class. Thus, the alien leaders sent their children to Russian schools, paving the way for their eventual Russification, acquisition of ranks, estates and even serfs. In so doing these leaders became virtually assimilated, in style of life and economic interest, with the Russian service nobility. This was true not only of the descendants of the ruling families of Tatar and Caucasian principalities, but also of their retainers, as well as of the chieftains of many a Siberian tribe or people.[14]

This process helps to explain in turn the greater difficulty experienced by the Russian "Establishment" in absorbing those elites that were not inferior to the Russians, possibly even superior to them, by contemporary standards. This was, for instance, the case of the German nobility and bourgeoisie in the Baltic provinces. Their integration—such as it was—followed a somewhat different pattern. Since their educational level was distinctly superior to that of the average Russian in government service in the eighteenth century, they could do well in the Russian military and civil services, rising to high positions. Having done so, such aliens became a part of the cosmopolitan milieu of the court. They were considered members of the Russian elite even though they retained their own culture, language, and religion, as well as their traditional role of local leadership in their province of origin. Their political loyalty, however, belonged unquestionably to the Russian Empire. They were truly a bilingual and bicultural segment of the imperial political, military, and intellectual elite.[15] Another illustration, showing opposite results, is supplied by the Jews. Incorporated into the empire at the partition of Poland, they did not feel, and were not, culturally inferior to the Russians. But to join the Russian governing elite would have required them to abandon their traditional way of life, their religion—and they could not abandon their separateness. The Jewish policy of the imperial government before the 1870s, when it became openly discriminatory and oppressive, reflected its ambivalence and bewilderment at such a situation. The government wanted to attract the Jews into Russian society, allowing them to retain their religion. But only on condition that the Jews abandon their way of life, their customs, everything that in a secular sense differentiated and separated them from Russian society. But the Jews would not accept this, since to do so was to desert their religion. The government was incapable of appreciating the close connection between religion and the way of life—Alexander I's attempts at liberal "emancipation" and acceptance of them into Russian society failed. In disgust, Nicholas I embarked on forced Russification and brutal repression.[16]

Economic conflicts that existed or developed between the Russian people and the outsiders also hampered the latter's social integration into the empire. Obviously the major instance of such economic conflict was provided by the struggle for land between cattle-raising nomads and Russian peasant settlers. The imperial government, too, was anxious to have the nomads settle down and till the soil, since, in its opinion, settled agriculture was the hallmark of a higher level of civilization. This was a common eighteenth-century Enlightenment notion based on the belief in a universal pattern of cultural progress leading upward from hunter and fisherman to nomad cattle raiser, and finally to the settled agriculturalist and trader. The government considered it important to assist in this evolution. All those who were not yet peasants or otherwise settled should be helped to adopt this higher, better way of life. We have here a conscious policy of assimilation and Russification by way of promoting a uniform way of life throughout the empire. Reports of local governors in the Volga and Ural areas, as well as in Siberia, confirm that they conceived it their duty to Russify the tribesmen by transforming hunters and nomads into settled peasants. The same effort would also facilitate administration, since the system of laws and regulations applicable to Russian peasants would then automatically be extended to the non-Russians who had taken up agricultural pursuits. Even in the course of writing down the traditional oral law of the tribes (for instance, during the codification of Siberian local customary law in the 1820s and 1830s), Russian officials would introduce new concepts which Russified such law and made it into an instrument of social and economic transformation along the lines we have been considering here.[17]

In this instance, too, the traditional leaders and the rich were the first to be persuaded to adopt the Russian pattern and then help to bring their fellow nomads along. To this end the tribal elite were offered rewards of money, land, medals, even ranks, and they were confirmed by the government in their position of authority. In cases like that of the Buryats the policy worked. But once a nomadic population had settled down, Russian law and administration were extended to it, and it found itself absorbed into the dominant Russian world, albeit in a lower status. The poor, who could not easily change their way of life, were disregarded by Russian officials; retaining the old patterns of beliefs and traditions, they came thus to be separated from their own natural leadership as well as from the Russian establishment. Little wonder that when a new leadership arose from their ranks it not only spoke up for their old traditions but also rejected completely the system that had resulted in the isolation, poverty, and backwardness of their fellows. The emerging leaders confronted the imperial government, and its Russified elite, with the demand that it recognize their "national" identity—a demand for which the establishment was psychologically unprepared and with which it could not cope.

In the early years of the nineteenth century romantic notions of historicism, respect for tradition, and the uniqueness of every culture and society led to a recognition in Russia that the transition from one way of life to another may follow different patterns. The goal remained the same—administrative and social homogeneity throughout the empire—but the methods became more flexible, gradualistic, and took into consideration local conditions and traditions. Mikhail Speransky, when a government official, tried to strike a practical compromise which balanced the recognition of separateness with the ultimate aim of uniformity. He was moderately successful with the Siberian tribes, whose organization was simple, numbers small, and economy poor. It proved almost impossible to apply this policy consistently among the more complex, advanced areas of the Caucasus, Finland, and Central Asia.

The goal of social, economic, and political uniformity remained constant in the policy of the imperial government with respect to non-Russian lands and people throughout the pre-1917 period. At no point was it conscious or aware of the dynamic force of nationalism and nationality. Yet, the Russian government did not aim at eradicating or destroying nations and nationalities.[18] It simply felt that their way of life should change in a process of natural evolution which their membership in the

empire could speed up and help along. That this might at the
same time lead to the destruction of traditional customs, language, or sense of identity which people held very dear did not
seem to enter into governmental expectations.

True, some of the people in Siberia, in some areas of the Caucasus, and along the upper Volga valley had no clear sense of
nationality or what could be called a genuine national consciousness. Their passive acquiescence to Russian domination rendered
the government even more impervious to the claims and opposition of those people that did have a strong sense of national
identity and who were not willing to give up their traditional
ways and values. As long as it was only a question of changing
ways of life there was some hope of enlisting the support of the
upper classes. But once national consciousness had begun to
spread and take firm hold, this limited goal, too, became im-
practicable. Faced by the rejection of its drive for uniformity in
way of life, the government turned to an active policy of Russification in the second half of the nineteenth century, just at the
time when self-awareness was beginning to take hold of the nationalities. The stubbornness and myopia expressed in this policy
paved the way for the mass disaffection of the nationalities that
proved a very strong element in the collapse of the imperial regime.

Of the major factors which determined the patterns of Russian
imperial policy, time—chronology—is the first to be kept in
mind. In the earlier stages of expansion (sixteenth and seventeenth centuries), traditional means were used to conquer and
integrate the new territories into the Russian polity. This was a
continuation of the "gathering in" of lands claimed by the Grand
Duke and Czar of Moscow as rightfully his own.[19] The process
of incorporation, too, followed methods suggested by the patri-
monial (votchinnyi) conception of authority, and it was inti-
mately bound up with the elemental expansion of Russian
peasant settlement. This was also the pattern that prevailed subsequently along the eastern borders of the empire—into Siberia
and the southeastern steppes—perpetuated as it was by the of-
fensively defensive tactics of the Cossack hosts. Both at the be-

ginning of this process in the sixteenth century and at its end in the second half of the nineteenth, territorial consolidation for the sake of security was hardly to be distinguished from outright expansion and seizure of sparsely settled lands held by nomadic people on a lower (from the Russian point of view, of course) level of cultural and economic development.

The military and diplomatic acquisitions of non-Russian territory in the eighteenth and at the beginning of the nineteenth centuries involved old, established social and political structures of a western European type in the Baltic provinces, Finland, and Poland. Russian conquest had to make allowance for this fact, and it started on the basis of a federal type of relationship. The privileges and traditional rights of the local ruling elites were respected at first. Gradually, however, by virtue of the growing modernization of Russia's culture and socioeconomic makeup, these privileges and rights became anachronistic, not to speak of their being antithetical to prevailing political and ideological conceptions. The government in St. Petersburg proceeded to erode and eventually abolish the privileged status of these areas, especially the traditional rights of their ruling classes. This was accomplished by acquiescing in the local economic and social relationships and the elite's cultural uniqueness, while enforcing political and institutional unification.

Finally, alongside the imposition of political and economic control by the central government, there took place a gradual but relentless process of social Russification. It introduced uniform institutions and power structures, and this automatically led to administrative Russification as well. In its drive for uniformity in the way of life of all its subjects, the imperial government ended up by actively promoting *de facto* institutional and political Russification, which in the case of the weaker nationalities brought with it cultural Russification. This had been the experience of the Ukrainians and the cossacks in particular, and in the eighteenth and nineteenth centuries it was also experienced by the people involved in more recent acquisitions in the south and east. With varying means, at different rates, Russian imperial policy toward the non-Russian people within the borders of the state was one of social and administrative assimilation, which in the nineteenth century was bound to carry in its wake strong suggestions of cultural Russification as well.

NOTES

No attempt will be made to provide a comprehensive coverage of the literature that may be relevant to the problem of nationalities in pre-1917 Russia. The titles cited below are those that the present author has found most helpful and that also contain useful suggestions about further literature, preference being given to those in Western languages.

1. The legal aspect of the unitary or federal nature of the empire is discussed by Boris E. Nol'de, *Ocherki russkago gosudarstvennago prava* (St. Petersburg: "Pravda," 1911); N. M. Korkunov, *Russkoe gosudarstvennoe pravo,* vol. I, 4th ed. (St. Petersburg: Tipografiia M. M. Stasiulevicha), (particularly, Obshchaia chast', otdel 1, glava I).

2. A laudable departure from the Kliuchevskii tradition appears in the recent syntheses by George Vernadsky, *Russia at the Dawn of the Modern Age* (New Haven: Yale University Press, 1959), and *The Tsardom of Muscovy* (New Haven: Yale University Press, 1969, 2 vols). Hugh Seton-Watson also allocates more space to the non-Russian territories of the empire than do run-of-the-mill textbooks in his *The Russian Empire, 1801–1917* (Oxford: Oxford University Press, 1967). The ideological and intellectual aspect of the problem is treated in the essays of Georg von Rauch, Russland: *Staatliche Einheit und nationale Vielfalt (Föderalistische Kräfte und Ideen in der russischen Geschichte)* (Munich: Veröffentlichungen des Osteuropa-Institutes München, 1953, Bd. 5).

3. Practically all general histories of the USSR contain separate chapters dealing with non-Russian territories and people. Naturally, the emphasis stresses the conquest, the economic exploitation, and the revolutionary movements. But much useful information may be gleaned from this literature: B. D. Grekov, S. V. Bakhrushin, V. I. Lebedev, *Istoriia SSSR,* 2 vols., 2d ed. (Moscow: Gospolitizdat, 1947–1949); *Istoriia SSSR s drevneishikh vremen do nashikh dnei,*

v dvukh seriiakh v dvenadtsati tomakh (Moscow: Izdanie Akademii Nauk, Institut Istorii, 1966), especially vols. 2–4 of the first series; *Ocherki istorii SSSR* (Moscow: 1953–1957). Naturally, the histories of the various constituent republics and territories of the USSR provide useful information and relevant documents. See Bibliography.

4. In recent years the major Soviet republics have been publishing source collections on the period of conquest and incorporation into the empire. For a sample list, see Bibliography, History II.

5. One case study, superficial but informative, is *The Russian Conquest of Bashkiria 1552–1740, A Case Study in Imperialism* by Alton S. Donnelly (New Haven: Yale University Press, 1968).

6. Boris Nolde, *La Formation de l'Empire russe—Etudes, Notes et Documents I* (Paris: Collection historique de l'Institut d'Etudes slaves, vol. XV, 1952).

7. Seymour Becker, *Russia's Protectorates in Central Asia: Bukhara and Khiva, 1865–1924* (Cambridge: Harvard University Press, 1968; Russian Research Center Studies no. 54).

8. Marc Raeff, "The Style of Russia's Imperial Policy and Prince G. A. Potemkin," in Gerald N. Grob, ed., *Statesmen and Statecraft of the Modern West: Essays in Honor of Dwight E. Lee and H. Donaldson Jordan* (Barre, Massachusetts: Barre Publishers, 1967, pp. 1–51; Nolde, *La Formation . . .* , II (Paris, 1953), part IV; Alan W. Fisher, *The Russian Annexation of the Crimea, 1772–1783* (Cambridge: Cambridge University Press, 1970).

9. David M. Lang, *The Last Days of the Georgian Monarchy, 1658–1832* (New York: Columbia University Press, 1957).

10. Nolde, *La Formation . . .* , vol. I.

11. Venedikt A. Miakotin, *Ocherki sotsial'noi istorii Ukrainy v XVII–XVIII vv.* (Prague: 1924–1926); H. Auerbach, *Die Besiedelung der Südukraine in den Jahren 1774–1787* (Wiesbaden: Veröffentlichungen des Osteuropa-Institutes München, 1965, Bd. 25).

12. For the Baltic provinces' institutional incorporation in the course of the eighteenth century, see Ia. Zutis, *Ostzeiskii vopros v XVIII veke* (Riga: VAPP, 1946). The literature about Finland and Poland is too vast to be cited here and properly takes up an important sector in the respective national historiographies of these countries. For Poland, there is a convenient introduction in *The Cambridge History of Poland* (Cambridge: Cambridge University Press, 1951). For Finland, see John H. Wuorinen, *Nationalism in Modern Finland*

(New York: Columbia University Press, 1931); Peter Scheibert, "Die Anfänge der finnischen Staatswerdung unter Alexander I," *Jahrbücher für Geschichte Osteuropas,* IV (1939), Nos. 3/4.

13. Edward L. Keenan, Jr., "Muscovy and Kazan, 1445–1552: A Study in Steppe Politics" (Cambridge: Harvard University, unpublished dissertation, 1966).

14. Marc Raeff, *Siberia and the Reforms of 1822* (Seattle: University of Washington Press, 1956).

15. Reinhard Wittram, *Drei Generationen, Deutschland–Livland–Russland 1830–1914* (Göttingen: Deurerlichsche Verlagsbuchhandlung, 1949); Friederich von Schubert, *Unter dem Doppeladler (Erinnerungen eines Deutschen in russischem Offiziersdienst 1789–1814)* (Stuttgart: K. F. Koehler Verlag, 1962).

16. S. M. Dubnow, *History of the Jews in Russia and Poland from the Earliest Times until the Present Day,* vols. 1 and 2 particularly (Philadelphia: Jewish Publication Society of America, 1916–1918, reprinted 1946).

17. For the Siberian case, see Marc Raeff, *Siberia and the Reforms of 1822,* ch. VI. Also, Aleksandr E. Nol'de, *Ocherki istorii kodifikatsii mestnykh grazhdanskikh zakonov pri grafe Speranskom,* 2 vols. (St. Petersburg: Senatskaia Tipografiia 1906–1914); Evgenii Iakushkin, *Obychnoe pravo—materialy dlia bibliografii* (Moscow: Universitetskaia Tipografiia, 1908).

18. A case study concerning the Volga Tatars in Alan W. Fisher, "Enlightened Despotism and Islam under Catherine II," *Slavic Review,* vol. XXVII, No. 4 (December 1968), pp. 542–53.

19. For a comprehensive description of Muscovite claims to eastern territories in the sixteenth century, see Jaroslaw Pelenski, "Muscovite Imperial Claims to the Kazan Khanate: A Case Study in The Emergence Of Imperial Ideology" (New York: Columbia University, unpublished doctoral dissertation, 1968).

HANS KOHN

SOVIET COMMUNISM AND NATIONALISM: THREE STAGES OF A HISTORICAL DEVELOPMENT

Seen structurally, the nationality problems of the Soviet Union are similar to those of the Habsburg Empire before the First World War or to those of Czechoslovakia or Poland before the Second World War. These problems, common to multinational states, have been solved relatively well in the Soviet Union for the very reason that Lenin refused to regard the Soviet Union as a Russian nation-state. Russia before 1917, Hungary between 1867 and 1918, Czechoslovakia and Poland between 1918 and 1938 could not solve their nationality problems because they insisted on their nation-state character. Soviet communism tried to preserve a political and economic unity above the various ethnic, linguistic, or religious groups, a way later followed by Yugoslavia and by India. Through its ancient roots and its neutralist foreign policy, Switzerland represents the most successful application of the federal principle in the attempt to solve problems arising from multiethnicity. Even there we find minor maladjustments; understandably the tensions between the nationalities in the Soviet Union, Yugoslavia, or India are much greater. Nevertheless, they represent workable experiments in the difficult task of facilitating the cooperation of various ethnic and linguistic groups. But Soviet communism had to face not only the problem of the national movements within its frontiers, but also that of survival and assertion in a world of nations, many of them better organized and economically more advanced than Russia.

More important than structural comparisons for an understanding of the role of Soviet communism in a world of nationalism will be an analysis of its historical and ideological background
and the changes which it underwent. Such an approach carries
the danger of isolating the Soviet case too thoroughly, of stressing
its special features (*Eigenart*) at the expense of what it has in
common with similar historical phenomena, and of underplay-
ing the question of how much is due to specific situations. The
historical approach, however, clarifies the great changes in Soviet communism over more than half a century, changes which
were partly caused by, or corresponded to, world-wide changes
in a period of unusually dynamic developments everywhere. We
have only to compare the British Empire or the United States of
1914 with their descendants of 1970 to understand the depth of
difference in the self-understanding and spatial awareness of a
nation which has undergone great changes in the recent decades.

Yet, in all these changes historical forces and attitudes perse-
vere. It was so in the French Revolution of 1789–1799 and has
been so in the Russian Revolution which started in 1917. How
far did revolutionary France at the end of the eighteenth century
follow and intensify, in domestic and foreign policy, the less dynamic trends of royal France? A conservative statesman and historian born in the last decade of the *ancien regime,* François
Guizot, stressed the continuity of history. "When nations," he
wrote in the preface to his *Essai sur l'histoire de France* (1824),

have lived gloriously for a long time, they are unable to break with
their past, whatever they do. They experience its influence at the very
time when they work to destroy it. In the midst of their outstanding
transformations, they remain in the essential aspects of their character and destiny the product of their history. Even the most daring and
powerful revolution cannot abolish national traditions which have
existed for a long time.

On the other hand, Ernest Renan, born about the time Guizot
wrote the lines quoted, was carried away by the enthusiasm of
1848. Looking back at the Revolution of 1789, he praised it as
opening up an entirely new chapter in the history of France and

of mankind. "One can call all preceding periods of history," he
wrote in *L'Avenir de la science,* "the irrational epoch of human
existence which one day will count as little in the history of mankind, and in that of our nation, as at present the chapter on the
history of Gaul counts in the history of France. . . . The year
1789 will be a holy year in the history of mankind." Lenin in
1917 was much nearer in his outlook to the Renan of 1848 than
to Guizot.[1]

I
The first stage of Soviet communism was determined not
only by Russian history but also by the specific cultural atmosphere of Europe in the early twentieth century. Never were
Russia and Europe culturally as close as then. It was also an age
overshadowed by thoughts of violence and of apocalyptic vision.
The Russo-Japanese War and the suppression of the revolution
of 1905, the Balkan conflicts and the unprecedented holocaust of
World War I, a new glorification of extremism by the Action
Française, the Black Hundreds and the Futurist Manifesto
(1909), Sorel's *Reflections on Violence* (1906) and Nietzsche's
misunderstood gospel of heroic vitality—all belong to the background of Lenin's revolution. Expressionism became the dominant movement among the nonconformist youth in Central Europe. Its leading periodicals were characteristically called *Der
Sturm* (1910) and *Die Aktion* (1911), its representative an-
thologies *Kameraden der Menschheit. Dichtungen zur Weltrevo-
lution* (1919) and *Menschheitsdämmerung* (1920) expressed
"hopes for world peace, world brotherhood and social revolution." Russian literature replaced the ineffectuality and boredom
of the superfluous man with Gorky's vagabonds (*bosiaki*) with
their vitality and rejection of the established order. "We sing a
song to the madness of courage," Gorky wrote in his "Song of
the Stormy Petrel" (1901). Soon, in the torment and corruption
of an apparently unending war, revolution appeared as a cleans-
ing blizzard. Alexander Blok expressed this vision in a poem
called "The Twelve." In the winter of 1917–1918, which was
unique for its horror and pregnancy, he suddenly saw Christ

emerge marching among twelve desperate Red soldiers, frightening and frightened in the dark and icy streets of starving Petrograd. Whether the Messiah walked only among the twelve or with them Blok did not say and did not know.

In April 1917 Woodrow Wilson entered World War I, the war to end all wars, to establish an era of lasting peace and national self-determination. He and Lenin each appealed to a worldwide audience and believed in a global applicability of their interpretation of war and history. The aggressiveness which characterized Lenin was not an isolated "Russian" or "Marxist" phenomenon. It was part of the upsurge of a revolutionary, elitist *élan vital,* glorified by part of Europe's youth just before 1914. Romain Rolland in his novel *La Nouvelle Journée* (1912), the final volume of his *Jean Christophe,* described this youth:

The new generation, robust and disciplined, was longing for combat and, before its victory was won, had the attitude of the mind of the conqueror. . . . Proudly, they exalted violent realism, trampling under foot the rights of others. . . . They were not content to despise, they regarded the gentle dotards, the humanitarian thinkers of a preceding generation, as public malefactors.[2]

In its first stage, Lenin's revolution bore traits of a secular universal messianism. It was rooted in Marxism, but it could also appeal to a Russian Slavophile tradition, though there was a deep gulf between the two conceptions. Marx and Lenin were internationalists whose universal philosophy of history was based upon common laws of social-economic development. For them the bearer of salvation was the industrial proletariat, created by modern technology and destined by its use to save all mankind from the miseries and frustrations of history. Because the proletariat suffered exploitation and humiliation, it also bore the older mark of messianic destiny, the one of Deutero-Isaiah's *ebed Yahveh,* servant of God.

The Slavophiles based their messianic hope on the Russian peasant people, its peculiar way of life, which isolated Holy Russia, as God's own people, from Europe. The purity of its truly Christian life would enable the poor and despised country to spread the gospel of peace and social justice to all men. Tiuchev's poem of 1855 shows some resemblance to the vision in Blok's "The Twelve" and the *ebed Yahveh*:

> Those poor villages,
> this sterile nature,
> homeland of patience,
> land of the Russian people!

> The proud glance of the foreigner
> can neither see nor observe
> that which pierces through and shines hidden
> in its humble nakedness.

> The King of Heaven under the guise of a serf,
> has traversed and blessed Thee,
> Thee, my native land,
> bowed down by the weight of the Cross.

In his novel *The Possessed* Dostoevsky expressed a different nationalistic and non-Christian messianism. Shatov, a former peasant and revolutionary, has become the spokesman of an extreme Russianism. "Every people is a people only as long as it has its own God, and excludes all other gods irreconcilably; as long as it believes that by its own God it will conquer and drive out of the world all other gods," Shatov declared.

If a great people did not believe that the truth is only to be found in itself alone, if it did not believe that it alone is destined to save all the rest by its truth, it would at once sink into being ethnographic material, and not a great people. But there is only one truth, and therefore only a single one out of the nations can have the true God. That is the Russian people.[3]

In his *Journal of an Author* (1877) Dostoevsky, who as a pacifist condemned other peoples' wars as imperialist, claimed an exception for Russia's war, because "Russia represents an exception in the present historical period," though Europe does not recognize it. Russia's war, Dostoevsky claimed, is a war for a sacred idea, the first step for the realization of perpetual peace. "So much that is new and progressive will begin in human relations that it would be useless to mourn and to hesitate on the eve of the last great struggle which will bring about the regeneration of all Europe." In his last lecture on Pushkin, which Dostoevsky delivered in Moscow in June 1880, he claimed that "our [Russian] mission is the embodiment of the universal idea on earth."

Lenin's rational internationalism had nothing in common with Tiuchev's and Dostoevsky's irrational nationalism. Yet, in their writings words like liberty, imperialism, national liberation were used in a similar ambiguous way. National self-determination played, of course, as little a role in Dostoevsky's thought as it did in Bismarck's. It did play a role in Lenin's and Wilson's thought. Born on the bank of the Volga, where many Turkic and Finnish groups live, Lenin witnessed the growth of nationalism among them. He went beyond Marx and Western socialists of the pre-1914 period in understanding the potential importance of the awakening of these underdeveloped peoples. After 1905 he was aware of their growing unrest. The workers of the West did not actively support the revolution of 1905. But the revolution influenced the national movements in Asia from Egypt and Turkey to China. The revolutionary movements there were certainly not proletarian. The situation was rather similar to that in Spain, the Kingdom of Naples, or Russia one century before, but the inherent dynamism of the European wars in the twentieth century accelerated the nationalist movements among the non-European people.

In his internationalism Lenin differed from most Russian socialists as Marx did from Lassalle. "We want to rebuild the world," Lenin wrote in his thesis of April 1917. "The socialists cannot reach their great aim," he emphasized in his *Socialism and War* in August 1915,

without fighting against all forms of national oppression. They must therefore demand that the Social Democrats of the *oppressing* countries [and here he included Russia] recognize . . . the right of the oppressed nationalities to self-determination. . . . A Socialist of a great nation or a nation possessing colonies who does not defend this right is a chauvinist. To defend this right in no way means to encourage the formation of small states, but on the contrary it leads to a freer, more fearless and therefore wider and more universal formation of governments. . . . On the other hand, the Socialists of the *oppressed* nationalities must unequivocally fight for the complete unity of the *workers* of the oppressed and the oppressor nationalities. . . . The struggle for a socialist international revolution against imperialism is impossible without the recognition of the rights of nations to self-determination. No proletariat reconciling itself to the least violation by "its" nation of the rights of other nations can be socialist.

To Lenin "Great Russian chauvinism" always represented an obstacle to the success of communism.

Lenin's communism did not bear a Russian coloring. Even in 1920, in his *Left-Wing Communism, an Infantile Disorder,* he called it a mistake to lose sight of the fact that, "after the victory of the proletarian revolution in at least one of the advanced nations, . . . Russia will cease to be the model country and will again become (. . . in the socialist sense) a backward country." Against Lenin's expectation, the proletarian revolution failed in every highly industrialized country, even in defeated and economically chaotic Germany, the homeland of Marx and Engels. The messianic mood of 1917–1918 quickly disappeared in the West or turned into a purely nationalist and nation-centered movement. Democratic institutions of a liberal representative type quickly lost their vigor in Central Europe, and the future seemed to belong to fascism, an extreme and exclusive form of aggressive nationalism.

As an anti-imperialist, Lenin appealed to the Islamic and Asian peoples and supported their struggle for independence. During his lifetime communism did not develop into a mass movement anywhere in the underdeveloped world. At the fourth congress of the Communist International, in the fall of 1922, several communist parties from the East were represented. According to their own figures, their adherents numbered in the low hundreds, and only Japan reported 1,300 members. A Dutch delegate to the congress remarked that

proletarian Russia is the friend of genuine self-determination and the freedom of Oriental nations. The international proletariat, therefore, acclaims the political aspirations of the Mohammedan nations toward complete economic, financial and political enfranchisement from the influence and domination of the imperialist states. It acclaims it as an aspiration which, even though it may not aim at the abolition of wage slavery and private ownership of the means of production in Islamic lands, nevertheless menaces the foundations of European capitalism.

In Lenin's time the Soviet government helped Turkey and Persia to achieve full independence; it concluded treaties of friendship with Persia on February 26, with Afghanistan on February 28, and with the Turkish Grand National Assembly in Ankara on March 16, 1921. Russia renounced all the privileges, concessions, and capitulations which, in common with other governments, Russia had imposed upon Oriental states. Soviet Russia returned the provinces of Kars and Ardahan, which Czarist Russia had gained in the war of 1878, to Turkey, and restored some islands and territories acquired in June 1893 to Persia. This attitude contrasted with the procedures which the Western powers wished to impose on Turkish and Arab lands at San Remo and at Sèvres in 1920. China unsuccessfully tried at Paris (1919) and in Washington (1922) to achieve recognition of its sovereignty and the abolition of the "unequal treaties" on the part of the Western powers. In that case, too, the Soviet government "discontinued and abominated the former policy of the Czarist government and declared null and void" all unequal treaties.

Yet, communism as a doctrine made no progress in the Islamic Middle East. It did in the Far East, where Soviet Russia concluded a treaty of friendship with the People's Republic of Mongolia on November 5, 1921, and a new nationalist era of modernization and education started there, the first official example of nationalist communism. West of Mongolia the sparsely populated territory of Tuva was organized in 1921 into a Tuvinian People's Republic, Tannu-Tuva, which in 1944 was incorporated into the Russian SFSR as the Tuva Autonomous Oblast.

More complex was the relationship with republican China. On January 26, 1923, the Soviet plenipotentiary Adolf Joffe agreed with Sun Yat-sen, China's revolutionary leader, that China offered no favorable soil for the introduction of communism, but needed national unity and full sovereignty, for which Russian help was promised. In the following two years little progress was made in this direction. On his deathbed in March 1925 Sun Yat-sen, in a letter to Moscow, later published in the *New York Times*, praised

the heritage left by the immortal Lenin to the oppressed peoples of the world. With the help of this heritage, the victims of imperialism will be able to escape from the international regime which is based upon servitude and injustice. I shall leave behind me a party [the Kuomintang] which as I have always hoped will be allied with you in the historic task of freeing China and other exploited peoples once and for all from the yoke of imperialism. . . . To that end I have commanded my party to remain in constant touch with you. . . . In taking leave of you, I wish to express the hope that the day may soon come when the USSR will welcome a free and powerful China as a friend and ally, and that in the great struggle for the liberation of the world's oppressed peoples these two allies may advance side by side from victory to victory.

Within the next few years the cooperation of the Kuomintang and the communists made the unification of China under Chiang Kai-shek, the leader of the Kuomintang's army, possible. But Sun's hope never became a reality. In 1927 Chiang broke with Soviet and Chinese communism; in 1949 the Chinese communists without Soviet help defeated Chiang and became masters of China. But there was no "fraternal unity" between Soviet and Chinese communists, and the rift between them has steadily deepened. This is certainly a strange and unpredictable outcome of a policy which seemed to Lenin and to Sun based on self-evident premises.

Before 1945 Soviet communism had little effect on nationalism outside Russia. Within its borders the Soviet government strove to equalize the rights of all nationalities and to abolish the linguistic and religious privileges of the Russians which existed under the Czar. To achieve some approximation of the new principle of equality, it was necessary to bring the more backward and neglected people up to the level of the more advanced ones. At the same time, unity above the diversity of languages and cultural traditions had to be imposed by the Party and the universal doctrine of communism.

For Lenin, nationalism was a secondary problem. He did not see in the nation, not even in the Russian nation, a determinant and life-giving force of history. Communism and nationalism belonged for him to two different planes. But under the concrete conditions of his time communism had to try to find a *modus vivendi* with nationalism, to fit it into its framework and so to dispose of it. Lenin always pointed out that it was of the utmost importance to recognize the full gravity of the problem of nationalism and not to belittle it from an "international" point of view. Lenin's goal was the cooperation of nationalities in economic units of maximum dimension, ultimately of global dimension. But he was aware of the fact that this goal could be effected only on the basis of voluntary cooperation, and that implied the equality and, within the very narrow limits allowed by the doctrine, the freedom of the various nationalities. Any oppression of one people by another was bound to arouse a combative nationalism and to wreck the main condition essential to a fraternal cooperation of the workers of all peoples in building the new society.

Even after the end of the capitalist order, Lenin believed, the nationality question would retain its importance for a long time, until the great differences in education and standard of living were wiped out and the peoples' historical hatreds and mutual distrusts gradually disappeared. In order that this goal might be achieved, and not for their own sake, national languages and cultures had to be fully taken into account. Such a recognition, Lenin hoped, would eventually divest nationalism of its present absolutist character. This was the background of the Declaration of Rights of the Peoples of Russia, November 15, 1917. Like the Declaration of the Rights of Man and the Citizen, August 26, 1789, the new Declaration often remained more of an intention than a reality, a guidepost open to ambiguous interpretation and incomplete fulfillment. These declarations were products of a concrete historical situation and of the ideas current at the time. Both exercised a wide influence on human thought.

The federative form of Soviet communism has been interpreted by Soviet scholars as a "new and decisive step along the road to the union of the workers of all countries in the Socialist World Soviet Republic." The banner of the Union dispenses with historical national emblems. Its symbols are a sickle and a hammer on a sunlit globe framed in ears of corn, interwoven with ribbons bearing in various languages the slogan, "Proletarians of all countries, unite!" Thus, the hope was expressed that in the former Russian empire socialism would serve as a supranational force, binding peoples together. Outside the Soviet Union nationalism in the coming decades was to prove itself everywhere a much stronger force than international socialism or any religious universalism. These years witnessed the rapid growth of an exclusive and arrogant nationalism. Was there a real chance for the success of Lenin's "realist" compromise in the former Russian empire? Lenin himself warned in his concluding speech at the eighth Russian Communist Party Congress on March 19, 1919:

It seems to me that the Finnish example and that of the Bashkirs show that in the question of nationality it is not possible to proceed from the assumption that economic unity is necessary at any price. Necessary, of course, it is. But we must attain it through propaganda, through agitation, through a voluntary union. The Bashkirs distrust the Russians, because the Russians are at a higher level of civilization and have used their civilization to rob the Bashkirs. Consequently . . . the name Russian means oppressor to the Bashkirs. . . . We must take this into account, we must combat it. But that takes a long time. We cannot get rid of it by a decree. We must go to work on it very cautiously. Above all, such a nation as the Russian who has aroused a wild hatred in all other nationalities must be particularly cautious. We have only now learned to manage better, and even that only some of us. There are still many communists who demand "uniform schools" and accordingly no instruction to be given except in Russian. In my view a communist who thinks in that way is a pan-Russian chauvinist. The tendency still exists in many of us and we must wrestle with it.[4]

These words by Lenin are, with necessary changes (*mutatis mutandis*), valid in the age of nationalism everywhere, whatever the ruling ideology. They apply in the United States to the relations with Blacks and Indians, in Israel to the relations with its Arab subjects, and of course to the relationship of nationalities and Russians within the Soviet Union and between communist states.

Under Lenin Soviet communism continued some of the progressive trends common to Europe at that time, in searching for new methods of education, of fighting illiteracy, of modernism in art and literature, in broadening the participation of the masses in the various aspects of cultural life. Literature and the arts preserved relative freedom. Anatoly Lunacharsky, the first People's Commissar for public instruction, was a man of wide culture, thoroughly familiar with Western intellectual trends. Gorky and Trotsky lent their support to maintaining a high critical level of artistic life. The first years of Soviet communism showed therefore a great wealth of significant developments in poetry and drama, in stagecraft and film. It was characteristic that some leading writers formed a group called the Serapion Brothers, taking the name from the tales of the German romantic writer and musician E. T. A. Hoffmann, who had died a century before. They emphasized not only their love of this master of playful and bizarre imagination but also their freedom from any commitment to time and place. Only after 1925 Soviet communism withdrew into a parochial attitude, firmly bound to its place and influenced in the arts more by the 1860s in Russia than by contemporary Europe.

II

In the second stage of Soviet communism, both ties with the outside world and its international and messianic aspects weakened. The vast Eurasian empire withdrew into itself. Its leadership represented by intellectuals like Trotsky and Lunacharsky, who had spent many years abroad, was replaced by a bureaucracy of Stalin's choice who were less in touch with the world at large and did not care much for it. The global revolution had failed in Central Europe and in the Far East. A *cordon sanitaire* of states separating Europe and Russia fell more and more under the sway of reactionary governments. Anti-communist and anti-Russian dictatorships replaced unfamiliar democratic regimes. In the Far East Japan's might was rising. The Communist International, founded in 1919 when unexplored roads into the future seemed open, lost its international character. The communist parties outside the Soviet domain became tools of Soviet Russia's foreign policy. All decisions were made by an executive committee in Moscow. After 1924 the Third International held only two "world" congresses, in 1928 and in 1935. Everywhere the situation became stabilized or changed in a reactionary, past-dominated direction. Soviet communism became, to a growing degree, Russian, and this "Russification" gained with the rapid rise of fascism in the 1930s. Many liberals saw the Soviet Union as backward, more Czarist in its origin than Marxist. Western contempt helped to reawaken the traditional, especially Slavophile, Russian suspicion of the West. Soviet communism began to resemble the "closed" society and world outlook of Russia under Nicholas I.

For the first time the Eurasian empire felt itself seriously threatened simultaneously on two fronts, by the advance of Japan in the East (occupation of Manchuria in 1931) and by the triumph of fascism in the West (the 1931 German parliamentary elections). The new German ideology based its expansionist policy on the view of communism as the embodiment of all evil and at the same time on a contempt for the Slavs. Stalin's tyranny and the strange, incomprehensible show trials in Moscow helped, on their part, to support the Western and fascist judgments.[5]

Two examples of the deep-seated anti-communism and anti-Russianism in the Western world in the early 1940s were the judgments by Lord Kennet and the Swiss Federal Council. In "Hitler and Pilsudski," Lord Kennet wrote, "two personal rulers faced each other with the game [!] in their own hands, no longer directly subject to the gusts of popular passion. . . . It was soon apparent that the German-Polish treaty [of January 26, 1934] was to be no mere gesture." In Switzerland The Federal Council, led by the administrators of the department of foreign affairs, Giuseppe Motta and after 1940 by Marcel Pilet, interpreted Swiss neutrality in a way friendly to Italy, Germany, and Vichy and contemptuous of and hostile to Soviet Russia, with which no normal ties were sought. As late as February 1945 a "harmless" poster by a private "Switzerland-Soviet Union Society" with the inscription "We strive for friendly and trustful relations between our country and the Soviet Union" was officially forbidden and removed. Motta made himself (and thereby Switzerland) the defender of Christianity and occidental civilization (*Abendland*) against communism.

Historiography is in modern times a good indicator of the trend of public opinion. The leading official Soviet historian until 1932, the year of his death, was Mikhail Pokrovsky, who had joined the party in 1905 and became Lenin's friend. The small Soviet encyclopedia described him in 1930 as "the most distinguished Marxist historian, not only in the USSR but in the whole world." Fritz Epstein wrote in 1933 that "Pokrovsky developed an orthodox Marxist interpretation of Russian history which serves today as the historical justification for the Soviet Union." [6]

Pokrovsky sharply rejected Czarist policy toward the non-Russian people of the empire and Czarist aggressive foreign policy in general. He was a declared foe of what Lenin called "Great Russian chauvinism." He regarded Russian rule over foreign peoples as oppression and exploitation. He was an internationalist and scorned the patriotic legends which adorned the works of other, and not only Russian, historians. At the first All-Soviet Conference of Marxist Historians he declared that the annexation of Georgia in 1801 was a crude imperialist grab and could not be defended as protection of Georgia against Turkey or Persia. Nor could, according to Pokrovsky, the war of 1877 against Turkey, which Dostoevsky regarded with such great hopes, be explained as altruistic support for Bulgaria. In reality, it was dictated by the appetite of Russian imperialism. "In the past we Russians—and I am a pure-blooded Great Russian— were the biggest robbers imaginable." Russian history, Pokrovsky emphasized, was not fundamentally different from other, especially Western European, history. It repeated with the time-lag a general development and this time-lag could be explained by Russia's backwardness.

In 1934 Soviet communist leadership quite suddenly and vehemently rejected Pokrovsky's Marxist historiography. In its place a new Russian-centered patriotic historiography was promoted and soon expressed itself in literature and all the arts. The historian Evgenii Tarlé, formerly attacked as "a class enemy, an imperialist and a foe of Bolshevism," was recalled from his enforced exile to write a history of the wars of 1812 and 1854, when Russia was invaded by the West. Special emphasis was now laid upon Russian national history and literature, on the glories of the feudal and Czarist past. A new dignity, unknown under Lenin, was bestowed upon the Russians as Russian people. Soviet communism changed in its outward relations by emphasizing patriotism more than internationalism and in its domestic relations by recognizing a leading position of the Russian people among the equal nationalities of the Soviet Union. It was not a turning back to Czarist times, but a difficult and precarious attempt to balance, in the interest of Soviet communism, and as it was then seen of communism in general, Soviet nationalism and proletarian internationalism, Soviet supranationalism and the reawakened vigor of Russian nationalism as the decisive support of Soviet communism in times of unprecedented danger. The balancing act led inevitably to many ambiguities: only an authoritarian regime could attempt it with some degree of credibility and success. The Soviet Union paid its respect to the rising tide of nationalism all over the globe.

The second German-Russian war in this century was not fought by Stalin to spread communism or world revolution, but to defend the homeland, though the accents were set differently from those in Czarist times. The war of 1914 had been, primarily, a war of German intention;[7] the war of 1941 was undoubtedly a war unleashed by German aggressiveness. In 1941 Soviet foreign policy followed a much more cautious and defensive line than that of the Czarist government in 1914. In his report to the Moscow Soviet on November 6, 1941, Stalin accused the Germans of a "perfidious" attack. Using, on the anniversary of the October revolution, a strange-sounding rhetoric, Stalin declared that Hitler was out "to exterminate the Slav peoples, the Rus-

sians, and Poles . . . ," and the following day he called upon
the Red Army to seek its inspiration in "the manly images of our
great ancestors—Alexander Nevsky, Dmitri Donskoy, Kuzma
Minin, Dmitri Pozharsky, Alexander Suvarov, Mikhail Kutuzov"
—accepting saints of feudal Russia and generals of reactionary
Czardom among the defenders of Russia against the West and
as the ancestors of the supranational army of the Soviet Union.
In his Order of the Day as National Commissar for Defense, on
February 23, 1942, Stalin stressed that the policy of racial equality of the USSR was a factor of strength in comparison to Hitler's
racial policy. When Mikhail Glinka's opera *A Life for the Czar*
(1836) was again performed a century after its composition,
the title was changed to *Ivan Susanin,* the name of the peasant
hero who sacrificed his life in von Rosen's original text, "for the
glory of Holy Russia and its Orthodox Czar" (the first Romanov
prince). Under the communists he sacrificed it for his "beloved
native land."

Soviet communism became, during World War II, Soviet patriotism. For the first quarter of a century the Soviet Union had
used the *International* as its anthem, a song written in French by
Eugène Pottiers in 1871. It was a song common to all socialist
parties in the pre-1914 period. In its Russian text it culminated
in the messianic futuristic vision: *"My nash, my novy mir po-
stroem: Kto byl nichem, tot stanet vsem"* (We are building our
world, the new world, and he who was nothing will become
everything). This vision was in common with the statement in
the *Communist Manifesto* that in the course of the revolution
"the most radical break will be made with the traditional ideas,"
and with the eschatological promise in *Matthew* XIX, 30: "The
first will become the last, and the last one will be the first."

The new Soviet anthem introduced in December 1943, the
year in which the Third International was dissolved, sounded
different. It did not refer to world revolution or to the international proletariat, but to the eternal federation of free republics
into which Russia had been turned. It praised the free fatherland
which was not called Russia but the "rampart" of the friendship
of nations. The song ended with the stereotyped wish of so many

national anthems that the Soviet flag might lead the Soviet people from victory to victory. The anthem has its own melody written by the Soviet composer A. V. Aleksandrov (1888–1946). But in spite of all the respect paid to the equality of the Soviet republics, Russian steadfastness provided the inspiration for the unexpected great victory of the Red Army against the German invaders who were supported by many "Occidental" fellow-soldiers who came from almost all over Europe, from Finland to Italy, from Spain to Rumania.

The primacy of the Russians among the various people of the Soviet Union was recognized by Stalin at the banquet for Red Army commanders on May 25, 1945:

I should like to drink to the health of our Soviet people . . . and first of all to the health of the Russian people. I drink first of all to the health of the Russian people because it is the most outstanding of all the nations forming the Soviet Union. . . . It has won in this war universal recognition as the leading force in the Soviet Union among all the peoples of our country. . . . The confidence of the Russian people in the Soviet government was the decisive force which ensured the historical victory over the enemy of mankind—fascism.

Fascism was identified with Germany and likewise Soviet communism was identified with the Russian people. The first autonomous Soviet state established in Soviet Russia was, in recognition of Marx and Engels, the republic of the Volga Germans, farmers settled there in the eighteenth century. Immediately after the German invasion in 1941 the autonomous republic was abolished, its German inhabitants, irrespective of their class character, were exiled into distant parts of the Soviet Union, and all cultural life was Russified. This example was followed in 1945 by the Czechoslovak and Polish regimes established after the liberation of their countries from German occupation. But in the Soviet Union this measure was taken—like the removal of American citizens of Japanese descent after Pearl Harbor—long before enemy armies approached the Volga region. Another, though very fleeting, moment threw even a stronger light on the attitude of Soviet communism in the desperate war fought for its existence. As late as 1941 textbooks published for the Soviet high schools read:

Lenin and the Bolsheviks worked for the defeat of the Czarist government in this predatory and shameful war [against Japan in 1904–5], because the defeat facilitated the victory of the revolution over Czarism. In one of the leaflets against the war, comrade Stalin wrote about the necessity of defeat: "Let us hope that this war will become a still greater disaster for the Czarist regime than was the Crimean war."

Beria had stressed the "imperialist predatory character" of the war, demanded defeat of the Czarist government, and called the Japanese a "brother people."

Only four years later, on September 2, 1945, the same Stalin broadcast to the Soviet people that

the defeat of the Russian troops in 1904 left grave memories in the minds of our people. It was a dark stain on our country. Our people trusted and awaited the day when Japan would be routed and the stain wiped out. For forty years have we, men of the older generation, waited for this generation, waited for this day. And now this day has come.

Such words would have appeared most improbable in 1920 and again in 1970, as improbable as the short flare-up of Pan-Slavism between 1942 and 1946.[8]

On April 4, 1942, a Slav congress met in Moscow. Dmitri Shostakovich greeted it with a statement: "I am proud to be a Russian, I boast of being a Slav. . . . May all the intellectuals of the glorious family of the Slavonic nations fearlessly fulfill the great mission entrusted to them by history." Pan-Slav propaganda was carried into the diaspora, and an American Slav Congress met in Detroit on April 25, 1942. By the end of 1945 all Slav peoples in Europe, including the Lusatians in eastern Germany, lived in an unprecedented situation: "Liberated" by Soviet communist armies, they potentially formed for the first time a union, based upon a common ideology, which however was not Slavophile, but rather strangely had a German paternity in Marx and Engels.[9]

In December, 1946, a Pan-Slav congress met in Belgrade, a city chosen because at that time Tito's Yugoslavia was regarded as the strongest pillar in the new Slav union under Soviet Russia's leadership. Belgrade seemed predestined to become the seat of the Pan-Slav movement and of the newly established Cominform. In his opening address to the congress Tito asked "What would have happened if the glorious Red Army had not existed?" He ended by a threefold toast, to "Slav solidarity,"—recalling Jan Kolár's interrelations (*Wechselbeziehungen*) in his book published in 1837 in German—then to the greatest Slav brother, which was in essence not Slav but a multiethnic union, and finally to its leader of genius, Stalin, who, of course, was not a Slav either.

But the situation quickly changed. In February, 1948, Czechoslovakia, which President Beneš regarded as a bridge between Soviet communism and Western democracy, between Slavs and other Europeans, became a communist people's republic, and, more significant for the future, in June, 1948, Tito's communist Yugoslavia broke with Stalin's Soviet communism and Cominform, and proclaimed its own road, no longer Moscow-directed, to socialism. The ghost of Pan-Slavism disappeared after 1948 as suddenly as it had reappeared after 1941. Stalin was unable to assert Moscow's formerly uncontested power among all the communist nations and parties, and a new third stage in the relationship of Soviet communism to nationalism, both within the USSR and beyond its frontiers, emerged in the 1950s.

III

The war of 1914 was not, as William II and Chancellor Bethmann Hollweg claimed, a war of the Germans against the Slavs. It was, at least as far as Central and Eastern Europe were concerned, a war to establish German hegemony over all the Slav and non-Slav peoples living between the Baltic and the Aegean seas. Movement toward this goal was resumed with greater clarity and brutality by Hitler in 1939. Even in its milder form this goal demanded a thorough German victory over Russia. It came in 1917–18, but was nullified by the unexpected defeat of Germany in 1918. In this situation, which in 1914 was unforeseeable, when both Germany and Russia did lose the war decisively, the various peoples of the disputed area found a possibility for maximum expansion, at the expense of German and Russian power. This expansion was limited only by the mutual jealousy and conflicting aspirations of those peoples, a state of disunity which provided Hitler with the opportunity for the march eastward and the undoing of the defeat of 1918. For a few years the whole of Central and East Central Europe was subjected to German domination. German hubris changed the situation in 1941. After great suffering the Soviet Union emerged as the victor and the unexpected happened: thanks to Hitler the boundaries of the influence of Soviet communism reached to the gates of Berlin and Vienna.

This unexpected turn of events made out of the Soviet Union, which in 1917 was still a backward country, a potential world power, soon second only to the United States in military armament and industrial technology. For a while (1946–1953), this achievement turned the head of Russian patriotism and of its leader, who succumbed more and more to a paranoia known among Roman caesars and Oriental despots. During that period the superiority of the Russians was emphasized, sometimes to ridiculous lengths, and a strange game was played with words like internationalism, cosmopolitanism, patriotism.[10] The Soviet Union demanded as its share in the worldwide victory the control of Persian Azerbaijan, naval and air bases in Eritrea and Libya, and a military foothold in the Straits of Constantinople. These demands were rejected by the West, whereas the United States established military bases, often storing places for nuclear weapons, in lands neighboring the Soviet Union and China. The Soviet leadership soon gave up demands for similar strategic advantages. With the death of Stalin in 1953, Soviet communism returned to a more realistic policy of restraint, as communist China did later, in not pressing its immediate claims to islands so near its mainland as Quemoy, Matsu, Hongkong, and Macao.

De-Stalinization, officially made manifest by Stalin's successor Nikita Khrushchev in February 1956 before the 20th Congress of the Communist Party of the Soviet Union, led to a policy of greater flexibility in relations with other nations, communist or

SOVIET COMMUNISM AND NATIONALISM

non-communist. No longer was the Kremlin the undisputed head of communists everywhere. Soon the Kremlin recognized, though reluctantly, that the insistence on Soviet communism as the only valid model for all communist theory and activity could not be enforced. The reason for this fundamental change was, strangely enough, the great triumph of communism on the world stage. No longer was the Soviet Union the only communist state, one which could be kept behind its narrow limits. As World War I had created the conditions for the rise of communism in the Russian empire, so World War II created the conditions for its expansion. By 1949 thirteen communist states existed and later, with Cuba, fourteen of them, each one with its own historical background, geographic situation, and national customs, which were fundamentally different from those of Russia.

Even before 1956 this situation had been tacitly acknowledged. The Union of Soviet Socialist Republics did not expand as a further step toward a world union. It was no longer even regarded as its center or nucleus. The fundamental messianic aspect of the early stage of Soviet communism was practically abandoned. Only those Ukrainian and Belorussian territories ruled before 1939 by Poland, Czechoslovakia, and Rumania were united with the Soviet Ukraine and Soviet Belorussia. Former component parts of the Russian empire, the Baltic provinces and Bessarabia, were incorporated as national republics into the Soviet Union, a "normal" though not always wise or generous procedure on the part of victorious states throughout history. These provinces had become part of Russia long before the awakening of a national movement. The attitude toward Finland proved more generous.[11]

On the other hand, Yugoslavia, Bulgaria, Poland, Czechoslovakia, Hungary, and Albania remained outside the Union, theoretically fully sovereign states, concluding economic treaties and military alliances with the Soviet Union as with other states. As early as May 26, 1955, Khrushchev had visited Yugoslavia, and immediately upon his arrival at the Belgrade airport expressed recognition of the right to separate development, of specifically national roads to communism, of "Titoism" or, as it became known, "national communism." Thus, Marxist-Leninist states, different in their methods and positions from Soviet communism, emerged as a characteristic factor in the third stage of the relationship between communism and nationalism. The Soviet model of federation as a solution to intrastate nationality problems was followed by Yugoslavia, to a certain degree by China, and finally in 1968 by Czechoslovakia. In 1956 the communist leadership in Poland and in Hungary was assumed by Wladyslaw Gomulka and by Janos Kadar, both of whom had been imprisoned for years as "Titoists."

In many ways the communist regimes, not only in Yugoslavia but also throughout Central and East Central Europe, followed their "own" line. The style of life varied from country to country. At the end of May 1970, a meeting of the Union of Hungarian Writers criticized, through its president Joszef Darvas, Stalinist cultural policy of the pre-Kadar years, and its dogmatic and narrow-minded interpretation of "socialist realism." In contrast to the Stalinist position, it was claimed, the present cultural policy was broad-minded. It had accepted the existence of rival trends, at the same time providing for "a quiet atmosphere" favorable to cultural achievements.[12] Except for what seemed to the Soviet leadership as valid strategic reasons (Hungary in 1956, Czechoslovakia in 1968), it refrained from open interference. The victory of 1945 and the new *cordon sanitaire* gave to the post-Stalinist Soviet regimes a feeling of greater security. All communist regimes sought new cultural and economic ties with the West and the emerging, so-called Third World. The isolationism of strictly closed societies gave way to more open systems.

Rumania under Nicolae Ceausescu set an example of "independent" foreign policy, while keeping the life of the country strictly on Marxist-Leninist lines. The visit by President Richard Nixon on August 2, 1969 was a "sensation" but did not change the course of policy. The variety and diversity in the communist camp continued, based upon national differences, contrary to the expectation that communism as an ideology "has a unique capacity of unifying mankind," claims formerly made for Christianity and Islam, and so far unfulfilled in every case.

Of the fast-growing, closer contact between communist and

non-communist nations, let us refer only to historiography, a field probably more exposed to divisive influences than other fields of scholarship. Soviet historians first participated in the tenth International Congress of the Historical Sciences in Rome in 1955. The differences then were still very marked. They diminished slowly in the following congresses (Stockholm 1960, Vienna 1965), and the thirteenth congress was held in late summer 1970 in Moscow. Communist and non-communist historians also met in several conferences dealing with the history of the Habsburg empire. I was present at the one held at the University of Indiana in 1966, and Professor R. John Rath of Rice University attended those at Bratislava (1967), Vienna (1968), and Austin, Texas (1969). He wrote about them:

During the past few years communications between historians of Eastern, Central and Western Europe, and the United States have continually improved. Almost entirely absent . . . were the ideological, political, and national polemics between Marxian-Socialist and Western historians which all too frequently hindered the free and honest exchange of ideas. . . . At Bratislava scholars from all ideological camps demonstrated much greater willingness to liberate themselves from the narrow confines of their own particular national and political (views). . . . In Vienna the next fall (1968), in spite of the . . . developments in Central Europe . . . , there seemed to be an even greater readiness to understand the other person's point of view than there had been in Bratislava.[13]

Neither within the Soviet Union nor in the relationship of the communist states with each other was the problem of nationalism successfully solved. In that respect the development within the communist dictatorships followed the general trend of nationalism, which has not been diminished but accentuated as the result of the war, and of the dissolution of the Western empires. To discuss the various definitions, with which communist theoreticians have tried to accommodate the development in European communism and in the Third World to dialectical insight bears hardly any fruit. National tensions remain in the Soviet Union and in the other European states which turned communist after 1945, though the general situation there has improved, compared with that after 1918. The *Herrenvolk* concepts of Poles, Serbs, and Czechs have disappeared, and that of the Russians has been wisely controlled since Khrushchev came to power. Naturally, tensions remained, for instance over Transylvania between Hungarians and Rumanians, over Macedonia between Serbs and Bulgarians. Among the Russians, a small group around the journal *Molodaia gvardiia* has revived Slavophile and populist (*Narodnik*) attitudes, praising the Russian peasant and despising Western technological civilization. National communism in a small and backward country like Albania could declare its complete independence from, and its contemptuous hostility to, the Moscow leadership. In this case the dialectic of nationalism and international relations can well be studied: originally a Yugoslav "satellite," Albania used the Stalin-Tito struggle to enhance its independence and with Soviet help joined the Warsaw Pact and the United Nations. With the improvement of Soviet-Yugoslav relations after 1953, Albania turned against both as revisionist or anti-Stalinist. It forced the Soviet Union to abandon its submarine base at Durrës, broke diplomatic relations with Russia, and later left the Warsaw Pact and instead signed a pact of military and economic assistance with China. In spite of its old hatred of Yugoslavia and of recent sharp condemnation of Tito's revisionism, fierce Albanian nationalism went so far in July 1969 as to declare that "the Albanian people will without hesitation help the Yugoslav people in their resistance to aggression" [by the Soviet Union].

On the other hand, Bulgaria offered the example of an emphasis on native nationalism entirely compatible with a pro-Soviet attitude in politics and ideology. At the Congress of the Bulgarian Writers in May 1968, the party leader Todor Zhivkov declared, "Today this national spirit is naturally emerging with the great cause of the Bulgarian communist party." The poet Dora Gabe called for "the unity of past and present," and the writer Stefan Dichev wished to encourage "the historical novel which, by unveiling the past, must stimulate patriotism." Professor Pavel Matev wrote in *Lituraturen Front* of May 24:

An art work is valuable to mankind when it is a national product. The poetry of each nation must have a national character and should not resemble the poetry of other nations. . . . Mankind is not composed of individuals . . . but of individual nations, each with its own specific psychology, mould and class structure, which are created and determined by historical circumstances.

The issue of June 4 features excerpts of a letter by Zhivkov, congratulating the painter Tsanko Lavrenov on his seventieth birthday for exalting "the beauties and grandiose past of our fatherland." [14]

On the whole, the relationship of Soviet communism to nationalism, at home and abroad, has changed not only from the attitude assumed in 1917 but also from that which prevailed under Stalin. Though the Soviet Union has grown into one of the two superpowers, by far the weaker one, it seems to have learned what could not be clearly seen from the Kremlin fortress—the limitation of power and of its power within the communist world. No longer could the Kremlin dictate. Like other powers in this world of diversity and limitations, it had to negotiate. The Soviet communist leaders, as did the leaders of other communist states, began to travel widely and to break the partly self-imposed isolation. One of the turning points in this process was the visit of Soviet leaders under Khrushchev to Poland in mid-October 1956 to influence the course of Polish communist policy. Khrushchev yielded; the Polish communists "were allowed to shape their own policy at their own pace," yet "when Gomulka's government obtained full sovereignty, Poland's alliance with the Soviet Union was strengthened." [15]

This "normalization" of relationships among communist parties was noticed by the old and experienced Italian communist leader Palmiro Togliatti, who was the first to use the word "polycentrism" for the post-Stalinist phase, replacing the former "monolithic" form. In a memorandum which Togliatti wrote just before his death in August 1964 in the Soviet Union, and which was published the following month by the Italian party, he insisted on the independence of all parties from central guidance and rejected any creation of a new centrally controlled International. He expressed his support for Khrushchev's anti-Stalinist revisionism and warned that the "regime of restrictions and suppressions of democratic and general freedom" had not yet entirely disappeared.

The complexity and fluidity of the relationship between Soviet communism and nationalism have been further, and very profoundly, influenced by the communist movement taking over China in 1949. That was not the work of Soviet communism. Indigenous Chinese forces under an indigenous leader who regarded himself, to say the least, as the equal of Soviet leadership, won against an ineffectual and corrupt Chinese government. In the course of the 1960s the competitive struggle between Soviet and Chinese communism became more and more embittered. On February 4, 1964, the Chinese official party organ *Jen Min Jih Pao* charged that the Soviet Union wished to arrive at an agreement with the United States to divide the world and that the men in the Kremlin "regard U.S. imperialism—the most ferocious enemy of the world—as their most reliable friend."

This struggle was not confined to the two communist giants. In many communist parties pro-Chinese groups were formed. Of the Asian communist states, the Mongolian People's Republic was an ally of the Soviet Union, whereas the Korean Democratic Republic and the Democratic Republic of Vietnam tried to maintain their neutrality as against both powers. The Soviet leadership made great efforts to call a communist world congress, originally with the intention of forming a united front against China and of reasserting Moscow's leadership. When this conference finally met in Moscow in June 1969, it was only a partial success for Soviet communism. Five communist governing parties (China, North Korea, North Vietnam, Albania, and Yugoslavia) were not represented, and Cuba sent only an observer. Nevertheless, sixty-nine parties signed the final declaration. There was unanimity about several obvious positions: the plans for celebrating Lenin's centenary in 1970, support of the North Vietnamese and Vietcong, condemnation of Israeli aggression, and retention of the present borders in Europe. China's right to Taiwan and to membership in the United Nations was recognized, but no communist party or trend was condemned or excommunicated and no central leadership was established. The relationship among communist countries and parties was defined as a "complex historical process," based upon recognition of proletarian internationalism, the equality and sovereignty of all countries, and noninterference in each others' internal affairs. It was stressed that the nonparticipation of some parties in the conference would not affect cooperative efforts with those in attendance. To a degree unknown in previous communist meetings, there was openness and freedom of discussion and avoidance of mutual vituperation.

Thus, in the last fifty-two years Soviet communism and the world at large have changed greatly. We have tried to distinguish three stages in the development of communism as a ruling power in Russia and as a missionary force in mankind. Like all historical divisions, the one which we presented is only an approximation of the perplexing complexity of reality. The last fifty-two years were full of astonishing changes, and this process, like history itself, has not come to an end. Communist leaders have not been more prescient or wiser than those whose loyalties belong to other ideologies or religions. All are undergoing more rapid changes today than ever before, and this on a much wider geographical basis. Arnold J. Toynbee concludes that "the factor that has played the greatest part in defeating communist hopes and expectations—and this both in the Soviet Union and everywhere else—has been the triumph of nationalism. Communism has been worsted by nationalism as decisively as liberal democracy has been." [16] This may be an overstatement, but it contains an undeniable truth.

NOTES

1. Ernest Renan, *L'Avenir de la Science. Pensées de 1848* (Paris: Calmann Lévy, 1890), pp. 25, 494.
2. Romain Rolland, *Jean Christophe* (Paris: 1926), Vol. X, p. 202; Hans Kohn, "A Turning Point," *Journal of the History of Ideas,*

Vol. XXX, No. 2 (April, 1969), pp. 283–90; Hans Kohn, "The Crisis in European Thought and Culture," Jack J. Roth (ed.), *World War I, a Turning Point in Modern History* (New York: Knopf, 1967), pp. 25–46.

3. F. M. Dostoevsky, *The Possessed,* Vol. VII, part II, ch. 1; Ernest J. Simmons, *Dostoevsky, The Making of a Novelist* (New York: Oxford University Press, 1940), pp. 296 ff.; Dostoevsky's letter to A. F. Blagonravov of Dec. 19, 1880; Hans Kohn, "Dostoyevsky and Danilevsky: Nationalist Messianism," Ernest J. Simmons (ed.), *Continuity and Change in Russian and Soviet Thought* (Cambridge: Harvard University Press, 1955), pp. 500–16.

4. *Vos'moi s"ezd RKP (b), 18–23 marta 1919 g.* (Moscow: Partiinoe Izdatel'stvo, 1933), pp. 107–108.

5. W. F. Reddaway *et al.* (eds.), *The Cambridge History of Poland* (Cambridge: Cambridge University Press, 1941), pp. 607 f.; Edgar Bonjour, *Geschichte der schweizerischen Neutralität,* Vol. V (Basel: Helbing & Lichtenhahn, 1970), pp. 399–409.

6. N. Meshcheriakov, "Pokrovskii," *Malaia sovetskaia entsiklopediia* Vol. 6 (1930), pp. 662–63; Fritz Epstein, "Pokrovsky, Mikhail Nikolaevich," *Encyclopedia of the Social Sciences* Vol. 12 (1934), pp. 181–82; Fritz Epstein, "Die marxistische Geschichtswissenschaft in der Sowietunion seit 1927," *Jahrbücher für Kultur und Geschichte der Slaven* n.s. VI, Heft 1 (Breslau: Priebatsch, 1930), pp. 78–203; Anatole G. Mazour and Herman E. Bateman, "Recent Conflicts in Soviet Historiography," *Journal of Modern History,* XXIV (March 1952), pp. 56–68; C. E. Black (ed.), *Rewriting Russian History: Soviet Interpretations of Russia's Past* (New York: Research Program on the U.S.S.R., F. A. Praeger, 1956).

7. Hajo Holborn, *A History of Modern Germany, 1840–1945* (New York: Alfred A. Knopf, 1969), p. 418.

8. I. V. Stalin, *O velikoi otechestvennoi voine Sovetskogo Soiuza* 5th edition (Moscow: Gosudarstvennoe Izdatel'stvo Politicheskoi Literatury, 1946), pp. 26 f., 36, 42; see also *Istoriia SSSR* III (for tenth grade) 2nd ed. (Moscow: 1941), p. 29. The new edition of this volume in 1946 changed the text and quoted Stalin's speech of 1945. See, for the original attitude, Lavrenti P. Beria, *On the History of the Bolshevik Organization in Transcaucasia,* tr. from the Russian (New York: International Publishers, 1939), pp. 44–46.

9. Hans Kohn, "The Impact of Panslavism on Central Europe,"

Reflections on Modern History (Princeton: Van Nostrand, 1963), pp. 164–74.

10. Georg von Rauch, "Die Sowjetische Geschichtsschreibung heute," *Die Welt als Geschichte* Heft 4, Vol. 11 (Stuttgart: W. Kohlhammel Verlag, 1951), pp. 249–62; Solomon S. Schwarz, "Revising the History of Russian Colonialism," *Foreign Affairs* (April 1952), pp. 488–93; M. H. Ertuerk, "Was geht in Turkestan vor?" *Ost Probleme* (1950), pp. 1010–16.

11. See on Finland, Marvin Rintala in Hans Rogger and Eugen Weber (eds.), *The European Right* (Berkeley and Los Angeles: University of California Press, 1965), pp. 408–42.

12. *Neue Zürcher Zeitung,* Fernausgabe (May 27, 1970), No. 143.

13. *Austrian History Yearbook* Vols. IV–V (Houston: Rice University, 1970), p. 517. See there pp. 487–97, the review of Pèter Hanàk (ed.), *Die nationale Frage in der osterreichisch-ungarischen Monarchie* (Budapest: Verlag der Ungarischen Akademee der Wissenschaften, 1966) and of Vladimir Dedijer, *The Road to Sarajevo* (New York: Simon and Schuster, 1966).

14. "Current Developments: Bulgaria," *East Europe* (New York, 1968), no. 7, pp. 43 f.

15. Hugh Seton-Watson, "Nationalism and Imperialism," Royal Institute for International Affairs, *The Impact of the Russian Revolution, 1917–1967. The influence of Bolshevism on the world outside Russia* (London: Oxford University Press, 1967), pp. 169, 177.

16. *The Impact of the Russian Revolution, 1917–1967, Ibid.*

ZBIGNIEW BRZEZINSKI

POLITICAL IMPLICATIONS OF
SOVIET NATIONALITY PROBLEMS*

Nationality problems are critically important in the evaluation of domestic Soviet reality today, and I feel very strongly that American scholarship on the Soviet Union as a whole has tended to minimize or simply to ignore them altogether. What I propose to do is raise four very general questions relating to political aspects of Soviet nationality problems.

The first of these questions, very simply put, is: What is the actual political situation in the Soviet Union, insofar as the nationalities are concerned? This prompts the subsidiary query: How is the political situation evaluated by the Soviet leaders themselves? What is the Soviet assessment of the political state of the Soviet nationalities? There is a great deal of evidence pointing to the fact that a rather active debate on these issues has grown up in the Soviet Union in the course of the last decade. The outlines of that discussion are probably well-known to every Soviet specialist. They involve the issue of whether the nationalities are merging or coming together. Obviously, there are very important, substantive differences between these two concepts.

In reviewing Soviet literature, it is striking to see the degree to which these sources emphasize the existence of nonantagonistic contradictions in relationships between Soviet nationalities. This implies that the possibility of antagonistic contradictions existed in the relatively recent past, certainly prior to the 1917 revolution, but perhaps even afterward. In considering Khrushchev's reforms

* This is an edited transcript of an informal presentation made to the Seminar on Soviet Nationality Problems, November 4, 1969.

developed for the Soviet Union, particularly those of the 1960s, I was also impressed by the degree to which some of Khrushchev's efforts to revamp Soviet political institutions were designed to blur the dividing lines between the Soviet nationalities. Certainly the schemes for establishing new party and governmental bodies in the Transcaucasus, in Central Asia, and in the Baltic republics seemed to move considerably beyond the framework of an international relationship based on the continuing existence of separate states. This would have been in keeping with the merger concept, the eventual communist solution of the nationality question in the Soviet Union, rather than with the notion of the coming together of more distinctive, more heterogeneous nations.

Another way of probing the question of the political situation is to try to make at least some tentative assessment, from the outside, of where the different nationalities of the Soviet Union might stand in terms of some highly generalized spectrum pertaining to the political expression of the sense of national identity. I can imagine such a spectrum involving four major stages: beginning at one extreme would be the biological assimilation by the dominant group, by the Russians. Next to it would come the absorption, by a superior, or more-developed, if you will, culture. Beyond that would appear some sort of social and economic integration on the basis of the preservation of a relatively exclusive, highly developed national culture. Then, at the far end of the spectrum, a nationalism, potentially secessionist in its political aspirations and attitudes, would be indicated.

In order to make some tentative preliminary and inescapably arbitrary judgment about where to range the different nationalities on the spectrum, we have to ask several subsidiary questions. Mainly, what is the level of economic development of a given nation or nationality? If it were highly developed we would most likely place it at a different point than if it were relatively underdeveloped and were being developed during the process of assimilation. How intensively and extensively has its national culture been developed? To what extent has the particular nationality a sense of art, history, tradition, and development of the national consciousness? What specifically is the degree of national tradition—nationalism in the political sense—possessed by the given nationality? What is the degree of geographic cohesion of such a nation or nationality? What evidence do we have of its secessionist aspirations in the past or present? If we may use these four or five categories, though there will doubtless be others, in making a judgment, perhaps we could say fairly arbitrarily that the Balts and the Ukrainians, by way of example, might be potentially the most secessionist of nationalities.

I would say by way of example, and again fairly arbitrarily and subjectively, that the Georgians might be considered an example of a relatively integrated, exclusive, national, cultural identity, not intensely secessionist—for a variety of historical as well as geographical reasons—but certainly much more self-contained than most. In many respects they have a subjective sense of intense superiority vis-à-vis the Russians. On the other hand, absorption by a more developed culture might apply, tentatively, to the Moldavians and the Belorussians, who, for linguistic and other reasons, may be absorbed by the Russians. Biological assimilation certainly threatens the Kazakhs, for today they comprise only one-third of the population of their own republic. So this may be one way of seeking the answer to the question of what the actual political condition of the nationalities in the Soviet Union is, but certainly it does not exhaust the process of finding the answer.

Beyond that, one has to ask himself, still concerning these nationalities—assuming that it is right to put the Ukrainians and the Balts at one extreme of the spectrum—what the groups are that press for such an attitude, what groups are less involved, less activist? Here, again by way of a tentative generalization, it can be suggested that the intellectuals, the humanists, the pseudo-intellectuals (school teachers, run-of-the-mill journalists, and the like), tend to be the more nationalistic elements in the different republics, across the entire spectrum. At the far end the most assimilationist, integrationist, or cooperative would be the engineers, technicians, scientists, those who might largely be called the modernizing elite. This could be particularly applicable to the less-developed countries.

The second general question which I would like to raise for

discussion is the elusive but highly important problem of the impact of the nationality dilemma on the political evolution of the Soviet system itself. What is the influence of the nationality question on the future prospects of political change, or perhaps of its absence in the Soviet Union? Here again evidence, though limited, elusive, and occasionally contradictory, nonetheless exists to an extent. The language debate of 1958 concerning the highly controversial Article 15 of the Soviet Constitution did involve, on an appreciable scale, the participation of the leading political elites of the different republics, with prime ministers and first secretaries participating actively, in addition to the more articulate elites of the societies, particularly in the literary and journalistic fields. So we do know that there is a potential for active political involvement in the process of change of the political elite itself, derived from national identification or self-identification of the political elite.

During the ill-fated Council of National Economy (*Sovnarkhoz*) era of Soviet economic organization (1957–1964), there was a great deal of evidence of localism (*mestnichestvo*), not only geographical localism, but of localism involving a more national orientation, including national claims on resources that were being distributed or consumed. Certainly in the Soviet press we have seen evidence of concern about this. One of the criticisms of the *Sovnarkhoz* arrangement was that it began to strengthen localism on a nationality basis. If there is economic decentralization in the future, I think it will quite deliberately not be allowed to coincide with regional, national boundaries, as, for example, it has in Yugoslavia, where major problems have arisen in economic planning and political relationships between the different republics.

The failure of the Soviet Union to proceed with the constitutional reforms which have long been promised is possibly associated with the complexity of the problem of central versus federal or national arrangements. Given the degree of conflicting aspirations, you would be opening a Pandora's box of nationality aspirations by trying to rewrite the constitution as a whole. Perhaps part of the Soviet reticence in dealing with this problem relates to the realization that a constitutional reform would reopen the entire issue of the distribution of power between central government and local republics or nationality institutions. This would occur in the context of perhaps a more legitimate claim than presently allowed, on the part of some of them, to a larger distribution of power. All of which leads to a hypothesis, that on the whole, the nationality question in the Soviet Union has a profoundly conservative influence upon the prospects of political evolution in the Soviet Union.

The nationality question acts as one of the major sources of restraint inhibiting the Soviet political elite and other relevant groups from embarking on a road of constitutional as well as broader political reform which many groups otherwise, for reasons specifically associated with their own character and identity, would be inclined to follow. Because the nationality question tends to make the political elite conservative, the effectiveness of appeals by any would-be Soviet liberalizer could be diminished very significantly by the impact of nationality problems on the state of mind and the political aspirations of the political elite itself. It induces in the political elite a considerable preoccupation with the maintenance of unity. It is this awareness which makes the Soviet—really Russian—political elite conservative. For them the nationality question is an extraordinarily sensitive one. This is quite understandable, because of the extraordinarily diversified mix of the population, and because population growth will soon leave the Russians in the minority. Russian leaders realize that to take the reform route now is potentially to jeopardize the preeminence and leadership which today, according to most statistics, is primarily in Russian and to some extent in Ukrainian hands. Therefore, they are less inclined than, say, the Serbs to release their hold on central instrumentalities. (For that matter, the Russians are in an infinitely superior political position vis-à-vis the nationalities in the Soviet Union in comparison with that of the Serbs vis-à-vis the Croats, the Slovenes, and others. Certainly in the Russian case both numbers and economic power reinforce political domination. In the case of the Serbs it can be argued that power in terms of such things as economic development and cultural development conflicted with their control of political power and was a source of major tension in the 1930s, and in fact continues to be to this day in Yugoslavia, even though in a setting far more elastic, far more flexible, far more decentralized than before.)

Thus, as an answer to the second large question, I would say that Soviet evolution, on the whole, is hampered by the persistence of nationality problems. In speculating about evolution in Soviet society, whatever framework one applies, ranging from the kind of economic determinism that has been characteristic of Isaac Deutscher or others, to more voluntaristic theories, it seems to me imperative to take into account—to a far greater extent than has heretofore been the case—in Western theories of Soviet political change the role, positive or negative, of the nationality factor. For reasons which I have tried to expound, this nationality consideration has a profoundly conservative impact, inhibiting the kind of change which is usually associated with the words democratization, liberalization, and decentralization. This operates very strongly in the psyche of the dominant political and even in the dominant national elites in the Soviet Union.

The third large question which I would like to raise is this: What are the long-range evolutionary prospects or, for that matter, even more than evolutionary—what are the long-range prospects? What are the alternative paths that one can really examine and consider in relation to Soviet political development? How far can it go? Let me ask the most sensitive question immediately. Under what conditions is secessionism possible in the Soviet Union? Under what conditions might the secessionist potential which is at one extreme on the spectrum be translated into political reality?

By way of seeking an answer, one has to ask some subsidiary questions. Is a domestic crisis a sufficient condition for allowing secessionism to become a reality? By domestic crisis I really mean something profound, a paralysis of leadership which incapacitates it from taking effective action on the domestic scene and, more than that, which forces it to abandon or drop control. This means a cross-institutional conflict, a conflict between the key institutions, the police, the army, a division in the elite as a whole, loss of values, ideological demoralization, and uncertainty about which way to head. All these are conditions normally associated with a prerevolutionary situation. I also mean by crisis a very significant economic stagnation in the Soviet Union, one involving loss of economic momentum, absence of innovation, perhaps indeed even conditions approximating those of Czechoslovakia in the early 1960s when there was a net decline in the actual growth of the gross national product.

Now, would these conditions suffice to activate and to make a secessionist aspiration politically significant? My judgment on the whole would still be negative. Even under such conditions it would be very difficult in any given nationality to mobilize the kind of activism on a popular level which would be necessary while avoiding the sort of reactive, defensive, response which I think secessionism would evoke, particularly from the dominant Russian majority.

Even in conditions of crisis, the framework of the Soviet system, the interrelationship, political and economic, between different republics, is sufficiently inflexible and tight to make effective secessionism extremely unlikely. Secessionism, as a realistic alternative for the future, is only likely in the condition of some form of a combination between domestic crisis and an international calamity. One has to make a personal judgment regarding the extent to which one considers that to be a realistic alternative. But, short of some major collapse combining domestic crisis with a major international conflict directly challenging perhaps even the existence of the Soviet system as a whole, I do not see in the next decade or so that sufficient degree of dynamism and viability, even among those groups which we have put on the extreme of the spectrum, for effective secessionist capability.

If this hypothesis is right, what is left? Is Czechoslovakia, or Yugoslavia, a model for the next twenty years? That is to say, will there be a redistribution of political power, redefinition of the constitutional order, a greater sharing of economic and political authority in the Soviet Union? What works against it, certainly, is a rather paramount coalition. First of all, the very tradition of the Soviet system in the last fifty years has a certain weight which cannot be disregarded. This tradition is contrary to a development like this, which would be far reaching and fundamental in scope. Certainly the vested interests of the elites seem on the whole to be against it, to be likely to oppose it. Second, and this is not to be discounted even though it is a highly intangible, elusive consideration, the imperial genius of the Russian people has to be taken into account. The Russians represent one of the several successful imperial nations in our contemporary history. Surely they stand on a par with the British, the French, and in many respects perhaps are superior to them in terms of skill, expansion of authority, capacity to rule effectively both directly, and, more important, indirectly with a certain subtlety and nuance which is very significant in effectively maintaining an imperial relationship. The Russians have not lost that talent. Clearly, they are effectively demonstrating it to this day, and one would have to envisage a very fundamental reversal in historic patterns and relationships in order to discount this factor, among others.

If the Soviet Union continues to grow economically, I would expect in more and more of its nations and nationalities an ascendancy of the scientists over the humanists. In assessing the present position of the different nationalities on our spectrum I suggested that in addition to assigning them positions on this spectrum it was important to define the different groups within the different nationalities which might press for secession versus the other extreme, assimilation. We saw that the non-Russian engineers and the technical modernizing elite were more likely than the humanists to be susceptible to close, interwoven relationships with the Russians. Hence, if economic development and scientific innovation continue, these elites may possibly become more ascendant within the different nationalities. Thus, in the foreseeable future we are going to observe more, rather than less, assimilation and perhaps more intensive rather than less Russification. Soviet leaders, under the circumstances, perhaps may be inclined to press even more rapidly for assimilation.

Nonetheless, I certainly would be very surprised if the Soviet Union were able to avoid altogether the kind of dilemmas posed by the need for a larger framework and the yearning for more intimate communities that other multinational societies are today facing. When you look at what is happening in England, Belgium, Canada, and Ireland, you see two trends which are seemingly contradictory, but in a sense are quite logically interrelated. One is toward larger cooperation in ever broader spheres of involvement. This is now possible, and modern communication and economic patterns dictate them.

Increasingly, you see Walloons and Flemish, or Scots and English seeking integration on a larger plane, for example, throughout Europe. At the same time such groups express their yearning for unity through more distinctive, more self-oriented, more linguistically and religiously formed narrow communities. And this could very easily happen in the Soviet Union as well, but if it did happen I would see it as a source of friction and tension rather than of fundamental change.

Let me conclude by posing the fourth general question for discussion: What are the implications of all of this for American policy? We must not spend too much time on this question, because we are not in the business of making policy, but to some extent the problem does have interesting, intellectual complications. In some of my advisory and governmental work I felt strongly that, on the whole, the formal position of the United States has tended to correspond fairly closely to the prevailing view in American scholarship. American scholars generally have minimized the significance of the nationality problems of the Soviet Union. Also, I was struck that in some of our broadcasting into the Soviet Union nationality problems had been treated with a tremendous degree of self-restraint, and in the American government planning process any discussion of nationality problems in the Soviet Union was almost nonexistent. Moreover, efforts to stimulate it would meet with enormous opposition which first operated on the level of denying that the problems did exist and, when that could no longer be sustained, by arguing that the problems had better not exist. Consequently, in the last twenty years, with the exception of a very short-lived period of the most intense cold war in the late 1940s and early 1950s, Soviet nationality problems tended to be swept under the rug in American thinking.

Continuing to ignore them seems unrealistic because the problems are becoming increasingly important, and in many respects are, I believe, crucial to the future evolution of the Soviet Union. Developments in the Soviet Union in turn are vital to the future pattern of American-Soviet relations. Given this integral relationship, it obviously affects American foreign policy very directly. Playing up anti-Russian feelings would entail extremely high risks for the expanding areas of American-Soviet accommodation. That would be a kind of belated equivalent to the totally unsuccessful Soviet efforts to identify the USSR, for example, with a separate black republic in the American South. These attempts characterized the Soviet position in the 1930s. Such attempts would certainly stimulate enormous Soviet resentment and, if they operated very directly on the overt level of aiding and encouraging various secessionist movements, would stimulate retrogressive tendencies in the Soviet Union. These in turn would jeopardize the rather limited areas of accommodation that have already been obtained, threatening their possible expansion and certainly stimulating among the dominant Soviet population group, the Russians, a feeling of intense resentment against the United States.

This leaves open, basically, a compromise approach to our relations with the USSR. Since the nationality question in the Soviet Union is fundamental, since the nationalities comprise 50 percent of the Soviet people or more, since a resolution of the nationality question is critical to the future evolution of the Soviet Union, the nationality problems have to be faced squarely. And eventually, if there is going to be gradual decentralization in the Soviet system, then a redefinition of the relationship between the center and the localities has to take place.

To the extent that the United States has a variety of informal means for stimulating a greater degree of responsible self-consciousness among the nationalities of the USSR, efforts in that direction seem to me justifiable. Obviously it need not involve encouragement of secessionism, but can involve very deliberate efforts to make the Soviet elites, both Russian and non-Russian, aware of the way in which different nations at a relatively high stage of their development have sought to resolve the problem of multinational existence. This suggests Switzerland, Yugoslavia, and a variety of other nations or relevant models. They have sought to solve their problems on the basis of far more complicated and elastic constitutional arrangements than those prevailing in the USSR, and this is the path that eventually—and we can certainly state it explicitly—the Soviet Union could pursue. This would not then be a direct, head-on attack, nor a revival of cold war strategy. But it would also no longer be a refusal to recognize a situation which, in my view, constitutes one of the crucial realities of the Soviet Union, one directly related to the problems of change on which much of the Soviet-American relationship depends.

JOHN N. HAZARD

STATUTORY RECOGNITION OF
NATIONALITY DIFFERENCES
IN THE USSR

The centenary of Lenin's birth provided an opportunity in 1970 for a review of the legislative activity of the member republics of the Soviet federation. Thirteen years had passed since the republics had regained authority to draft codes of law. Although Stalin's federal constitution of 1936 remained in force, its provisions centralizing the legislative process had been amended in 1957 to reinstate the powers granted the republics by the first federal constitution of 1923.

The 1936 constitution as originally promulgated provided in Article 14 that "The jurisdiction of the USSR, as represented by its higher organs of state power and organs of state administration, covers: (u) legislation concerning the judicial system and judicial procedure; criminal and civil codes." The 1957 amendment changes the 1936 text to read in section (u) "Definition of the fundamentals of legislation on the judicial system and judicial procedure and the fundamentals of civil and criminal legislation." Under the 1957 reformulation, the federal parliament was again to establish only "fundamental principles" for the various branches of law, and the republics were empowered to enact codes establishing details. The 1923 constitution, in its Article 1, had authorized the federal authority "(m) to establish fundamental principles of exploitation and use of the land; (o) to establish the fundamentals of the judicial system and procedure as well as the civil and criminal legislation of the union; (p) to establish the fundamental laws regarding labor." [1]

To contemporary Soviet jurists the revision is understood as recognition that differences in the cultures of the various nationalities making up the Soviet Union require distinctive legislation in each republic.[2] While the federal parliament, its executive, and the judiciary it appoints establish the norms necessary to the preservation of socialism and the evolution to communism, the national forms are not identical and need not be. The legislative relationship between the central authorities and those of the republics embodies the implementation of Stalin's time-honored Marxist-Leninist formula, "National in form and proletarian in content." [3]

A Soviet writer cited Lenin in reviewing legislative practice during preparations for the leader's centennial of 1970.[4] Lenin had declared that implementing the concepts of nationality policy and democratic centralism would constantly involve more active realization of "the possibility of complete and unimpeded development, not only of distinctive local characteristics but also of opening matters for discussion locally, of asserting local initiatives, of establishing differing roads, methods and means of moving toward the common goal." [5]

The centennial year was well suited to reconsideration of the place of the republics in the legislative process. Thirteen years had passed since constitutional restitution of the codification authority of the republics, and six since Nikita Khrushchev had been ousted from his position as First Secretary of the Communist Party and Chairman of the Council of Ministers. His removal had represented, in part, a repudiation of his policy of transferring to the republics most of the operating functions and some of the planning functions previously performed by the economic ministries of the central government.[6] Recentralization of much of the economic life of the country in 1965 [7] had strengthened simultaneously the hands of those who had shared Stalin's predilection for centralization of other aspects of Soviet policymaking. It was no secret that, as skilled cadres had been developed in increasing numbers in the republics, some of them had become restless at what they perceived to be a trend toward curtailment of their opportunities.[8] Outsiders can hardly measure the extent of restlessness which emerged, but events suggest that the nationalities, and especially the Ukrainians, thought the time had come for a reformation of the partnership with the Russians to permit a broader sharing of policymaking functions.

Theorists within the USSR had been trying for several years to redefine the relationship between the center and the republics.[9] They had sought to describe just what was the sovereignty of the republics so as to give substance to the formula that the special interests of each nationality should be recognized without departure from the basic premise that in a working class state there can be no irreconcilable conflicts of an ethnic nature. The year 1970 became an occasion again to update Karl Marx's formula that the workers can know no "fatherland," for class interests must take precedence over those of the "nation."

A reading of history suggests that Lenin, in facing the nationality aspirations of his time, gave clear indication of his order of priorities.[10] He was a centralist without compromise when it came to creating his revolutionary party. From 1903 he had fought doggedly for a party with a centralized structure, knowing no semiautonomous substructures based upon national affinity.[11] There was to be no independent Jewish Bund within his revolutionary party. Later, when he was forging his new society on the anvil of experience as the German armies withdrew from what had been the Russian Empire, he had his party congress reject the proposals of some of the border people living around the Russian core to have national communist parties linked in federation with the Russians.[12]

Further, when the first Soviet state apparatus was created with the seizure of power from the Provisional Government in November, 1917, Lenin had moved cautiously in creating his new Russian "federation." He seems to have recognized that his party's long espousal of "self-determination" designed to release the ethnic minorities from what it had called the Czar's "prison of peoples" had required recognition in the new state of some subordinate administrative regions formed on ethnic lines. Lenin had even felt the need to recognize the right of the largest ethnic minorities to withdraw from the federation to create their own republics, independent under international law and with full authority to legislate as their parliaments might wish.

Lenin's policy of federation, as applied to the smaller ethnic minorities that were kept within his new Russian state, had been to provide very few of the governmental institutions commonly associated with federations elsewhere. He had created no upper chamber of the legislature to provide the ethnic units with representation without regard to size. His Russian federal parliament, called a Congress of Soviets, included only deputies chosen on the basis of population. His one measure recognizing this problem of potentially hostile ethnic minorities was creation of a People's Commissariat of Nationalities on the day after seizure of power.[13] Headed by Joseph Stalin, who as a Georgian had been Lenin's chosen spokesman prior to the revolution on the ethnic problem,[14] this Commissariat was to serve as "the initiator of the entire Soviet legislation on the national question. . . ." To perform the function it was divided into national departments working in close cooperation with communists living within the ethnic units concerned.

By stages the work of the Commissariat was broadened until in July 1922 the various ethnic groups were authorized to delegate representatives to constitute within the Commissariat a Council of Nationalities, presided over by the Commissar and assisted by a collegium of nine. It was charged with "supervision over the execution of the nationality policy of the Soviet government." Thus, the ethnic minorities had a channel through which to exert influence on the formulation and execution of policy, but they had no formal, direct part in the legislative process.

Lenin fostered his concept of centralized leadership, even when establishing relations with the leaders of republics which had been withdrawn from the federation to become independent states. Through the Communist Party members in each of these, he stimulated activity expected to bring the newly independent states back into the federation. The communists in one of them, independent Belorussia, provided him with his most notable success, for in the process of legislating, the Belorussian Commissar of Justice, to whom the task of drafting legislation for enactment by the Belorussian Congress of Soviets was given, kept an eye focussed directly on Moscow. He telegraphed to the Russian Republic's Commissar of Justice in December 1918 to praise him for his authorship of the People's Court Act of 1918, and Belorussian judges were examined on the provisions of this Act, although it had not been adoped formally as Belorussian law. Later in 1920 the Belorussian Congress of Soviets sent delegates to meetings of the Russian republic's legislature, and the BCS united its purely administrative ministries with those of the Russian Republic.[15]

Even the Ukrainian communists, who were more numerous than the Belorussians and who had demonstrated some inclination to take steps different from those of the Russians, conformed to Russian legislative models. The Ukrainian statute on the civil courts of February 19, 1919, was almost identical with that of the Russian Republic, the modification permitting the council of people's judges itself, which in the Russian Republic was limited in performing the reviewing function to remands for retrial, to sit as a court of first instance for the rehearing. Other Ukrainian statutes of 1919 closely paralleling those of the Russian Republic were the decrees on marriage and divorce, the decree forbidding the sale of immovables, and the decree abolishing the Czarist inheritance system. When the Ukrainian Commissar of Justice issued a first circular defining the principles of criminal law to be applied by the courts, there was no effort to disguise the Russian source of the circular similarly adopted in the Ukraine.

The conclusion is compelling that in the formative years of 1917–1920 Lenin had anticipated that his new Russian federal republic would stimulate the reunion of Ukrainians, Belorussians, Armenians, Georgians, and Azerbaijanians and perhaps even of the citizens of the Baltic states when they came to appreciate their military and economic impotence. He expected them eventually to place more emphasis upon centralization of political and economic authority than upon ethnic autonomy, and cer-

tainly so when it came to innovating in legislation. His formula
emphasized "local initiative," but it could not be read without
regard to what was transpiring in practice and also without regard to the formula's concluding phrase. The final words assume
that in the exercise of local initiative there must be evident a
desire to achieve a common goal.

The new type of federation proposed in 1922 to replace the
Russian federation as a central authority came as something of
a surprise, for it was to give more recognition to ethnic claims
of identity than had the 1918 constitution of the Russian federation. For the first time a bicameral legislature was created by
moving to the law-making level of the state structure the advisory council of the original Commissariat of Nationalities. The
new chamber was to be a fully equal legislative partner with a
second chamber, the latter to be representative of population
alone and favoring, in consequence, the numerous Russians.
Further, the new constitution authorized the republics joining in
federation to enact their own codes, as the minority ethnic groups
joined in the Russian federation of 1918 had not been permitted
to do. In spite of these changes the emphasis of the formative
years upon centralized policymaking was retained, albeit in a
new form.

Under the constitution of 1923, which implemented the treaty
of union of 1922, the federal legislature was granted the right to
enact federal "fundamental principles" to which the republics'
codifiers were required to adhere. That no such fundamentals
were enacted before the various republics moved to legislate for
the neo-capitalist conditions established by Lenin's New Economic Policy suggests that the Ukrainians, at least, were feeling
entirely competent to do their own drafting without formal direction from the center.

The first civil code to emerge before the new USSR had been
formally constituted came from the Ukrainian republic during
the summer of 1922, while the Communist Party was preparing
the steps to be taken toward federation. It seems to have been
the result of independent thought on the part of Ukrainian legal
scholars, for in a review published thirty-eight years later two

Russian authors informed their readers that the Russian republic's draftsmen of 1922 had profited from Ukrainian experimen-
tation.[16]

Similarity of thinking, presumably inspired by the unifying
factor of the centralized Communist Party functioning through
branches in each republic, produced not only civil codes but
criminal as well in 1922. These were similar but not identical in
character. The federal authorities followed to establish "fundamental principles" only in 1924 and then only for the judicial
system and for criminal law and criminal procedure.[17] Not until
the early stages of the drive for collectivization of agriculture
was there publication of a statute for land use,[18] while the new
model for collective farm charters throughout the entire USSR
appeared only as the drive reached its peak in 1930.[19] No fundamentals binding upon the republics in drafting codes of civil
law and procedure were published during Stalin's lifetime. Family law was also left solely to the republics until Stalin's surprise
reform of 1944 when he put a stop to recognition of unregistered
marriage and divorce in an effort to strengthen the family and
reduce juvenile delinquency.

The historical record suggests that Stalin's main interest was
state security, and that beyond maintaining the principle of state
ownership of productive resources he had little interest in civil
law and its associated law of the family and of labor. He rarely
intervened to legislate a principle binding on the republics in
these fields, while he was always alert to the need for suppressing
dangerous activity through the criminal law and manipulation of
criminal procedure. His most dramatic exercise of federal authority came in 1934 when he unexpectedly required the republics to amend their codes of criminal procedure to simplify and
speed the handling of security cases.[20]

The 1934 federal action was later shown to have been but the
harbinger of a move to strengthen the federation's central authorities in all legislative fields. The second federal constitution
of 1936 put an end to the rights of the republics to enact the
major codes of law.[21] The republics were no longer to be controlled in the major fields through the instrumentality of federal

"fundamental principles." There were to be federal codes in criminal and civil law and criminal and civil procedure. Codification was immediately begun in committee, and drafts were circulated privately, but the war suspended the process. After its termination, codification was begun again, but it moved slowly. Those who ought to know have suggested that the delay was not because Stalin was changing his view on the federal relationship but because those charged with the drafting process were so frightened by his temper during his declining years that they feared to put before him the issues which had divided the experts, and without resolution of these matters no codes could issue.

The first hint of a reversal of Stalin's policy of centralized codification reached the outside world in 1956 with abolition of the federal government's Ministry of Justice.[22] As motivation, the decree declared that its purpose was "to eliminate excessive centralization in guidance of the work of the courts and legal institutions of the republics and to strengthen the role of the latter." The decree coincided with the 20th Congress of the Communist Party, when Khrushchev and some of his colleagues were violently criticizing Stalin's dictatorship. Later, criticism reached even the surviving Ministries of Justice in the republics for intervening in the affairs of the courts by way of audit of their activities, and proposals were heard which would give the auditing function only to higher courts.[23] Republic Ministries were abolished by the republic legislatures in 1960. Their administrative functions were transferred to the respective republic supreme courts and their legislative drafting functions were transferred to newly created Juridical Commissions to be attached to the various Councils of Ministers. But the auditing function did not relate directly to legislation, although centralization of the legislation process was vitally affected by abolition of the federal government's Ministry, for it had been performing the function of drafting the various all-union codes under the mandate of the 1936 Constitution.

The news that the republics were to regain the legislative authority they had lost in 1936 came to the outside world quite informally when a young American exchange student interviewed Soviet law professors in December 1956 to learn that a change in policy on centralized codification was in the offing.[24] Within six weeks the nature of the change became evident when the agenda for the February 1957 session of the USSR Supreme Soviet was published. It included the item, "The question of referring to the jurisdiction of the Union Republics legislation on the structure of courts of the Union Republics and adoption of civil, criminal and procedural codes." [25]

When the chairman of the Council of Nationalities rose to explain the item, he declared that it had been inserted to follow the decision of the 20th Congress of the Communist Party to decentralize the housekeeping and cultural work of the state, already begun in public administration.[26] He reviewed the cultural differences which could be noted between republics, especially the contrast between the Baltic and Central Asian Republics, choosing for special mention the contrast between rain-soaked and desert areas, a situation which he found necessitating a difference in the law of water rights. He quoted Lenin to the effect that the change would strengthen the republics by giving their legislative committees something to do. He added that time had changed the cadre situation since 1936, in that most of the republics had established faculties of law, and there were thus available a number of legally trained persons to proceed with codification.

The reporter in the other chamber, the Council of the Union, added some detail in justifying the proposal, referring to the economic growth of the republics and the transfer to them under the decision of the 20th Congress of many administrative functions relating to industry.[27] He did not mark a complete retreat to parochialism, however, for he re-emphasized the necessity of preserving common principles of law in the republics, and quoted Lenin again, this time in support of the necessity of preserving uniformity of law, while fostering at the same time local initiative exercised to meet the special requirements of local situations.

The amendment was accepted and the codification process

began, but without the aid of a Ministry of Justice of the USSR. Work was centered in a committee of experts attached to the Council of Ministers of the USSR at the time of abolition of the Ministry. Its task was to submit proposals to the legislative committees of the two chambers of the Supreme Soviet of the USSR.[28] These drafts were, of course, to be only of "fundamentals," for the codes themselves were to be drafted and promulgated by the republics under the revised constitutional provisions.

The linking of the decentralization of codification to the decentralization of industrial administration suggests that it was related in 1957 more to a desire to achieve efficiency than to the necessity of meeting incipient demands of the ethnic minorities for recognition of aspirations for greater independence within the federation. The outsider cannot but wonder whether the transfer to the republics of the codification process was not an effort to overcome the stultification of local initiative which had occurred during Stalin's epoch, when republic soviets lost so much authority that they failed to create in citizens' minds the sense of participation which Lenin had fostered as necessary to Soviet-type democracy. There is much evidence that the stultification process had proceeded so far at the provincial and city level that deputies simply did not appear for meetings of their soviets since they found nothing interesting to do. If this interpretation is accurate, it is possible that in 1957 Khrushchev and his colleagues hoped to revitalize political interest outside of Moscow, thereby gaining increasing popular support and at the same time, perhaps, ideas which could be tried out in one or another republic before becoming the subject of a nation-wide policy move from which there might be extensive unanticipated social damage before it was possible to assess the results.

The decentralization policy posed little danger, for the federal system retained its control over "fundamentals." The drafting of these fundamentals indicated the extent to which the center was prepared to delegate to the republics the authority it had previously assumed under Stalin's leadership. In formulating the fundamentals of criminal law, the federal authorities established what has been traditionally the "general part" of the code, that part which establishes over-all policy by stating the purpose of criminal law, the types of penalties which may be utilized to punish crime, and the importance of intent as measured in the treatment of negligence, attempts, mistakes, and acts committed by the intoxicated, the insane, and minors.

It was the matter of crimes by minors that attracted the attention of outsiders, for a change in policy occurred during the period of drafting. At the outset, the age at which minority was to terminate for purpose of criminal penalty was to be left to the republics to determine, it being supposed that the age of reason might come earlier in some regions than in others.[29] When the fundamentals were finally adopted in 1958, they reversed the thinking of the previous year and established a rule for all republics to adopt.

Generally, the republics were left free to define their own concepts of crime, and to establish penalties, so long as they were chosen from the list of those prescribed by the federal fundamentals. Yet, to this principle, there was established an immediate exception, for simultaneously with enactment of the fundamentals, there was enactment of a federal statute on crimes against the state.[30] This enactment continued Stalin's practice of defining acts threatening state survival on a uniform basis, and of doing so in detail, but the list was less inclusive than in Stalin's law. Evidently, the draftsmen of 1958 intended to leave with the republics greater authority than before in defining crime.

The restraint shown by the fundamentals was not, however, to last, for in 1962 the federal government enacted a common increase in penalty for gang rapes[31] and for bribe taking.[32] Clearly old attitudes die hard in the USSR, as elsewhere, and on these issues, perceived to be of great social concern, those who were conservative within the Communist Party seem to have regained sufficient influence to deny the making of criminal policy to the republics. The republics were permitted to keep their individual codes of criminal law, but on vital issues had to conform in every detail with federal policy, as enunciated by federal statutes.

Studies have been made of the extent to which the codes of the fifteen union republics differ on various matters. The Russian

and Latvian republics' codes enacted in implementation of the
1958 fundamentals, have been statistically compared. Examined
article by article,[33] the general parts show an over-all conformity
of 59 percent because they are based on the "fundamentals," being verbatim the same in the general chapters on "Crime," but
having a conformity index of only 40 and 47 percent respectively
in the chapters on "Punishment," and "Assignment of Punishment and Relief from Punishment." Such disparity as was found
was authorized, however, by the fundamentals, for in seven instances the federal statute had expressly empowered the republics to introduce variations. The republics' chapters on "Crimes
against the State" and "Military Crimes" conformed to the fundamentals without variation, as might have been expected, since
the federal law allowed no variation. As the federal authority
created new definitions of crime, indicated earlier, the republics
conformed their codes.

— The same study shows that the major initiative of the republics has been taken in defining specific crimes, other than state
and military, and that there has been considerable divergence.
Thus, the Russian and Latvian criminal codes showed only 38
percent conformity where freedom had been given to act without
federal models, some of the divergence being the introduction in
one or the other republic of crimes not defined in its partner's
code. But for the others there were different definitions and different penalties. Only about 15 percent of the provisions were
found to be identical both in terms of proscription and penalty.

Greatest conformity in the definitions was found to occur
when strong federal interests were concerned, while crimes which
were primarily of personal concern showed a very low conformity index. A noticeable difference was found in the tendency of
the Latvian code to establish milder penalties than that of the
Russian Republic, except where strong state interest was discerned. There was one notable exception to this general rule:
crimes against the personal property of citizens, where the Latvian code provided stiffer penalties than the Russian, perhaps
because the latter had inherited a revolutionary tradition which
showed little interest in personal ownership.

The study has concluded that the two codes differed sufficiently to permit its author to draw an inference of independent drafting. He believed it likely that the identity which did appear emerged more from preliminary inter-republic conferences or proposals of legal authors, than from dictation by the federal authorities.

Another study of variation, confined to examination of a single crime, indicated the same situation. The crime chosen for study was the crime of homosexuality.[34] The crime was selected because it had not been proscribed by Soviet criminal codes until Stalin's personal intervention in 1934 to strike a blow against a practice which had expanded presumably without his knowledge throughout the USSR. His intervention took the direct form of a federal statute. Previously, only one republic, the Uzbek, had concerned itself with the matter by defining as criminal in 1929 the corruption of minors and the conduct of schools of homosexual activity. Stalin's federally defined crime went well beyond the narrow definition of the Uzbek code in exercise of Article 3 of the 1924 federal fundamentals of criminal law to which reference has been made. This article authorized the federal authority to define crimes "when the USSR thinks it necessary to follow a single line through establishment of a single court practice."

Stalin's statute was not all-inclusive, for it limited the definition of homosexuality to men. But it did establish two grades: (1) the act in simple form, for which imprisonment up to five years was authorized; and (2) the act accompanied by taking advantage of the dependent position of the victim, or if force was used or payment made, or if it was conducted as a profession or publicly. In such an event, the penalty might be increased to eight years' imprisonment. All republics were required to insert the federal statute unchanged in their codes. In a sense homosexuality was raised by this act to the level of a matter of state security, constituting a peril to the moral fabric of the socialist community.

The first signs of a reawakening of independent thinking on this matter appeared when the federal statute was amended by federal authorities to establish minimum as well as maximum penalties, and to simplify grade two by limiting its application to circumstances when force was used or the victim had been dependent. These provisions were not incorporated by the Ukrainians into their code; the Tajiks only introduced the first federal amendment on minimum penalties; and the Uzbeks preserved their 1929 provisions on homosexual schools as an addition to the amended federal statute. What caused Stalin to permit these variations by the republics in adopting the federal statute is unknown.

When the republics were released (in 1958, with the publication of new fundamentals) from the obligation to follow the federal definitions of all but state and military crime, the republics demonstrated wide divergence in regard to homosexuality as a crime. All chose to retain recognition in some form of homosexuality as criminal, in contrast to their position before adoption of the 1934 federal law. Only the Russian and Belorussian republics re-enacted the original features of the superseded 1934 federal law. The others introduced variations in either or both the definitions and the penalties.[35]

Considerable difference also appears in the approach of various republics to religious and tribal customs, largely because they are to be found in socially dangerous form in only a few of them. In 1928 the Russian republic had introduced a chapter entitled "Crimes constituting relics of tribal order," but it was declared applicable only in areas of tribal custom, that is, the non-Slavic areas. These prohibitions were incorporated within a few months in the Central Asian republics to discourage Islamic marriage practices, but they were poorly enforced.[36] Since the non-Islamic and nontribal republics found no need, they refrained from adopting such provisions, thus creating a classic example of differing provisions occasioned by differing social conditions. The same situation prevailed after adoption of the 1958 fundamentals, so that current codes show that republics with Muslim and tribal cultures have retained the provisions and those without such cultures have ignored them.

The possibility of using the republics to fly trial balloons before a policy position has been firmly established was offered by

legislation defining the crime of "parasitism." A study surveying
the situation has noted that the idea of exiling persons found
"committing antisocial acts permitting them to lead a parasitic
way of life," following a hearing and sentence by a "social assembly," emerged first in the form of statutes enacted in the
Central Asian Soviet republics.[37] In 1965 the practice was modified in the Georgian republic to permit sentence only by a local
soviet's executive committee, sitting in judgment on the petition
of a "social assembly." [38] Finally, in revised form, a "parasite"
statute was enacted by the Russian republic in 1961 [39] to provide a more orderly and formal procedure for determining most
circumstances of parasitism. The hearing and sentence were
made the work of a people's court if the accused was not working at all. The "social assembly" could function only if the accused had been employed while committing his parasitic acts,
and then only if the procurator thought the procedure more
suitable under the circumstances than the procedure of a formal
court.

As soon as the Russian republic had provided a model, the
other republics brought their statutes into conformity with it,
although there was no published legal requirement that they do
so. Seemingly, the idea had been tried out, modified as a result
of experience, and after a second modification introduced in
final form by some process of coordination and recommendation
to all republics to take identical action. The technique of 1961
differed sharply from Stalin's technique of 1934 with homosexuality, for no federal statute had been issued.

The priority given republic initiative over federal initiative in
the parasite situation was to survive Khrushchev's ouster in spite
of reversion to centralism in economic administration. A third
revision of the parasite laws was instituted in 1965 by the Russian republic. It reduced greatly the power of the "social assembly," and in its new form it was later adopted by the other
republics.[40]

In the field of civil law a similar division between federal and
republic authority has emerged. The federally adopted "fundamentals" of December 8, 1961,[41] introduced some novelty into

the relationship, as there had been no civil law federal fundamentals under Stalin. Still, they created no shock, for the civil
codes of the various republics had never evidenced divergence
in principle since enactment in 1922. Drafts had been shared at
that time. Later, when the Baltic republics were brought into the
USSR in 1940, the Russian republic's civil code was enacted in
each without amendment, presumably to save time in drafting
legal codes for restructuring their social systems along Marxian
socialist lines at a moment when there was no opportunity for
reflection and drafting.

The 1961 fundamentals of civil law are relatively short, about
half the length of the civil codes enacted by the republics in their
amplification. They treat the matter of capacity of citizens and
legal persons, provide a definition of "transactions," as well as
of "agency," establish a statute of limitations on the commence-
ment of civil suit, define the over-all property rights of citizens,
state, cooperative and public organizations in terms similar to
the broad provisions of the federal constitution, create general
principles for the recognition of the law of contract and tort, as
well as of copyright, patent, and inheritance.

When the outsider turns from the federal fundamentals to the
codes themselves,[42] he finds considerable amplification and very
little difference between republics in this amplification. The
wording of many articles of the codes in the various republics is
identical. Sometimes a long article in one republic will be divided into two in another, thus creating a numbering system that
differs, but the words will be the same, or modified only to introduce what the draftsmen of the diverging code think makes for
greater clarification. Comparison of the law of sales in the various codes indicates that the principles appear in all republics in
the same order, and present identical rules, even as to such matters as had previously aroused debate, such as the age at which
a child may bind himself by contract. This debate had reason to
occur under the formula accepted as justifying divergence, for
it was based on the assumption that the age of maturity came at
different times for youths in various weather zones and culture
patterns. The important subject of offer and acceptance of con-

tracts, which is not treated at all in the fundamentals, is established in the same way in all codes.

With inheritance, there is more difference verbally, although the principles are generally the same. An example of variation is to be found in defining the responsibility of heirs for the payment of debts of the decedent. Both the Russian and Kazakh republic codes use a general phrase creating the responsibility with regard to an "heir." The Ukrainian and Latvian republic codes are more specific, for they add a supplemental paragraph to leave no doubt in the multiple-heir situation. They say that multiple heirs are liable for debts only in proportion to the share of the estate received. All but the Ukrainian code provide for the extinction of a creditor's right against the estate if a claim is not presented within six months of the declaration that claims may be filed. The Ukrainian code requires filing within six months but is silent on the consequences of failure to file.

Similarity in the wording of the civil codes is not currently cloaked in mystery. An explanation has been given[43] which supports the conclusion that there is no dictation from the center but rather a cooperative drafting procedure engaged in by the experts of all republics to create at least the skeleton of a code. The specialists are assembled in conference to discuss a draft, the draft having been prepared in Moscow after experts have traveled to the various capitals of the republics to learn of desires. These are then discussed at the conference and the draft returned to the specialists in the various republics for final revision and enactment. Under this procedure, some republics take longer in adding their details than others, a fact that made possible the enactment of the first civil code under the new fundamentals by the Uzbek republic rather than the Russian or Ukrainian. In conversation, some Soviet specialists have explained this event by noting the remarkable personality of the late woman Minister of Justice of the Uzbek republic, Suleimanova, who directed her staff to move quickly and who seems to have had a desire to be first to enact the draft.

In spite of the similarity in civil code provisions, some variation appears, and this has been made the subject of a monograph by a Soviet author,[44] who, in describing the codes, focuses on differences caused by "national" characteristics, and chooses as an example the provisions on the leasing of premises in city-owned and ministry-owned multiple dwellings. The federal fundamentals leave details on this subject to the republics. Eleven republic codes establish a five-year term for such leases and prohibit the parties from establishing any other. The codes in the Azerbaijan, Ukrainian, and Latvian republics provide that as a general rule a lease shall be without a stated period of time, but the parties may agree to establish one. The Kazakh code establishes a maximum period of five years, and permits the parties to establish anything less than that or even to provide for no fixed term. According to the monograph, this variation is caused by local conditions but it does not say what these are.

It presents as another example of variation the inheritance of leased dwelling space, repeating again that this is closely linked to national tradition. Most republics are said to include grandparents among "heirs" in a second category which permits inheritance of space if there are no closer heirs, but the Azerbaijan code goes one generation back to include great grandfathers and great grandmothers "because many citizens reach [the age of] 100 or more." The Kazakh and Moldavian codes expand the group permitted to inherit premises. The Kazakh code places brothers and sisters of the deceased tenant in a third category, even when they are able to work, so that they may inherit if there are no grandparents or brothers and sisters unable to work. The Moldavian code substitutes in the third category incapacitated nephews and nieces. The explanation is said to lie in the differing conceptions in national custom of the "family" unit.

Other differences are laid to geographical or climatic variations, these being reflected in varying sizes of dwellings permitted to remain in private ownership. All republics maintain a 60-square-meter limit on the space in the dwelling actually used for living purposes, although this may be increased in the event of large families to whatever is set as the maximum permitted by the standard norm of occupancy for any given city, but all allow variation in the size of the non-living space in the dwelling—that

is, the size of the kitchen, storeroom, halls, bathroom, and ve-
randa. The author notes that in the cold climates the porches
must be screened with glass and thus become part of a living unit,
while in warm climates they are relatively inconsequential ap-
pendages.

Differences in water use occur. In the rainy republics, the
right to use is governed by the civil codes, but in the dry republics, the Uzbek, Kazàkh, Azerbaijan, Georgian, Armenian, and
Kirgiz, a separate law on use of water has been enacted to provide for maximum conservation and equitable distribution.

Differences are also laid to varying difficulty of communication. In the republics having good roads and railroads, these
being listed as the republics on the Baltic, the Ukraine, Moldavia, and Azerbaijan, a contract of sale must be certified by a
notary if the sale concerns a private dwelling, wherever located,
while in the Russian, Kazakh, and Central Asian republics, in
which there might be great difficulty in reaching a notary, the
parties are permitted if they live outside of a city to obtain the
certification of the executive committee of the local soviet.

Differences are also laid to degree of economic development.
These appear in the differing rights granted to a tenant in a
privately owned dwelling to bring into his rented premises without the consent of the owner additional members of his family.
The republics with the least housing shortage place the greatest
limitations on the tenant. Thus, in the Baltic republics, if the
space concerned is not isolated from the rooms of the owner, no
one may be introduced without his consent, and if the space is
isolated, only minor children and spouse may be introduced
without the owner's consent. The republics with most severe
shortages permit the introduction of minor children whether the
space is isolated or not, and permit the introduction of a spouse
and even of parents unable to work if the space is isolated from
the owners, these being the Russian and Turkmen republics. The
Georgian and Azerbaijan republics offer a slight variation in
permitting the introduction of parents into isolated space even
if they are able to work, presumably because the housing shortage is more severe than in the Russian and Turkmen republics.

The republics with moderate housing shortages, namely the Ukrainian, Uzbek, Kazakh, Moldavian, Kirgiz, Armenian and Tajik, take an intermediate position permitting only minor children to be introduced without the owner's consent, whether the space is isolated or not. Belorussia is a variation on this group, permitting not only the minor children but also the spouse to be introduced under such circumstances.

As to the right to execute a contract, there is some difference. All republics but Georgia provide that the local authorities may limit the right of a citizen to execute a contract if he is determined to be a spendthrift or because of "systematic drunkenness" or other reasons which result in depriving his family of the means of survival. Georgia seems to have felt no such need to protect the family.

Family law was brought under federal fundamentals for the first time in 1968,[45] although there had been some uniformity introduced in 1944 by Stalin's surprise decree requiring registration of marriage.[46] Because of the recent enactment of fundamentals, it is yet too early to determine what variation will appear in the various family codes eventually to be enacted in amplification of the basic principles, but in the codes presently remaining in force, except as modified by the new fundamentals, the variations are numerous. There is a difference in age of the parties entering upon marriage. It is eighteen in the majority of republics but is subject to reduction by one year (or in Belorussia, two) in exceptional cases by the executive committee of the local soviet. In some of the warmer republics, the Ukraine, Armenia, Moldavia, and Azerbaijan, the age of the woman is set at sixteen.

With regard to nullity of marriage, the majority of republics provide for nullity if both parties were under marriageable age at the time of the ceremony, but to this there are three exceptions: if both parties are over marriageable age at the time of the examination of the case, if there is offspring, or if the wife is pregnant as a result of the marriage. Georgia adds a fourth exception: if one of the spouses has become ill or disabled as a result of the marriage.

On the naming of children, Belorussia permits a child to follow custom and to take a double name to represent each parent. Elsewhere, the father's name is used if the child was born in wedlock, although there is no requirement that this practice be followed.

Maintenance is treated in a varied manner: in all republics there is a mutual obligation on the spouses to provide each other assistance in the event of incapacity to work or need. The variation on the rule is found only in the length of time the obligation continues after termination of a marriage by divorce. Maintenance by a stepfather is set in most republics as applying only to minors, or incapacitated or needy children regardless of age, but not if the child has one natural parent able to support him. Belorussia narrows the rule to require maintenance by a stepfather only of a minor, regardless of capacity or need.

Adoption is provided for by all codes, but there is a variation in age after which it is denied: eighteen in most republics, but in Georgia twenty, and in Azerbaijan the adopter must be at least eighteen years older than the adopted person. Guardianship likewise varies in its provisions as to age. Generally it may continue until the age of fourteen, but the Ukrainian code sets the age at eighteen.

Centralized direction of policy is maintained not only by legislation but also by its interpretation and application by the judiciary. The Supreme Court of the USSR is given by statute[47] not only the right to "review materials generalizing on judicial practice," but also to examine protests of its President or of the Procurator General of the USSR against decisions of republic courts "if these judgments and sentences are in conflict with all-union legislation or violate the interests of other union republics." The generalizing function is performed through the issuance of orders binding on all republic courts. Some of these concern, as a student of federal structures elsewhere might expect, the interpretation to be given laws enacted by the federal Supreme Soviet, as for example Order No. 2 for 1969 [48] on the application by republic courts of the USSR statutes on railroad and water transport and the USSR Air Code as well as the federal funda-

mentals of civil legislation. The order detailed the treatment to
be given disputes concerning the transportation of baggage and
freight, if one of the parties is a collective farm, an enterprise
owned by two or more collective farms, or a citizen. Order No.
4 for 1969 [49] instructs republic courts to include in their opinions
the motives for their decision and to state their finding of facts
more clearly and their conclusions of law more logically. Order
No. 4 went farther than Order No. 2 in that reference was made
not only to the federal fundamentals of criminal procedure but
also to the codes of criminal procedure of the various republics
expanding upon the fundamentals. The order constitutes a brief
essay on how to draft a judgment and sentence, presumably to
make certain not only that the trial is conducted in accordance
with standards established by the fundamentals and the codes but
also to facilitate review by the federal court of the decisions.

The deficiencies in the examination of cases of minors coming before republic courts were made the subject of Order No. 8
for 1969.[50] The federal court states its concern for the fact that
varying interpretations are appearing in the republic courts of
Article 210 of the Criminal Code of the Russian Republic and
of corresponding articles in the codes of other republics, an article
providing for punishment of adults who entice minors into crime.
Second, the federal court is concerned because it finds that republic courts are failing to apply a procedural requirement of
the codes of criminal procedure of the various republics requiring that the court in examining the case determine the causes and
conditions facilitating commission of the crime and notify the
agencies concerned of these conditions. Since Article 210 of the
Criminal Code of the Russian Republic is not one that has been
transposed from the federal fundamentals of criminal law, the
court is not interpreting federal law but rather unifying practice
in a field where all republics have enacted a similar provision
under the guidance established during the codification process
to which attention has been directed above.

Through these three Orders, the work of the court is seen to
have passed from (1) interpretation of federal statutes having
no counterpart in the republics, to (2) interpretation of federal

fundamentals and the republic codes expanding upon them, to (3) the interpretation of republic codes for which there is no formal federal model adopted by the federal legislature but only the informal coordination of republic policy in drafting committees. The court seems in the third case (Order No. 8) to be making itself the official interpreter of an unofficially adopted Union-wide policy on the instigators of juvenile crime.

The three orders examined are, as indicated, "generalizations" of practice without reference to any specific case. They constitute an important part of the federal Supreme Court's work, being issued about once a month after considerable study followed by a plenary meeting attended by the Presidents of the various republics' Supreme Courts. The substance of the discussion at the meeting is reported in a resumé prior to the pages of the Supreme Court's official report of the Order. The form, at least, is not that of dictation from above, but rather of common resolution of a Union-wide problem achieved in the presence of judges from both federal and republic courts.

The federal Supreme Court conducts other notable functions with regard to specific cases, and it is these which attract the attention of specialists in other federal systems accustomed to the preservation of rigid lines of jurisdiction between federal and state authority. Since these opinions concern specific cases, the law being applied is usually that of the republic concerned, although that law may have a base in federal fundamentals from which it was taken. Those cases where the republic law concerned is of federal origin require little comment in the light of the explanation already given of federal authority.

One such was the Case of "Z," [51] tried by a court in the Russian Republic under its Articles 108 and 112 (Intentional infliction of light bodily injury on one victim and intentional infliction of grave bodily injury from which death of another victim resulted). The issue chosen by the federal court was the defendant's claim that he had committed the harmful acts in self-defense. Since the self-defense principle included in the criminal code of each republic is taken from the federal fundamentals, the federal court was performing a clearly recognizable federal function in determining how it should be applied, even though it chose to implement its unifying role by acting in a specific case by examining the evidence and providing a concrete example of the principles it wished to impart.

Much more difficult cases for a specialist on less-centralized federations are offered by those USSR Supreme Court decisions which neither cite federal law nor rest on uncited principles of federal fundamentals known by all to have been incorporated by the republics in their codes. If the court is seeking to unify practice by deciding the cases and publishing its decisions, it must be seeking to create an unwritten standard somewhat similar to the standard of "due process of law" applied by the Supreme Court of the United States without benefit of a written definition. The decisions present interest, however, because the court makes no reference to any unwritten standard, and there is no phrase in the Soviet federal constitution or in the federal court's statute, such as that in the Fourteenth Amendment to the United States Constitution, to establish a formal basis for such a decision.

Two cases concerning the evaluation of evidence present the matter in sharpest outline. In one, a conviction for theft of state property in large quantities was set aside by the federal court, although it had been affirmed by the Supreme Court of the Tajik Republic.[52] The federal court concluded that the evidence set forth in the trial court's record could support no more than a conviction for theft in small quantities.

The second evidence case was a conviction for intentional killing, issued by a Leningrad provincial court, and reviewed by the Russian Republic's Supreme Court.[53] It was set aside because the federal Supreme Court concluded from the record that a fisherman who was trying to protect his catch from theft through use of an electrified device had demonstrated no intent to kill the youth who had been electrocuted while trying to steal the fish.

Another type of federal supreme court opinion examines the classification of crime chosen by republic courts as the legal basis for punishment. The articles concerned are not those placed in the republic code by formal direction of the federal legislature but are articles drafted by the republics' legislative committees and enacted by the republics' legislatures, albeit with the help of consultations among the specialists of the various republics as coordinated by the specialists in Moscow. The articles are, therefore, in a form selected by the republic authorities after listening to the proposals of others from sister republics and specialists from Moscow, but with consideration of the applicability of these outside proposals to the specific conditions of the republic that has adopted them.

In one such case a road inspector was convicted for killing a bystander who put his head into the truck's cab just as the inspector started to drive it to an inspection parking place after the truckdriver had refused to do so.[54] The Armenian courts had concluded that the crime should be classified as committed while exceeding authority, and they subjected the inspector to a severe penalty. The federal Supreme Court disagreed and declared that the act could not be classified as such since the driving of the truck to the inspection zone, although unusual, clearly did not exceed the limits placed on the rights and powers of a road inspector.

In a companion case, the Supreme Court of the USSR refused to accept a conviction in the Russian republic for an official's taking bribes, for which the maximum penalty may be capital punishment. The federal court declared that the record showed that the official in a factory had used his position to induce two employees subordinate to him to share with him their royalties on a rationalizing proposal to which he had directed their attention but for which he was not registered as a co-inventor. In the federal court's view the act should have been classified as misuse of a position for mercenary motives, and not the more serious crime of bribetaking.[55]

In some cases the federal Supreme Court has felt called upon to interpret a republic's code so as to add to its very general provisions sufficient precision to permit the republics' courts to apply the article in a manner deemed correct by the federal court.

Thus, when a protest was filed against a conviction for killing "under exacerbated circumstances" when two villagers followed a third to the fields and beat him mercilessly, finally killing him by stuffing his mouth with earth, the federal court supported the interpretation of this act by the republic's court as killing "under exacerbated circumstances," even though the federal court's president had protested the Moldavian court's interpretation as erroneous. The protester had thought the crime on the facts no more than ordinary killing.[56] Again, when the crime of "malicious hooliganism" was found by the Turkmen courts in another case, the federal court defined the crime more precisely, explaining that to establish the commission of such a crime a court had to establish that the action complained of had been a manifestation of a "clear lack of respect for society as a whole." It was not enough that the disorder had been the result of personal animosity between two parties.[57] In this case a federal interest was more evident since the crime of hooliganism as defined in all republics had been made the subject of an intense nation-wide campaign in 1966. At that time the Presidium of the federal Supreme Soviet had established a common definition of the crime and had instructed the republics to amend their codes accordingly.[58]

The cases concerning articles of the civil codes of the republics are fewer. Some have to do with failure to present evidence properly, as when a civil suit was brought to recover from a member of a dwelling cooperative association the balance due on his membership obligation. The federal court concluded that the Belorussian courts had not computed the debtor's admitted obligation in accordance with the requirements of appropriate legislation and remanded the case for new trial and the presentation of properly prepared evidence.[59]

In another, the federal court found error in interpreting the effective date of a Russian republic's regulation permitting a village soviet's executive committee to certify the signature of a testator in a village where no state notary's office existed. When the Russian Republic courts refused to give this regulation retroactive effect to validate a will executed before it was promulgated by a testatrix who died after the date of promulgation, the federal court upheld the will as validly executed.[60] Seemingly, the federal court thought its interpretation more reasonable than that of the courts of the republic which had promulgated it.

Disputes over housing rights have given rise to several federal interpretations. The federal court held that members of a family do not lose their right to space in a municipal dwelling when the principal tenant is ousted temporarily for misconduct, and it returned the civil suit brought by other claimants to the space for retrial in a Belorussian court.[61]

When members of a family claimed a property interest in a newly purchased dwelling because they had pooled their savings to buy the house and had executed a contract to purchase the house together, the Supreme Court of the USSR overruled the Belorussian Supreme Court's denial of the claim on the ground that the denial violated a federal Supreme Court general order of 1962 creating a right of co-ownership in this type of situation.[62] A violation of a similar type of general order on the treatment by republic courts of tort claims resulted in the setting aside of a judgment of the Russian republic's courts in which a plaintiff who had been injured as a minor was not permitted to use as a measure of damage her average wage on reaching majority.[63] The matter was one which had plagued the courts for some time because of the general rule that damages for injury are to be computed on the basis of wages at the time of the injury, and the Supreme Court of the USSR had wished to unify the interpretation of the rule when persons were injured as minors before their working potential had been determined.

Labor codes have been brought before the federal court in several cases. Two had to do with dismissals. In one an employee had been dismissed on the grounds that, since the place of employment had been liquidated in a general reorganization, it was proper to dismiss its employees under provisions of the Tajik republic's labor code.[64] The federal court agreed with the republic's court that this was a proper interpretation of the code, the more so since it conformed to a general order of the federal court instructing republic courts to apply this article of the code to dismissals on reorganization, even though the function previously performed was transferred to a new public enterprise arising out of the reorganization.

In another case in the Armenian republic a senior inspector of personnel had been dismissed without the consent of the trade union's official in the plant. The Armenian courts rejected the suit, but the federal court's president filed a protest with his court against the decisions. The court agreed with its president on the ground that the republic's courts had failed to investigate the case sufficiently to determine the reasons for dismissal, which were not set forth in the record and which might have justified dismissal under one of the exceptional provisions of the code.[65]

In a fourth labor law case, suit had been brought under the labor code to recover from a worker damages for harm he had caused a state enterprise. A State Arbitration Tribunal had heard a dispute between two state enterprises which had been shipper and buyer over a shortage of goods on arrival of a freight car sealed by the shipper, and had held for the buyer. Thereafter the shipping enterprise brought suit against its employee with whom it had in his employment contract a clause making him fully responsible for losses caused in performance of his work. The trial court gave judgment for the enterprise on the basis of the Kirgiz Labor code. The civil chamber of the republic's supreme court affirmed the judgment, and the presidium rejected a protest against its civil chamber's decision when it was filed by the republic's deputy procurator. Then the president of the federal court protested the decision, and the plenary sitting of his court agreed with him on the ground that a contract for full liability may be concluded only with certain categories of employees, and that the validity of the contract under scrutiny should have been investigated.[66] The categories of persons with whom such contracts may be concluded are established by the republic's Council of Ministers in agreement with the Central Council of Labor Unions and with the USSR State Committee on Labor and Wages. The position litigated in this case was not on the list, so that the contract was held to be illegal. This made the judgment on the basis of the republic's Labor Code unfounded. Further, even assuming the various judgments and affirmances in the republic's courts correct, the evidence was thought to be inadequate to prove liability, for there had been no investigation of the official's responsibility for the shortage. The decision of State Arbitration in the suit between the enterprises was not considered proof of an employee's specific liability for the shortage.

Reviewing the multitude of detail which inevitably must be sifted if one attempts to pass beyond the general provisions of the various Constitutions of USSR on the relationship between federal and republic authority, the conclusion is impelling that under Stalin the pressure for uniformity of legislative policy increased progressively over the years. This was noted especially in the field of criminal law and procedure, but even in civil law and its closely related fields of family and labor law, centralization of policymaking was on the increase by virtue of the activities of the experts of the Institute of Law of the USSR Academy of Sciences, notably while it was directed by Academician Andrei Y. Vyshinsky.

Under Nikita Khrushchev the emphasis changed when he introduced his policy decentralizing the process of economic administration. Accompanying this emphasis upon republic participation in direction of the economy, the Supreme Soviet of the USSR introduced decentralization in other branches of activity, including legislation. Amendment of Stalin's 1936 constitution to restore the codification authority to the republics, albeit subject to federal establishment of "fundamentals," was evidence of the change.

After Khrushchev's ouster in 1964, and even before that time when he and his colleagues began to show their concern over the expansion of certain types of serious crime, the pendulum was swung back part way. Federal statutes introduced in 1960 and 1961 increased penalties for crimes not previously included among those involving the security of the state, and the republics conformed their codes.

The Supreme Court of the USSR has increased its supervisory activity over the work of republic courts, developing a policy not unlike that of the United States Supreme Court when it determines what is "due process of law," and requires the courts of the members of the federation to conform to it. It has even gone further to define with some precision some of the crimes established by republic legislation even though there is no federal fundamental principle seemingly involved. In short, it is establishing a uniformity in application of republic codes, when the texts need not, in principle, be conformed.

Soviet authors praise this "flexibility" as it emerges in the relationship between central authorities and those in the republics, noting that the USSR was not formed by states fearful of domination by the central authorities. While this lack of distrust may have existed and may remain among members of the Communist Party, which has always refused to accept the concept of federation in its own structure, the distrust of centralized direction has not been completely overcome among the population generally. There has been constant, although undramatic, pressure from citizens of the republics for recognition of greater policymaking authority. This has emerged in committees drafting a new constitution for the USSR. One of the promised changes from the 1936 constitution is an enlargement of the powers of republics. While this enlargement is not expected to be drastic, it is being talked about as "notable." It is possible, therefore, that the division of powers between center and republics will change before long, and that a new chapter in the relationship will be opened.

NOTES

1. James H. Meisel and Edward S. Kozera, *Materials for the Study of the Soviet System: State and Party Constitutions, Laws, Decrees, Decisions, and Official Statements of the Leaders in Translation* (2d ed.; Ann Arbor, Mich.: George Wahr Publishing Co., 1953), pp. 242, 153; *Zasedaniia Verkhovnogo Soveta SSSR chetvertogo sozyva (shestaia sessiia). Stenograficheskii otchet.* (Moscow: Izdanie Verkhovnogo Soveta SSSR, 1957), p. 735.

2. V. M. Chkhikvadze, ed., *The Soviet State and Law* (Moscow: Progress Publishers, 1969), p. 106.

3. Frederick L. Schuman, *Soviet Politics at Home and Abroad* (New York: Knopf, 1946), p. 305.

4. R. M. Ramanov, "Sovershenstvovanie respublikanskogo pravotvorchestva," *Sovetskoe gosudarstvo i pravo* No. 1 (1970), p. 23.

5. *Ibid.,* citing V. I. Lenin, *Polnoe sobranie sochinenii* (5th ed.; Moscow: Gosudarstvennoe Izdatel'stvo Politicheskoi Literatury, 1962), Vol. 36, p. 152.

6. For the Khrushchev "theses" and the decrees of 1957, see English translation in *Current Digest of the Soviet Press,* Vol. IX, No. 18 (June 12, 1957), p. 3, and *Ibid.,* No. 20 (June 26, 1957), p. 14.

7. For the 1965 Kosygin speech, the Communist Party Resolutions, and the decrees, see *Current Digest of the Soviet Press,* Vol. XVII, No. 38 (Oct. 27, 1965), p. 12.

8. Zbigniew Brzezinski, this volume.

9. M. G. Kirichenko, "Problemy razgranicheniia konstitutsionnogo zakonodatel'stva Soiuza i respublik," *Sovetskoe Gosudarstvo i Pravo,* No. 11 (1967), p. 53, partial Eng. trans. in John N. Hazard, Isaac Shapiro and Peter B. Maggs, *The Soviet Legal System* (2d ed.; Dobbs Ferry: Oceana Publications, 1969), p. 32.

10. This conclusion is documented by Ramashamian Vaidyanath's study, "Soviet Autonomy in Theory and Practice," developed during his visit to Columbia University's Research Institute on Communist Affairs.

11. Leonard Schapiro, *The Communist Party of the Soviet Union* (New York: Random House, Inc., 1960), p. 50.

12. Resolution of 8th Communist Party Congress "Po organizatsionnomu voprosu," section A, paragraph 5. *KPSS v rezoliutsiiakh i resheniiakh s'ezdov, konferentsii i plenumov TsK.* (7th ed.; Moscow: Gosudarstvennoe Izdatel'stvo Politicheskoi Literatury, 1959), Vol. 1, p. 443.

13. Julian Towster, *Political Power in the U.S.S.R. 1917–1947* (New York: Oxford University Press, 1949), pp. 70–71.

14. Stalin's major work in this field is "Natsional'nyi vopros i Sotsial Demokratiia" (1913). Eng. trans. in Joseph Stalin, *Marxism and the National and Colonial Question* (Moscow: Cooperative Publishing Society of Foreign Workers in the U.S.S.R., 1936), p. 3.

15. For details on the formative years, see John N. Hazard, *Settling Disputes in Soviet Society* (New York: Columbia University Press, 1960), p. 59 (footnote 62), pp. 113, 206.

16. N. I. Avdeenko and M. A. Kabakova, "Grazhdanskoe protsessual'nogo prava," pub. in *40 let sovetskogo prava* (Moscow-Leningrad: Izdatel'stvo Leningradskogo Universiteta, 1957), Vol. 1, p. 653 (footnote 36).

17. Orders of Oct. 29 and 31, 1924 [1924] 23 *Sobranie zakonov SSSR*, Pt. 1, item 203, and 24 *Ibid.,* item 204.

18. Decree of Dec. 15, 1928 [1928] 69 *Ibid.,* item 642.

19. Decree of March 1, 1930 [1930] 24 *Ibid.,* 255.

20. Decree of Dec. 1, 1934 [1934] 64 *Sobranie Zakonov SSSR,* Pt. 1, item 459.

21. Article 14 (u).

22. Edict of May 31, 1956 [1956], *Vedomosti Verkhovnogo Soveta SSSR,* No. 12 (854) item 250.

23. N. Morozov and I. Perlov, "Ob organizatsii sudebnoi sistemy," *Izvestiia* (May 18, 1958), p. 4.

24. Darrell P. Hammer communicated his unpublished interview orally to me; I made it known in "Soviet Codifiers Receive New Orders," *American Journal of Comparative Law,* Vol. 6, No. 4 (Autumn 1957), pp. 541, 544.

25. "Informatsionnoe soobshchenie o zasedaniiakh Verkhovnogo Soveta SSSR 5 fevralia 1957 goda," *Izvestiia* (Feb. 6, 1957), p. 1.

26. Speech by M. A. Gedvilas, *Zasedaniia Verkhovnogo Soveta SSSR chetvertogo sozyva (shestaia sessiia). Stenograficheskii otchet* (Moscow: Izdanie Verkhovnogo Soveta SSSR, 1957), p. 449 at 450.

27. Speech of M. A. Iasnov, *Ibid.,* at pp. 491, 492.

28. *Supra,* footnote 24.

29. Article 21 of the draft established no age limits on responsibility of minors. See draft in *Biulleten' Verkhovnogo Suda SSSR,* No. 4 (1958), p. 1.

30. Law of Dec. 25, 1958 [1958] *Vedomosti Verkhovnogo Soveta SSSR,* No. 1, item 8.

31. Edict of Feb. 15, 1962 [1962] *Ibid.,* No. 8, item 84.

32. Edict of Feb. 20, 1962 [1962] *Ibid.,* No. 8, item 85.

33. Zigurds L. Zile, "Soviet Federalism in Criminal Law—A Case Study" in A. Sprudzs and A. Rusis, eds., *Res Baltica, A Collection of Essays in Honor of the Memory of Dr. Alfred Bilmanis* (Leyden: Sitjhoff, 1968), p. 152.

34. John N. Hazard, *Communists and Their Law* (Chicago: University of Chicago Press, 1969), p. 457.

35. The codes of all republics are published in *Ugolovnoe Zako-*

nodatel'stvo Soiuza SSSR i Soiuznykh Respublik, 2 vols. (Moscow: Iuridicheskoe Izdatel'stvo, 1963).

36. Gregory J. Massell, "Law as an Instrument of Revolutionary Change in a Traditional Milieu: The Case of Soviet Central Asia," *Law and Society Review,* Vol. 2 (1968), p. 179.

37. R. Beerman, "The Parasite Law," *Soviet Studies,* Vol. 13 (1961), p. 191.

38. Decree of Sept. 5, 1960, *Zaria Vostoka,* Sept. 6, 1960. Eng. trans. in *Current Digest of the Soviet Press,* Vol. XII, No. 44 (Nov. 30, 1960), p. 12.

39. Decree of May 4, 1961 [1961] *Vedomosti Verkhovnogo Soveta RSFSR,* No. 18, item 273.

40. Decree of Sept. 20, 1965 [1965], *Ibid.,* No. 38, item 932.

41. [1961] *Vedomosti Verkhovnogo Soveta SSSR,* No. 50, item 525. English translation in *Soviet Civil Legislation and Procedure, Official Text and Commentaries* (Moscow: Foreign Language Publishing House, 1964).

42. For Eng. trans. of RSFSR civil code of 1964, see Whitmore Gray and Raymond Stults, *Civil Code of the Russian Soviet Federated Socialist Republic* (Ann Arbor: University of Michigan Law School, 1965).

43. S. G. Novikov, "Uchastie nauchnoi obshchestvennosti v rabote Komissii Zakonodatel'nykh predlozhenii Verkhovnogo Soveta SSSR po podgotovke zakonproektov," *Sovetskoe Gosudarstvo i Pravo,* No. 12 (1963), pp. 56, 61–64.

44. S. V. Polenina, *Osnovy grazhdanskogo zakonodatel'stva i grazhdanskie kodeksy* (Moscow: Iuridicheskaia Literatura, 1968).

45. Law of June 27, 1968 [1968] *Vedomosti Verkhovnogo Soveta SSSR,* No. 27, item 241.

46. Law of July 8, 1944 [1944] *Vedomosti Verkhovnogo Soveta SSSR,* No. 37. No item number.

47. Statute of the Supreme Court of the USSR, Feb. 12, 1957, as amended Sept. 30, 1967 [1957] *Vedomosti Verkhovnogo Suda SSSR,* No. 4, item 85 and [1967] *Ibid.,* No. 40, item 526. Articles 9 (*b*) and (*c*) and 11.

48. [1969] *Biulleten' Verkhovnogo Suda SSSR,* No. 3, p. 11.

49. *Ibid.,* No. 4, p. 9.

50. *Ibid.,* No. 5, p. 14.

51. *Ibid.,* No. 1, p. 17.

52. Case of M. K. Tskaev, *Ibid.,* No. 1, p. 21.

53. Case of N. I. Shibanov, *Ibid.*, p. 22.

54. Case of N. G. Oganesian, *Ibid.*, No. 2, p. 13.

55. Case of A. M. Sukhanov, *Ibid.*, p. 14.

56. Case of I. P. Bondarenko, *Ibid.*, p. 9.

57. Case of A. Saparkopekov, *Ibid.*, p. 11.

58. Edict of July 26, 1966 [1966] *Vedomosti Verkhovnogo Soveta SSSR*, No. 30, item 595.

59. Dwelling Construction Cooperative No. 45 vs. I. B. Dets *et al.*, [1969] *Biulleten' Verkhovnogo Suda SSSR*, No. 5, p. 19.

60. A. A. Fateeva vs. V. A. Traksin, *Ibid.*, No 2, p. 8.

61. V. I. Ladokha vs. N. A. Ladokha, *Ibid.*, No. 4, p. 26.

62. L. I. Shpakovskaia vs. A. L. Mikheichik and L. N. Mikheichik, *Ibid.*, No. 5, p. 23.

63. V. P. Bakulina vs. Construction Administration No. 164 of Trust "Fundamentstroi" No. 2, *Ibid.*, No. 4, p. 24.

64. T. Kh. Dedkova vs. Dushanbe City Administration of Trade, *Ibid.*, p. 23.

65. A. A. Mekinian vs. Erevan Jewelry Factory, *Ibid.*, No. 1, p. 13.

66. Frunze Electrotechnical Factory vs. I. M. Labanov, *Ibid.*, p. 15.

ROBERT A. LEWIS

THE MIXING OF RUSSIANS
AND SOVIET NATIONALITIES
AND ITS DEMOGRAPHIC IMPACT

Spatial distributions are basic to geographic knowledge, and the distribution of population especially has been a central theme in human geography since at least the beginning of the nineteenth century. Much of the current work in the field is either directly or indirectly focused upon this topic.[1] The distribution of population has a discernible impact upon society. Regardless of the regime governing what is now the USSR, internal forces related to population distribution will shape that society in the 1970s. These forces include sharp regional differentials in rates of population growth, low Slavic and generally high non-Slavic fertility, severe regional labor shortages, widespread rural depopulation, rapid urbanization, and the maldistribution of population relative to industrial resources.

Another force related to the distribution of population seems to be causing increasing strain in Soviet society and may well become the dominant one. This is the multinational character of the USSR and Russian mixing with Soviet nationalities. An adequate understanding of Soviet nationality problems requires a sufficient knowledge of the geography (the spatial distribution and interrelationships) of Russians and Soviet nationalities.

The purpose of this essay is to study the mixing of Russians with Soviet nationalities. In particular, it is to ascertain to what extent mixing has occurred regionally since the end of the nineteenth century, and to learn about some of the effects of this mixing. Mixing occurs when the proportion of the total regional population comprised by a nationality approaches that of the entire country.

The chief premise underlying this study is that there are no unique "communist" demographic processes. People throughout the world tend to react in the same manner to forces which influence their demographic behavior, whether they live under capitalistic or communistic regimes—or anything in between. Demographic processes are largely related to socioeconomic conditions, rather than to the types of government under which they develop. To understand demographic processes in the USSR, one must relate Soviet developments to general theory whenever possible and make international comparisons of population trends and processes. In short, the problems of the USSR cannot properly be understood solely through studying the USSR.

The first section of this three-part study will be devoted to a discussion of data sources, problems, evaluation, and definitions. This discussion is important, because the present study is based primarily upon the various Czarist and Soviet censuses. These censuses provide the chief source of nationality and other socioeconomic data concerning the USSR. Unfortunately, they have been used and evaluated relatively little. We have worked with data problems in these censuses for a number of years and have solved the chief problems of data comparability. The resulting statistical series provides the basis for this study.

The second part of the paper will treat the mixing of Russians and Soviet nationalities between the years 1897 and 1959. Aggregate trends in the distribution of nationalities will be discussed, and indices of mixing and redistribution of select nationalities will be presented. The third section of the paper deals with an attempt to establish relationships between the Russian mixing, in particular, and such socioeconomic variables as Russification, urbanization, and labor-force characteristics.

Data and Definitions

The chief sources of data analyzed for this paper will be the Czarist and Soviet censuses of 1897, 1926, and 1959.[2] All population data used in the study are *de facto*. Data from the 1939 census were excluded, because only aggregate nationality data were published from this enumeration, except for the data, relating to a few union republics and autonomous republics, that have recently been published.[3] Nationality data from the 1970 enumeration had not been published at the time this paper was being written. The chief data deficiency for the nationalities was the lack of information about Khiva and Bukhara in the 1897 census. Inhabitants of those two khanates constituted about 40 percent of the Central Asian population. To compensate for this and other similar shortcomings in the data, we assumed that the composition of the total estimated population matched that of the area for which we have nationality data.

To study the mixing or redistribution of Soviet nationalities, the socioeconomic variables related to such mixing, or any kind of population change, it is necessary to make accurate regional comparisons over time. Despite the great array of nationality data presented in various Soviet censuses, such comparisons have been impossible to make, because among the censuses there has been no territorial, and very little definitional comparability. Because the territory of the USSR has changed several times since the latter part of the nineteenth century, it was different in all census years. Consequently, in order to provide data for the contemporary territory of the USSR,[4] it was necessary to gather data from East European censuses and other sources for the border areas formerly outside but currently within the USSR.

Because the Soviet Union has a large, diverse population, aggregate population data for the USSR are too gross to be meaningful. Moreover, frequent and drastic changes in the internal administrative divisions over the past hundred years have made it very difficult to compare regional demographic and other data from one point in time to another. This is because census and other data are normally collected for such divisions. To solve the problems, it was necessary to reorder the data of each census into a common set of territorial units.

Careful selection of territorial units (regions) is important in order to avoid biasing the data excessively. Unfortunately, popula-

ECONOMIC REGIONS, 1961

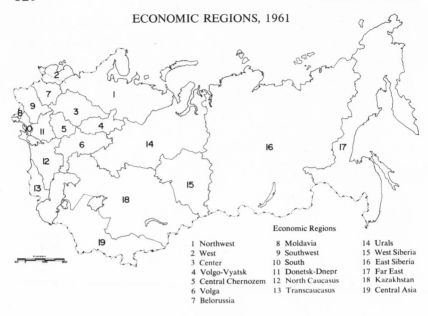

Economic Regions		
1 Northwest	8 Moldavia	14 Urals
2 West	9 Southwest	15 West Siberia
3 Center	10 South	16 East Siberia
4 Volgo-Vyatsk	11 Donetsk-Dnepr	17 Far East
5 Central Chernozem	12 North Caucasus	18 Kazakhstan
6 Volga	13 Transcaucasus	19 Central Asia
7 Belorussia		

Figure 1

tion data are not available for the USSR, or most other countries, in sufficient detail to permit construction of a unique set of uniform regions for every analytical purpose; consequently, the existing rather gross units into which data have been collected must be used. Regionalization is the spatial aspect of the classification problem.[5] There is no adequate, all-purpose, multivariable set of uniform regions for a country, just as there is no all-purpose statistical interval. Ideally, we should have a different set of regions for each problem studied. They should be delimited on a comparable basis, maximizing external variation and minimizing internal variation. However, when making comparisons over a long period of time, the problem of establishing such a set of uniform regions is virtually insoluble. So much socioeconomic change has occurred in all areas of Czarist Russia or the USSR between 1897 and 1959 that it is impossible to delimit a set of regions that continued to be homogeneous throughout this period on the basis of any socioeconomic criterion.

Even though the "major" (*krupnye*) Soviet economic regions of 1961 (Figure 1) are not ideal, we chose them as the basic statistical units for population data about the USSR for the following reasons: (1) The Soviet government often presents data in these units. In fact, data for the 1959 census have already been presented in these units. (2) Except for a few changes that have occured since 1961, the boundaries of the economic regions conform to those of the present administrative divisions; consequently, additional data can be presented in these units easily and accurately. (3) These are not true economic regions, because they have been delimited on the basis of political and administrative decisions and include political-administrative units in their entirety. Since nationality plays such a dominant role in political and administrative decisions, these regions are best suited for purposes of studying the nationalities. Because other population characteristics relate closely to nationality, these economic regions also serve adequately for population study in general.

In order to allocate population data into comparable territorial units (the economic regions), we have assumed that, except for urban concentrations, population is evenly distributed within each administrative unit; therefore, a variation in area would result in a proportionate variation in population. The "rural" population and rural population characteristic of the political divisions in 1897 and 1926 were allocated to the various economic regions on the basis of the area of each administrative division which fits into the appropriate economic region. All centers with a population of 15,000 and over were individually allocated to the appropriate economic region. By combining rural and urban components, it was possible to allocate the total population and total population characteristics into the economic regions for the various census years. Available tests indicate that our error was not great.[6]

Still another problem to be faced was the lack of comparable definitions. With the exception of sex and age, definitions among the various Soviet censuses were not comparable. Therefore, it was necessary to make major statistical adjustments in order to obtain comparable data. We did not always succeed in producing

122   ROBERT A. LEWIS

the very best definition of a particular population characteristic, but it was made as nearly comparable as possible.[7]

The derivation of comparable nationality definitions posed a special question, because no reasonable adjustment could be made. Data representing nationality and native language are available from the 1926 and 1959 censuses, but only data about native language were collected in the 1897 census. However, it is probably reasonable to assume that the Russian language had not been widely adopted by non-Russians by the end of the nineteenth century, and consequently that native language provided a good indicator of nationality in 1897.

Thus, for the first time comparisons based on comparable territorial units and definitions for the 1897, 1926, and 1959 censuses can be made for the contemporary territory of the USSR employing a wide variety of census variables. The end product of this statistical work is three data matrices, each 19 by 58. The 19 refers to the official Soviet economic regions of 1961, and the 58 refers to census variables, which pertain primarily to urbanization, labor force, sex, age, nationality, fertility, and literacy. These matrices provide the chief source of data for this study.

Table 1 presents data for Russians, Ukrainians, Belorussians, East Slavs, non-Russians, and non-East Slavs, the groups studied in this paper. "Non-East Slav" is a gross category comprising many diverse nationalities. The forty-three most numerous Soviet nationalities plus the Russians in 1959 included all but about

NOTES TO TABLE 1 (below):
(A) The distribution of a variable is the percent of a variable's Union-wide total that is found in each region.
(B) The level of a variable is the percent of a region's total population that is comprised by that variable. (NA) Not Applicable.

SOURCES FOR TABLES 1–5:
Pervaia vseobshchaia perepis' naseleniia Rossiiskoi Imperii 1897 g. (St. Petersburg: Izdanie Tsentral'nago Statisticheskago Komiteta Ministerstva Vnutrennikh Diel, 1905), 89 Vols.; *Vsesoiuznaia perepis' naseleniia 1926 goda* (Moscow: Izdanie Tsentral'nogo Statisticheskogo Upravleniia SSSR, 1929), 66 Vols.; *Itogi vsesoiuznoi perepisi naseleniia 1959 goda* (Moscow: Gosstatizdat, Tsentral'noe Statisticheskoe Upravlenie SSSR, 1962–1963), 16 Vols.; *Annals of the Association of American Geographers* (December 1969), p. 777, note 3.

Table 1. Nationality Data: 1897, 1926 and 1959

Regions	Russians as % of Total Russians			Ukrainians as % of Total Ukrainians			Belorussians as % of Total Belorussians		
DISTRIBUTION (A)	1897	1926	1959	1897	1926	1959	1897	1926	1959
Northwest	10.4	10.9	8.7	0.0	0.1	0.9	2.7	0.8	3.4
West	0.6	0.4	0.9	0.0	0.0	0.2	13.3	2.6	1.3
Center	25.6	25.4	20.5	1.7	0.5	1.0	5.0	1.3	1.2
Volgo-Vyatsk	8.7	7.1	5.5	0.0	0.0	0.2	0.0	0.0	0.0
Central Chernozem	12.2	11.7	7.3	5.7	4.7	0.8	0.1	0.2	0.0
Volga	11.4	10.8	8.3	2.2	1.4	0.8	0.1	0.2	0.3
Belorussia	0.6	0.5	0.6	1.5	0.4	0.4	73.9	82.9	84.4
Moldavia	0.2	0.3	0.3	1.7	0.9	1.1	0.0	0.0	0.1
Southwest	1.6	0.6	1.1	46.6	44.3	47.8	2.9	2.8	0.7
South	1.3	1.1	1.4	7.4	5.8	7.7	0.4	0.4	0.7
Donetsk-Dnepr	2.6	2.2	3.8	23.9	26.4	30.8	0.9	0.6	1.9
North Caucasus	5.0	5.0	7.9	7.3	8.7	1.0	0.4	0.8	0.5
Transcaucasus	0.4	0.4	0.8	0.1	0.1	0.2	0.1	0.1	0.1
Urals	11.9	11.0	12.0	0.4	0.8	1.5	0.1	1.0	1.5
West Siberia	3.0	6.1	7.6	0.4	2.0	1.2	0.1	2.7	0.9
East Siberia	2.5	3.3	4.9	0.1	0.3	0.6	0.0	2.4	0.7
Far East	0.3	0.9	3.1	0.2	1.0	1.2	0.0	0.7	0.7
Kazakhstan	1.4	1.7	3.5	0.5	2.4	2.0	0.0	0.4	1.4
Central Asia	0.2	0.6	2.0	0.1	0.3	0.7	0.0	0.1	0.3
TOTAL	99.9	100.0	100.2	99.8	100.1	100.1	100.0	100.0	100.1

Table continues

Table 1. (*continued*)

Regions	East Slavs as % of Total East Slavs			Non-East Slavs as % of Total Non-East Slavs			Non-Russians as % of Total Non-Russians		
DISTRIBUTION (A)	1897	1926	1959	1897	1926	1959	1897	1926	1959
Northwest	7.0	7.2	6.6	5.2	3.5	1.9	3.2	1.9	1.6
West	1.3	0.4	0.8	11.7	11.1	9.7	7.8	6.0	5.3
Center	17.4	16.8	15.0	0.8	1.3	1.8	1.5	1.0	1.4
Volgo-Vyatsk	5.7	4.7	4.0	3.3	3.4	3.8	1.9	1.8	2.1
Central Chernozem	9.6	9.0	5.4	0.3	0.1	0.1	2.1	2.0	0.4
Volga	8.0	7.5	6.1	7.2	7.1	5.5	4.9	4.3	3.2
Belorussia	5.7	4.6	4.6	4.0	4.4	1.5	8.8	8.2	7.8
Moldavia	0.6	0.5	0.5	2.5	3.2	4.4	2.0	2.0	2.7
Southwest	14.4	13.6	12.0	13.2	10.7	2.4	24.0	23.8	20.1
South	3.0	2.4	2.8	3.0	3.5	1.1	4.3	4.2	3.7
Donetsk-Dnepr	8.5	9.2	10.0	1.4	1.6	1.2	9.2	11.6	12.9
North Caucasus	5.4	5.9	5.9	4.2	4.7	4.8	4.9	6.0	2.9
Transcaucasus	0.3	0.3	0.7	11.0	11.9	17.0	6.3	6.3	9.0
Urals	7.8	7.5	9.0	6.1	6.0	8.6	3.6	3.5	5.2
West Siberia	2.1	4.7	5.8	0.5	1.2	2.0	0.5	1.6	1.6
East Siberia	1.7	2.4	3.7	1.7	1.6	2.2	1.0	1.1	1.4
Far East	0.3	0.9	2.5	0.5	0.9	0.7	0.3	0.9	0.9
Kazakhstan	1.1	1.8	3.0	9.9	8.6	9.0	5.8	5.5	5.6
Central Asia	0.2	0.4	1.6	13.5	15.3	22.4	7.7	8.1	12.1
TOTAL	100.1	99.8	100.0	100.0	100.1	100.1	99.8	99.8	99.9

Regions	Russians as % of Total Regional Population			Ukrainians as % of Total Regional Population			Belorussians as % of Total Regional Population		
LEVEL (B)	1897	1926	1959	1897	1926	1959	1897	1926	1959
Northwest	72.4	83.9	86.6	0.1	0.2	2.9	1.9	0.5	2.3
West	5.9	6.3	17.1	0.2	0.0	1.0	13.1	2.8	1.7
Center	93.3	96.0	94.5	2.7	0.8	1.5	1.9	0.4	0.4
Volgo-Vyatsk	78.5	78.4	76.4	0.0	0.1	0.7	0.0	0.0	0.0
Central Chernozem	82.0	84.3	96.0	16.6	15.1	3.3	0.1	0.1	0.0
Volga	65.0	69.4	75.6	5.5	4.1	2.3	0.1	0.1	0.2
Belorussia	5.3	5.6	8.2	5.6	1.8	1.7	64.8	66.2	81.1
Moldavia	8.5	11.8	10.2	27.1	15.5	14.6	0.2	0.0	0.2
Southwest	4.9	2.3	6.0	64.4	74.0	87.9	0.9	0.8	0.3
South	19.6	19.0	30.9	48.0	45.3	56.9	0.6	0.5	1.0
Donetsk-Dnepr	18.1	14.6	26.1	74.1	78.9	69.4	0.6	0.3	0.9
North Caucasus	44.8	42.6	76.4	28.4	33.7	3.1	0.3	0.6	0.4
Transcaucasus	4.3	5.7	10.2	0.4	0.6	0.9	0.1	0.1	0.1
Urals	72.4	73.7	73.3	1.2	2.4	3.0	0.1	0.5	0.6
West Siberia	84.1	77.4	85.3	5.1	11.4	4.3	0.2	2.7	0.7
East Siberia	66.6	72.8	80.4	1.6	3.2	3.3	0.1	4.0	0.7
Far East	43.6	47.2	81.2	13.4	22.8	9.9	0.2	2.9	1.2
Kazakhstan	16.0	22.0	42.7	2.6	13.6	8.2	0.0	0.4	1.2
Central Asia	2.2	5.8	16.4	0.5	1.3	2.0	0.0	0.1	0.1
	45.2	46.9	54.6	19.8	21.3	17.8	4.6	3.6	3.7

Table continues

Table 1. (*continued*)

Regions	East Slavs as % of Total Regional Population			Non-East Slavs as % of Total Regional Population			Non-Russians as % of Total Regional Population		
LEVEL (B)	1897	1926	1959	1897	1926	1959	1897	1926	1959
Northwest	74.5	84.6	91.8	25.5	15.4	8.2	27.6	16.1	13.4
West	19.2	9.2	19.8	80.8	90.8	80.2	94.1	93.7	82.9
Center	97.8	97.1	96.4	2.2	2.9	3.6	6.7	4.0	5.5
Volgo-Vyatsk	78.6	78.5	77.1	21.4	21.5	22.9	21.5	21.6	23.6
Central Chernozem	98.6	99.5	99.3	1.4	0.5	0.7	18.0	15.7	4.0
Volga	70.5	73.6	78.1	29.5	26.4	21.9	35.0	30.6	24.4
Belorussia	75.7	73.7	91.0	24.3	26.3	9.0	94.7	94.4	91.8
Moldavia	35.8	27.5	25.0	64.2	72.5	75.0	91.5	88.2	89.8
Southwest	70.2	77.0	94.2	29.8	23.0	5.8	95.1	97.7	94.0
South	68.2	64.8	88.8	31.8	35.2	11.2	80.4	81.0	69.1
Donetsk-Dnepr	92.8	93.9	96.4	7.2	6.1	3.6	81.9	85.4	73.9
North Caucasus	73.5	76.8	79.9	26.5	23.2	20.1	55.2	57.4	23.6
Transcaucasus	4.9	6.4	11.2	95.1	93.6	88.8	95.7	94.3	89.8
Urals	73.6	76.6	76.9	26.4	23.4	23.1	27.6	26.3	26.7
West Siberia	89.4	91.5	90.3	10.6	8.5	9.7	15.9	22.6	14.7
East Siberia	68.3	80.0	84.4	31.7	20.0	15.6	33.4	27.2	19.6
Far East	57.2	72.9	92.3	42.8	27.1	7.7	56.4	52.8	18.8
Kazakhstan	18.6	36.1	52.1	81.4	63.9	47.9	84.0	78.0	57.3
Central Asia	2.7	7.1	18.5	97.3	92.9	81.5	97.8	94.2	83.6
	69.5	71.8	76.3	30.5	28.2	23.7	54.8	53.1	45.4

1,000,000 of the Soviet population. The non-East Slavs made up about 24 percent of the total population, and of this the Turkic nationalities comprised 46 percent. Finno-Ugrians, Balts, Armenians, Georgians, Jews, Moldavians, Germans, Tajiks, and Poles accounted for the bulk of the remainder. However, as will be demonstrated, this category reflects the major trends at work in the distribution and redistribution of Soviet nationalities and Russians, and reflects very well the demographic relationship between the East Slavs and other Soviet nationalities.

In addition, it is necessary to attempt an evaluation of the nationality data in the various censuses, bearing in mind that for no aspect of society do we possess completely accurate information. Even though census data are gathered more systematically than most other socioeconomic data, they too are susceptible to error. The first consideration is to determine how precise the Soviet census definition of nationality is. Nationality can be broadly defined as a sense of community characterized to *different degrees* by such variables as language, territory, history, culture, religion, and national character. Because the importance of these component variables differs considerably from one nationality to another, it is impossible to use them in a census to define nationality. If there were a uniquely correct definition of nationality, uniquely correct data could be gathered according to this definition. In the absence of this definition, the best way to determine nationality for our purposes is through self-identification. Soviet census takers asked each person's nationality in the 1926, 1939, 1959, and 1970 censuses.

Moreover, how the nationality question is asked or worded and the sort of instructions given to the census taker can also bias the responses. In the 1926 census the question was asked, "to what subnationality (*narodnost'*) do you belong?" In the 1939, 1959, and 1970 censuses, the query concerned the nationality (*natsional'nost'*) to which the person belonged. In this sense, nationality refers to nation (*natsiia*), and not every ethnic group has officially acquired the status of *natsiia* or *natsional'nost'*. At least in theory these two are defined in terms of literary language, economy, territory, history, and number (at least 300,-

000). To prevent confusion and error on this point, a very pene-
trating Soviet analysis of the subject had recommended that both
terms (*narodnost'* and *natsional'nost'*) be used in the 1970 census,
but the recommendations were not heeded by the government.[8]
In the census question about spoken language, it was also recommended that the term "conversational language" (*razgovornyi
iazyk*) be used in place of "native language" (*rodnoi iazyk*),
which can be confused with the language of one's nationality. This
suggestion was also rejected.

Instructions to the census takers for the 1897 census were weak
in failing to provide instructions with respect to the native language question. The 1926 census supplied fairly detailed instructions respecting both the nationality and native language questions. The 1959 census was weaker than that of 1926 but still
stronger than that of 1897.[9] The "disappearance" of several rather
populous Soviet nationalities between 1926 and 1959 has been
blamed on inadequate census instruction, changes in the wording
of the key question, and some census takers' lack of knowledge
about ethnic terminology and the roster of Soviet nationalities.[10]
Despite these shortcomings, Czarist and Soviet censuses provide
a wealth of reasonably accurate data about the nationalities of
the country.

Mixing the Russians and Nationalities

The measurement of Russian and nationality mixing will be
accomplished primarily by analyzing the comparable data presented in Table 1. Tables 2, 3, and 4 derive from Table 1. They
show percentage point changes in the distribution and level of the
nationality variables for the periods 1897–1926, 1926–1959, and
1897–1959. These tables will be analyzed very generally to determine trends related to mixing and redistribution; they also provide insights and suggest problems for future study. We will first
look briefly at the nationality distribution recorded in 1897, then
investigate changes over time, and finally survey the situation
in 1959. To further this analysis, several indices have been calculated, and the chief characteristics of the Russians, the main
group that is mixing, were mapped.

Table 2. Change in Nationality Data: 1897–1926

Regions	Russians	Ukrainians	Belorussians	East Slavs	Non-East Slavs	Non-Russians
DISTRIBUTION (A)						
Northwest	0.5	0.1	−1.9	0.2	−1.7	−1.3
West	−0.2	0.0	−10.7	−0.9	−0.6	−1.8
Center	−0.2	−1.2	−3.7	−0.6	0.5	−0.5
Volgo-Vyatsk	−1.6	0.0	0.0	−1.0	0.1	−0.1
Central Chernozem	−0.5	−1.0	0.1	−0.6	−0.2	−0.1
Volga	−0.6	−0.8	0.1	−0.5	−0.1	−0.6
Belorussia	−0.1	−1.1	9.0	−1.1	0.4	−0.6
Moldavia	0.1	−0.8	0.0	−0.1	0.7	0.0
Southwest	−1.0	−2.3	−0.1	−0.8	−2.5	−0.2
South	−0.2	−1.6	0.0	−0.6	0.5	−0.1
Donetsk-Dnepr	−0.4	2.5	−0.3	0.7	0.2	2.4
North Caucasus	0.0	1.4	0.4	0.5	0.5	1.1
Transcaucasus	0.0	0.0	0.0	0.0	0.9	0.0
Urals	−0.9	0.4	0.9	−0.3	−0.1	−0.1
West Siberia	3.1	1.6	2.6	2.6	0.7	1.1
East Siberia	0.8	0.2	2.4	0.7	−0.1	0.1
Far East	0.6	0.8	0.7	0.6	0.4	0.6
Kazakhstan	0.3	1.9	0.4	0.7	−1.3	−0.3
Central Asia	0.4	0.2	0.1	0.2	1.8	0.4
TOTAL	NA	NA	NA	NA	NA	NA

Table continues

Table 2. (continued)

Regions	Russians	Ukrainians	Belorussians	East Slavs	Non-East Slavs	Non-Russians
LEVEL (B)						
Northwest	11.5	0.1	−1.4	10.1	−10.1	−11.5
West	0.4	−0.2	−10.3	−10.0	10.0	−0.4
Center	2.7	−1.9	−1.5	−0.7	0.7	−2.7
Volgo-Vyatsk	−0.1	0.1	0.0	−0.1	0.1	0.1
Central Chernozem	2.3	−1.5	0.0	0.9	−0.9	−2.3
Volga	4.4	−1.4	0.0	3.1	−3.1	−4.4
Belorussia	0.3	−3.8	1.4	−2.0	2.0	−0.3
Moldavia	3.3	−11.6	−0.2	−8.3	8.3	−3.3
Southwest	−2.6	9.6	−0.1	6.8	−6.8	2.6
South	−0.6	−2.7	−0.1	−3.4	3.4	0.6
Donetsk-Dnepr	−3.5	4.8	−0.3	1.1	−1.1	3.5
North Caucasus	−2.2	5.3	0.3	3.3	−3.3	2.2
Transcaucasus	1.4	0.2	0.0	1.5	−1.5	−1.4
Urals	1.3	1.2	0.4	3.0	−3.0	−1.3
West Siberia	−6.7	6.3	2.5	2.1	−2.1	6.7
East Siberia	6.2	1.6	3.9	11.7	−11.7	−6.2
Far East	3.6	9.4	2.7	15.7	−15.7	−3.6
Kazakhstan	6.0	11.0	0.4	17.5	−17.5	−6.0
Central Asia	3.6	0.8	0.1	4.4	−4.4	−3.6
TOTAL	1.7	1.5	−1.0	2.4	−2.4	−1.7

For explanatory notes, see Table 1.

In 1897, in the present-day territory of the USSR, East Slavs comprised 69.5 percent of the population; and the Russians were the largest group among the East Slavs, accounting for over 45 percent of the total population (Table 1). The non-East Slavs in this breakdown, of course, made up the remaining 30 percent. In terms of the level, defined as the proportion of a region's total population that a nationality comprised, East Slavs constituted the highest proportion in the western areas and in Siberia, as might be expected. There were relatively few East Slavs located in Central Asia, the Transcaucasus, Kazakhstan (Kazakhstan is separated from southern Central Asia here for statistical purposes), and the West. Belorussians outside Belorussia were found in appreciable numbers only in the West, whereas Ukrainians outside the Ukraine constituted a significant proportion of the population of the North Caucasus, Moldavia, Central Chernozem, and the Far East, although in the Far East their absolute number remained small. Outside the traditional Russian areas, Russians spread eastward into Siberia, where, in every area except the Far East, they comprised a majority. In the North Caucasus, South, and Donetsk-Dnepr, they were also proportionately strong, indicating a significant movement to the western steppe, mainly during the nineteenth century. The highest levels of non-East Slavic population, of course, were found in Central Asia, the Transcaucasus, Kazakhstan, the West, and Moldavia. They also constituted significant proportions of the total population in many other regions.

Expected patterns of distribution, defined as the percent of the total nationality population located in a region, likewise prevailed (Table 1). Only a small proportion of the East Slavs were found in Central Asia, the Transcaucasus, Kazakhstan, Moldavia, and the West. The greatest proportion of Russians was found in the Center, Central Chernozem, the Urals, Volga, the Northwest, and Volgo-Vyatsk. Almost 80 percent of the Ukrainians lived in the Ukraine and nearly three-fourths of the Belorussians in Belorussia. The non-East Slav population concentrated itself mainly in Central Asia, the Southwest (largely Jews), the West, the Transcaucasus, and Kazakhstan.

Table 3. Change in Nationality Data: 1926–1959

Regions	Russians	Ukrainians	Belorussians	East Slavs	Non-East Slavs	Non-Russians
DISTRIBUTION (A)						
Northwest	-2.2	0.8	2.6	-0.6	-1.6	-0.3
West	0.5	0.2	-1.3	0.4	-1.4	-0.7
Center	-4.9	0.5	-0.1	-1.8	0.5	0.4
Volgo-Vyatsk	-1.6	0.2	0.0	-0.7	0.4	0.3
Central Chernozem	-4.4	-3.9	-0.2	-3.6	0.0	-1.6
Volga	-2.5	-0.6	0.1	-1.4	-1.6	-1.1
Belorussia	0.1	0.0	1.5	0.0	-2.9	-0.4
Moldavia	0.0	0.2	0.1	0.0	1.2	0.7
Southwest	0.5	3.5	-2.1	-1.6	-8.3	-3.7
South	0.3	1.9	0.3	0.4	-2.4	-0.5
Donetsk-Dnepr	1.6	4.4	1.3	0.8	-0.4	1.3
North Caucasus	2.9	-7.7	-0.3	0.0	0.1	-3.1
Transcaucasus	0.4	0.1	0.0	0.4	5.1	2.7
Urals	1.0	0.7	0.5	1.5	2.6	1.7
West Siberia	1.5	-0.8	-1.8	1.1	0.8	0.0
East Siberia	1.6	0.3	-1.7	1.3	0.6	0.3
Far East	2.2	0.2	0.0	1.6	-0.2	0.0
Kazakhstan	1.8	-0.4	1.0	1.2	0.4	0.1
Central Asia	1.4	0.4	0.2	1.2	7.1	4.0
TOTAL	NA	NA	NA	NA	NA	NA

Regions	Russians	Ukrainians	Belorussians	East Slavs	Non-East Slavs	Non-Russians
LEVEL (B)						
Northwest	2.7	2.7	1.8	7.2	−7.2	−2.7
West	10.8	1.0	−1.1	10.6	−10.6	−10.8
Center	−1.5	0.7	0.0	−0.7	0.7	1.5
Volgo-Vyatsk	−2.0	0.6	0.0	−1.4	1.4	2.0
Central Chernozem	11.7	−11.8	−0.1	−0.2	0.2	−11.7
Volga	6.2	−1.8	0.1	4.5	−4.5	−6.2
Belorussia	2.6	−0.1	14.9	17.3	−17.3	−2.6
Moldavia	−1.6	−0.9	0.2	−2.5	2.5	1.6
Southwest	3.7	13.9	−0.5	17.2	−17.2	−3.7
South	11.9	11.6	0.5	24.0	−24.0	−11.9
Donetsk-Dnepr	11.5	−9.5	0.6	2.5	−2.5	−11.5
North Caucasus	33.8	−30.6	−0.2	3.1	−3.1	−33.8
Transcaucasus	4.5	0.3	0.0	4.8	−4.8	−4.5
Urals	−0.4	0.6	0.1	0.3	−0.3	0.4
West Siberia	7.9	−7.1	−2.0	−1.2	1.2	−7.9
East Siberia	7.6	0.1	−3.3	4.4	−4.4	−7.6
Far East	34.0	−12.9	−1.7	19.4	−19.4	−34.0
Kazakhstan	20.7	−5.4	0.8	16.0	−16.0	−20.7
Central Asia	10.6	0.7	0.0	11.4	−11.4	−10.6
TOTAL	7.7	−3.5	0.1	4.5	−4.5	−7.7

For explanatory notes, see Table 1.

Between 1897 and 1926, the East Slavs increased their proportion of the total population in the present-day territory of the USSR to 72 percent, or about two percentage points, which, of course, means there was a proportionate relative decline in non-East Slavs (Table 2). Not all of the East Slavs increased their proportion; the Belorussians decreased. Two major occurrences during this period affected the levels of the various nationality groups. These were the emigration of a large proportion of the Jewish population, the loss of the western border areas, with the consequent emigration of many, mainly East Slavs, and the in-migration to the border areas of non-East Slavs. According to the 1926 census, 1,867,020 persons, 1.3 percent of the total Soviet population, were born in foreign areas. Of these persons, 68.9 percent were born in territory that was formerly a part of the Russian Empire, but did not constitute a part of the USSR in 1926.[11] From 1890 to 1915 the net outflow from the Russian Empire, which included a large part of Poland, reached 3,300,000 persons. The emigrants came predominantly from western Russia, and the largest single group was Jewish.[12] The decline in both the level and distribution of non-East Slavs in the southwest reflects the emigration of the Jewish population. The in-migration of Poles and Moldavians (Rumanians) masked the effect of this loss of Jewish population in Belorussia and Moldavia. The decline in the level and distribution of East Slavs in Belorussia, Moldavia, the Southwest, and South resulted from the loss of the western border areas and the consequent in-migration of foreigners.

There was no significant redistribution of the population during the 1897–1926 period. Slight declines were evident in the proportion of the East Slavs located in western areas, and slight gains appeared elsewhere. The only significant gain for the non-East Slavs, and that represented only 1.8 percentage points, was registered in Central Asia. The non-East Slav gains in the western border areas had largely been cancelled by the Jewish emigration.

Between 1926 and 1959, the East Slavs once again increased their proportion of the total population, but only the Russians registered a significant relative gain (Table 3). The Belorussians barely increased, and the Ukrainians declined 3.5 percentage

Table 4. Change in Nationality Data: 1897–1959

Regions	Russians	Ukrainians	Belorussians	East Slavs	Non-East Slavs	Non-Russians
DISTRIBUTION (A)						
Northwest	−1.7	0.9	0.7	−0.4	−3.3	−1.6
West	0.3	0.2	−12.0	−0.5	−2.0	−2.5
Center	−5.1	−0.7	−3.8	−2.4	1.0	−0.1
Volgo-Vyatsk	−3.2	0.2	0.0	−1.7	0.5	0.2
Central Chernozem	−4.9	−4.9	−0.1	−4.2	−0.2	−1.7
Volga	−3.1	−1.4	0.2	−1.9	−1.7	−1.7
Belorussia	0.0	−1.1	10.5	−1.1	−2.5	−1.0
Moldavia	0.1	−0.6	0.1	−0.1	1.9	0.7
Southwest	−0.5	1.2	−2.2	−2.4	−10.8	−3.9
South	0.1	0.3	0.3	−0.2	−1.9	−0.6
Donetsk-Dnepr	1.2	6.9	1.0	1.5	−0.2	3.7
North Caucasus	2.9	−6.3	0.1	0.5	0.6	−2.0
Transcaucasus	0.4	0.1	0.0	0.4	6.0	2.7
Urals	0.1	1.1	1.4	1.2	2.5	1.6
West Siberia	4.6	0.8	0.8	3.7	1.5	1.1
East Siberia	2.4	0.5	0.7	2.0	0.5	0.4
Far East	2.8	1.0	0.7	2.2	0.2	0.6
Kazakhstan	2.1	1.5	1.4	1.9	−0.9	−0.2
Central Asia	1.8	0.6	0.3	1.4	8.9	4.4
TOTAL	NA	NA	NA	NA	NA	NA

Table continues

Table 4. (*continued*)

Regions	Russia	Ukrainians	Belorussians	East Slavs	Non-East Slavs	Non-Russians
LEVEL (B)						
Northwest	14.2	2.8	0.4	17.3	−17.3	−14.2
West	11.2	0.8	−11.4	0.6	−0.6	−11.2
Center	1.2	−1.2	−1.5	−1.4	1.4	−1.2
Volgo-Vyatsk	−2.1	0.7	0.0	−1.5	1.5	2.1
Central Chernozem	14.0	−13.3	−0.1	0.7	−0.7	−14.0
Volga	10.6	−3.2	0.1	7.6	−7.6	−10.6
Belorussia	2.9	−3.9	16.3	15.3	−15.3	−2.9
Moldavia	1.7	−12.5	0.0	−10.8	10.8	−1.7
Southwest	1.1	23.5	−0.6	24.0	−24.0	−1.1
South	11.3	8.9	0.4	20.6	−20.6	−11.3
Donetsk-Dnepr	8.0	−4.7	0.3	3.6	−3.6	−8.0
North Caucasus	31.6	−25.3	0.1	6.4	−6.4	−31.6
Transcaucasus	5.9	0.5	0.0	6.3	−6.3	−5.9
Urals	0.9	1.8	0.5	3.3	−3.3	−0.9
West Siberia	1.2	−0.8	0.5	0.9	−0.9	−1.2
East Siberia	13.8	1.7	0.6	16.1	−16.1	−13.8
Far East	37.6	−3.5	1.0	35.1	−35.1	−37.6
Kazakhstan	26.7	5.6	1.2	33.5	−33.5	−26.7
Central Asia	14.2	1.5	0.1	15.8	−15.8	−14.2
TOTAL	9.4	−2.0	−0.9	6.8	−6.8	−9.4

For explanatory notes, see Table 1.

points. The Ukraine and Belorussia suffered most during World War II. Our rather gross projections indicate that during the War total Soviet direct and indirect population losses came to at least 55,000,000. Russification constitutes also an important factor in the greater relative increase of Russians.

The decline in the level of non-East Slavs can largely be attributed to the deaths of large numbers of Jews during the War and the considerable loss suffered by the Kazakh population during collectivization and the resulting famine. In the census of December 1926, 3,968,289 Soviet Kazakhs were counted, but in January 1939 there were only 3,098,764, revealing a loss of about a million, not taking into account natural increase. Only a few Kazakhs are found in surrounding foreign countries. Within 1926 boundaries, the censuses recorded about 2,500,000 Jews in both 1897 and 1926 and slightly more than three million in 1939. In 1959, within 1959 boundaries, there were some 750,000 fewer than in 1939. Considering the larger area, their decline in number, and even a low rate of natural increase, it is probable that in the contemporary territory of the USSR there was a loss upwards of 2,000,000 Jews, not taking into consideration the Jewish immigration to the USSR that occurred during World War II.

Between 1926 and 1959, a sharp rise occurred in the level of East Slavs living in the South, Belorussia, and the Southwest. This was attributable largely to the loss of much of the Jewish population and the emigration of foreigners out of the western border areas reacquired by the USSR. There was also a significant increase in the East Slavic proportion of Kazakhstan. This growth was partially related both to the decline in the Kazakh population and to in-migration taking place in conjunction with the exodus from western areas during the War, the New Lands Program, and expanding industrialization. The Far East, Central Asia, and the West also experienced increases in their proportion of East Slavs. The greatest increase, from 20 to 34 percentage points, in the level of Russians occurred in the Far East, North Caucasus, and Kazakhstan. The level of Russians increased generally in Siberia, reflecting wartime migrations, displacement of industry, and the

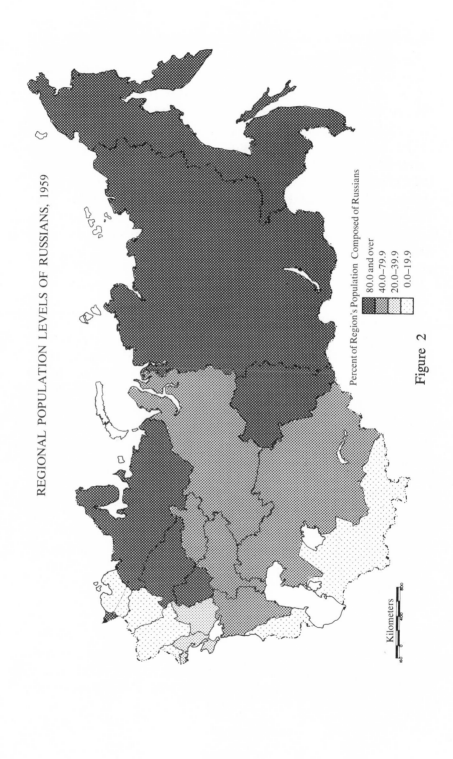

REGIONAL POPULATION LEVELS OF RUSSIANS, 1959

Percent of Region's Population Composed of Russians

80.0 and over
40.0–79.9
20.0–39.9
0.0–19.9

Kilometers

Figure 2

postwar economic development which occurred in the eastern region.

A dramatic redistribution of the Ukrainian population occurred between 1926 and 1959, when the proportion of all Ukrainians living in the Ukraine rose by 10 percentage points to reach almost 86 percent. Most of the decline in Ukrainians outside the Ukraine occurred in the North Caucasus and Central Chernozem. The number of Ukrainians in the North Caucasus dropped sharply from slightly over 3,000,000 in 1926 to somewhat above 300,000 in 1959. In the Central Chernozem their number fell drastically from 1,671,000 to 286,000. Ukrainians were replaced by Russians in both of these regions. Much, if not most, of this Ukrainian loss can probably be explained by Russification. As early as 1926 a large proportion of the Ukrainians living in the North Caucasus spoke Russian as their native language. A similar situation prevailed in 1926 in the northeast Ukraine and south Central Chernozem, particularly in Bryansk Guberniia. Furthermore, there is no evidence that large numbers of Ukrainians have moved out of these areas. A relative decline occurred in the level of Belorussians located in Siberia and the West, and a large increase in Belorussia. The proportion of Belorussians living in Belorussia rose slightly. Some of the decline in numbers of Belorussians found outside Belorussia could also be related to Russification.

In respect to redistribution, between 1926 and 1959 East Slavs declined in traditional East Slav areas and increased elsewhere; this was partially due to the greater loss of population from the western areas during World War II. The Russian pattern was similar, declining relatively in traditional Russian areas and increasing elsewhere. The non-East Slavs declined in the western border areas, except in Moldavia, and increased sharply in Central Asia and the Transcaucasus.

Table 4, which depicts nationality changes from 1897 to 1959, reflects the general trends that have been briefly surveyed for the other periods. Of the groups represented in this table, it is notable that only the Russians increased their proportion in the total population between 1897 and 1959. The Russians increased at a

CHANGE IN REGIONAL POPULATION LEVELS OF RUSSIANS, 1897-1959

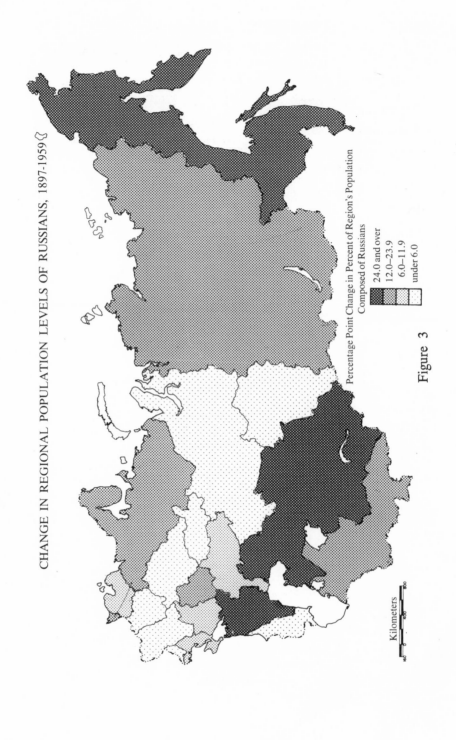

Percentage Point Change in Percent of Region's Population
Composed of Russians

24.0 and over
12.0–23.9
6.0–11.9
under 6.0

Kilometers

Figure 3

rate faster than the Ukrainians and Belorussians, probably because these two nationalities suffered greater war losses and most likely because of Russification. The Russians grew faster than the non-East Slavs, because the groups that comprise this category were generally the last to receive the benefits of modern medicine and economic development with the concomitant reduction in mortality rates. In addition, relatively greater population losses were suffered as a result of the 1917 revolution and emigration affecting especially Kazakhs and Jews.

The 1970 census, however, should show that, since 1959, this pattern of decline has been reversed, and that the non-East Slavs grew much more rapidly than the East Slavs. This is because the current rate of natural increase is generally much higher in non-Slavic areas than in Slavic areas. They will probably increase their proportion of the population by several percentage points.

East Slavs by 1959 made up 76 percent of the Soviet population, and Russians alone accounted for 55 percent (Table 1). In contrast to 1897, 1959 found Russians in significant numbers all over the USSR (Figure 2). Notice also that the greatest increase in the level of Russians took place in the Far East, North Caucasus, and Kazakhstan, areas of considerable economic development. The Southwest and Belorussia, situated adjacent to traditional Russian areas, accommodate the lowest proportion of Russians in their population. The relative lack of economic development there, along with the rural, rather densely settled character of these regions probably accounts for this.

The change which occurred in the population level of the Russians since 1897 is depicted in Figure 3. The Russian population changed least in the traditional Russian areas and most in the southern, northeastern, and parts of the eastern areas of the country. These became the major areas of in-migration during this century. However, in the aggregate, the population level of Russians changed about the same in Russian and non-Russian areas. The level of Russians in regions outside the contemporary Russian SFSR was 8.4 in 1897, 8.6 in 1926, and 17.8 in 1959. In the Russian SFSR the corresponding percentages were 75.1, 76.4, and 83.3. There was, however, a significant dispersal of Russians within the RSFSR.

REGIONAL DISTRIBUTION OF RUSSIANS, 1959

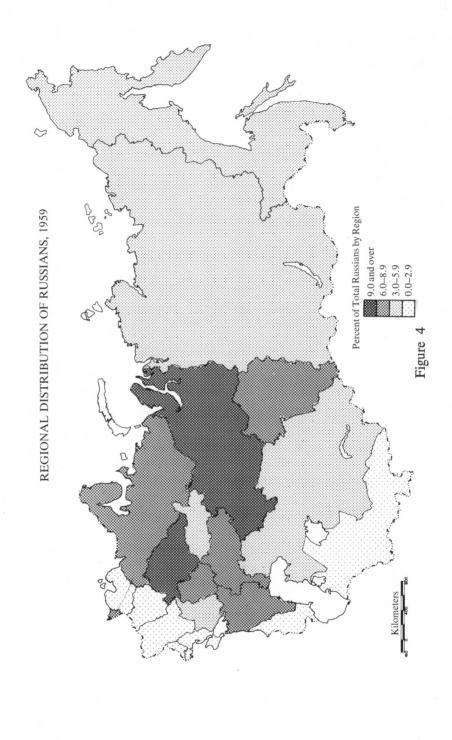

Percent of Total Russians by Region

9.0 and over
6.0–8.9
3.0–5.9
0.0–2.9

Figure 4

Kilometers

Belorussians comprised a relatively insignificant proportion of the population in all regions outside Belorussia. Ukrainians away from their union republic are found in appreciable numbers only in Moldavia, the Far East, and Kazakhstan. Moreover, in Moldavia and the Far East their proportion has declined sharply since 1897. The proportion of the population that is composed of non-East Slavs has declined since 1897 in all regions, except the Center, Volgo-Vyatsk, and Moldavia.

Despite considerable dispersion, 62 percent of the Russians were still to be found in 1959 in such traditional Russian areas as the Center, Central Chernozem, Volgo-Vyatsk, the Northwest, the Urals, and Volga (Figure 4). In 1897, 80 percent of the Russians lived in these regions. The sharpest decline occurred in the Center and Central Chernozem regions. The change in Russian distribution between 1897 and 1959, showing the decline in the proportion of Russians in traditional Russian areas and the gains in non-Russian areas, is illustrated in Figure 5. Belorussia, Moldavia, the South, the Transcaucasus, the West, and the Urals sustained only slightly positive values, even though they are represented by a rather high category on this map.

The 1970 census undoubtedly will record a continued dispersal of Russians. Because most people migrate for economic reasons, there is widespread depopulation of rural Russian areas. Conversely, industrial and urban growth is currently occurring at a greater rate in most non-Russian regions than in Russian ones.[13] Only preliminary results of the 1970 census as yet have been published (see end sheets and appendix),[14] but from these we can deduce much about the dispersal of the Russians since 1959.

We have calculated net migration rates between 1959 and 1970 for economic regions, major cities, and all *oblasts,* and autonomous and union republics. The general patterns which emerge from this analysis support the view that the Russians have continued to disperse. Virtually all of the administrative units located in Russian areas showed negative net migration. The Urals, Volgo-Vyatsk, West Siberia, and Central Chernozem together suffered a net loss of over 3,000,000 persons. Most of the loss has resulted from rural out-migration. Since 1959 the rural popu-

CHANGE IN REGIONAL DISTRIBUTION OF RUSSIANS, 1897-1959

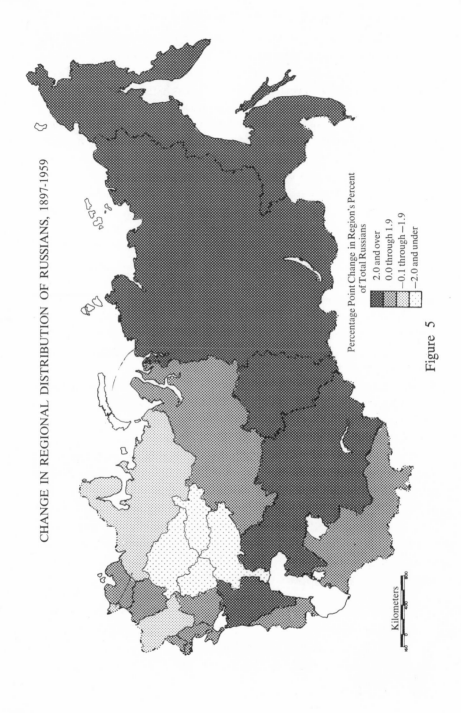

Percentage Point Change in Region's Percent
of Total Russians

2.0 and over
0.0 through 1.9
−0.1 through −1.9
−2.0 and under

Kilometers

Figure 5

lation of the USSR has decreased by more than 3,000,000 people. Urban population, as defined in the census, increased by 36,000,000. Forty-four percent of this came from rural in-migration, and 14 percent resulted from reclassification of rural settlements.

Non-Russian regions experienced positive net migration, except for the Southwest, Belorussia, and the Transcaucasus, which together lost over 1,000,000 through migration. Central Asia and Kazakhstan gained 1,375,000; the South and Donetsk-Dnepr picked up slightly over 1,000,000, and the West rose about 250,000. All regions saw an increase in their urban population, but in this respect the non-Russian regions grew the fastest by far.

In short, Russian areas are generally experiencing rapid rural depopulation, declining rates of urbanization and industrialization, together with low-fertility, and out-migration. Non-Russian areas are experiencing a growth in rural population, rapid urbanization, increasing industrialization, generally high fertility except in the Slavic and Baltic areas, and considerable in-migration. Russians have probably migrated mainly to Kazakhstan and Central Asia, to the North Caucasus and in smaller numbers to the West. The eastern regions continue to lose population, despite government plans to the contrary.

In contrast to the Russians, the nationalities seem to have concentrated since 1897. In 1897 about 78 percent of the Ukrainians lived in the Ukraine, and by 1959, 86 percent. The corresponding figures for the Belorussians were 74 and 84. This percentage, which comes from Table 1, does not agree with the one for Belorussia, given in Table 5, because of computational difficulties. Central Asia, the Transcaucasus, Kazakhstan, the West, and the Urals had in 1897 slightly more than a half of the non-East Slavs, and by 1959, two-thirds. The greatest relative increases occurred in Central Asia and the Transcaucasus, the two most populous non-Slavic areas; this change also indicates a concentration. Furthermore, many of the non-East Slavs living in such Slavic areas as the Urals, West Siberia, East Siberia, and the North Caucasus were, in 1959, concentrated in or near their own nationality units (Table 5 and Frontispiece).

Table 5. Nationality Administrative Units: Selected Characteristics, 1959

Key to Map, Frontispiece	Administrative Unit	Total Population in 1000s	% of Titular Nationality Living in Own Admin. Unit	% of Titular Nationality Living in Contiguous Admin. Unit	Titular Nationality as a % of Total Population	Russians as a % of Total Population	% of Non-Russians Speaking Russian as Native Language
	UNION REPUBLIC						
1	Armenian	1,763.0	55.7	32.1	88.0	3.2	1.0
2	Azerbaijan	3,697.7	84.9	10.2	67.5	13.6	4.5
3	Belorussian	8,054.6	82.5	1.3	81.1	8.2	8.8
4	Estonian	1,196.8	90.3	2.6	74.6	20.1	3.0
5	Georgian	4,044.0	96.6	0.9	64.3	10.1	3.0
6	Kazakh	9,309.8	77.2	18.7	30.0	42.7	11.4
7	Kirgiz	2,065.8	86.4	11.9	40.5	30.2	7.4
8	Latvian	2,093.5	92.7	0.8	62.0	26.6	7.1
9	Lithuanian	2,711.4	92.5	1.4	79.3	8.5	1.4
10	Moldavian	2,884.5	85.2	8.9	65.4	10.2	5.3
11	*Russian SFSR	117,534.3	85.8	5.7	83.3	83.3	23.9
12	Tajik	1,979.9	75.2	21.1	53.1	13.3	2.8
13	Turkmen	1,516.4	92.2	4.7	60.9	17.3	3.5
14	Ukrainian	41,869.0	86.3	2.4	76.8	16.9	9.2
15	Uzbek	8,105.7	83.8	15.2	62.2	13.5	3.2
	TOTAL	208,826.4	85.3	5.9	76.7	54.6	10.8

AUTONOMOUS REPUBLIC

16	Abkhaz	404.7	93.5	2.6	15.1	21.4	5.5
17	Adzhar[E]	245.3	—	—	—	13.4	3.7
18	Bashkir	3,341.6	74.6	17.5	22.1	42.4	6.2
19	Buryat	673.3	53.7	43.7	20.2	74.6	11.0
20	Chechen-Ingush[D]	710.4	55.7	3.6	41.1	49.0	6.4
21	Chuvash	1,097.9	52.4	13.8	70.2	24.0	3.2
22	Dagestan[A]	1,062.4	78.0	17.5	69.3	20.1	2.4
23	Kabardin-Balkar[B]	420.1	91.2	0.8	53.4	38.7	4.6
24	Kalmyk	184.9	61.2	12.0	35.1	55.9	3.7
25	Karakalpak	510.1	90.4	1.4	30.6	4.5	1.1
26	Karelian	651.3	51.1	4.3	13.1	63.4	30.6
27	Komi	806.2	85.4	5.2	30.4	48.4	15.3
28	Mari	647.7	55.4	13.1	43.1	47.8	3.6
29	Mordvin	1,000.2	27.9	21.0	35.8	59.0	3.6
30	Nakhichevan[F]	141.4	—	—	—	2.2	0.4
31	Severo-Ossetin[C]	450.6	52.2	36.5	47.8	39.6	7.3
32	Tatar	2,850.4	27.1	25.0	47.2	43.9	3.1
33	Tuvin	171.9	97.9	0.0	57.0	40.1	2.8
34	Udmurt	1,336.9	76.2	14.7	35.6	56.8	8.1
35	Yakut	487.3	95.5	1.7	46.4	44.2	7.0
	TOTAL	17,194.6	48.7	19.0	38.7	42.7	5.7

Table continues

Table 5. (*continued*)

Key to Map, Frontis- piece	Administrative Unit	Total Population in 1000s	% of Titular Nationality Living in Own Admin. Unit	% of Titular Nationality Living in Contiguous Admin. Unit	Titular Nationality as a % of Total Population	Russians as a % of Total Population	% of Non- Russians Speaking Russian as Native Language
	AUTONOMOUS OBLAST						
36	Adygei	284.7	82.8	13.0	23.2	70.4	10.2
37	Gorno-Altay[G]	157.1	84.0	8.1	24.2	69.8	11.6
38	Gorno-Badakhshan[K]	73.0	—	—	—	1.9	0.3
39	Karachay-Cherkess[H]	278.0	82.2	1.7	33.1	51.0	3.8
40	Khakass	411.0	85.7	8.9	11.8	76.5	22.0
41	Nagorno-Karabakh[J]	130.4	—	—	—	1.4	1.7
42	Evrei	162.9	0.6	0.4	8.8	78.2	58.3
43	Iugo-Ossetin[I]	96.8	15.4	71.0	65.8	2.5	0.8
	TOTAL	1,593.9	10.8	10.8	20.0	56.4	9.3
	NATIONALITY OKRUG						
44	Aga Buryat[L]	49.1	9.2	6.6	47.6	48.6	2.6
45	Chukchi	46.7	85.1	1.1	21.4	60.7	21.7
46	Evenki	10.3	38.1	38.5	33.7	57.9	10.7
47	Khanty-Mansi[O]	123.9	66.0	44.4	13.8	72.5	31.1

48	Komi-Permyak	217.0	87.5	7.3	58.0	32.9	11.0
49	Koryak	27.5	81.1	3.5	18.5	60.6	20.3
50	Nenets	45.5	21.5	62.3	10.9	68.8	23.4
51	Taimyr^M	33.4	8.2	60.8	9.0	65.3	23.3
52	Ust Orda^N	133.1	17.7	10.2	33.7	56.4	6.9
53	Yamalo-Nenets^P	62.3	60.8	29.7	22.4	44.6	10.2
	TOTAL	748.8	51.3	22.4	33.5	52.3	13.3

* Although the term "the Soviet nationalities" employed in this study excludes the Russians, the Russian SFSR is entered in the table for comparative purposes. Furthermore, it must be noted that every nationality administrative unit listed does not represent a titular counterpart. Letters B, D, H, and O denote units composed of two titular nationalities. Letters A, C, G, L, N, and P designate units including groups for whom the nationality administrative units are named, but these particular units do not completely correspond to the names of these nationalities. From "A" through "P," these nationalities are the following: people of Dagestan, Ossetins, Altays, Buryats, and Nenetses, respectively. Letters E, F, J, K, and M demark units including groups which are the dominant non-Russian nationalities in their administrative units, but do not serve as titular groups, simply because the government has specified no such thing there. These groups, from "E" through "M," are Georgians, Azerbaijanians, Armenians, Tajiks, and people of the North (*Sever*).

Such concentrations of nationalities located in alien administrative units contiguous to their own units indicate the relative degree of mixing experienced by a nationality. This evidence can be derived from the sources by determining what proportion of each nationality lives in its nationality administrative unit as well as the proportion in the *oblasts, krais,* autonomous republics (ASSRs), and in some instances the union republics (SSRs), autonomous *oblasts* (AOs), and nationality *okrugs* (NOs) immediately adjacent to it. The proportion of the population in its own nationality unit that the titular group comprises, considered with the proportion that the Russians make up, indicates the extent to which mixing has occurred in a unit (see Table 5 and Frontispiece). It also shows the role the Russians have played in this mixing. In calculations of the contiguity index, AOs and NOs were included only when no other part of the administrative division to which they were subordinate was contiguous to the nationalty administrative unit. SSRs were used in the computation only when they were not broken down into subordinate administrative units.

Over 90 percent of the nationalities associated with union republics are found in, or immediately adjacent to, their republics. In this regard the Belorussians, Ukrainians, and Armenians fall slightly below average. Armenians, Tajiks, and Kazakhs evidenced the largest proportions living in contiguous areas. Inside the republics, there was greater variation in the proportion that the titular group and Russians comprised of the total population. Over three-fourths of the titular nationalities of SSRs live in their own republics; the lowest values on this scale are registered by Kazakhstan and Kirgiziia, whose titular nationalities do not constitute majorities in their own republics. Armenia, the Russian SFSR, Belorussia, Lithuania, the Ukraine, and Estonia stand highest on the same scale. Aside from the Russian SFSR, Russians comprise more than a fourth of the total population in Kazakhstan, Kirgiziia, and Latvia. Outside the Russian SFSR, they average 17.8 percent of the total population.

Thus, the major nationalities have not mixed very much; they generally make up a large proportion of the population of their own republics. The significant and growing proportion of Russians present in most republics testifies to Russian mixing. For the Russian SFSR, the high values, in respect to variables that indicate mixing, obscure the considerable mixing of the Russians that has occurred throughout the many nationality administrative units inside the Russian republic.

On the average, smaller proportions of the titular ASSR groups lived in their own autonomous republics than did the titular SSR groups. But a larger proportion of titular ASSR nationalities than SSR groups lived in contiguous administrative units. The sum of these two categories, however, is much less than the sum of the same two in the SSR group. In addition, the titular group comprises, on the average, a much smaller proportion of the total population in the ASSR, despite the fact that Russians constitute a smaller proportion of the ASSR population. One explanation for the appearance of these lower values on the mixing scale is that the nationalities located in the Volga-Ural regions continue to be more dispersed than many others; but they have mainly remained settled in this general area. The Tatar proportions are low, because population figures reported in the 1959 census combined data for the Crimean Tatars, who had been forcibly dispersed during World War II, with information about the Volga Tatars, who were not exiled. Significant numbers of the other nationalities who were dispersed by the Soviet government during the War but later repatriated, such as the Kalmyks and the Chechen-Ingush, apparently had not returned to their nationality areas by 1959. A small proportion of the Karelians, Mari, Mordvinians, Tatars, and Chechen-Ingush lived in the titular ASSRs. They made up a relatively slight proportion of their units' population. These units possessed a high proportion of Russians. Thus, the variables listed in Table 5 indicate considerable mixing in the autonomous republics.

Even though Table 5 shows the average of the first two variables for the autonomous *oblasts* to be very low, the values on the mixing scale for all AOs, except the Evrei (Jewish) AO, are

high. This contrast appears because the Jewish population constitutes such a large proportion of the total population of these
nationalities and thus depresses the average. Yet, these nationalities made up a relatively small proportion of the total population
of their units, and the Russians a high proportion. Again, there is
evidence of considerable Russian mixing.

The proportions of the titular groups living in or immediately
adjacent to the NOs generally reflect two facts: some of these
nationalities are scattered in northern areas of low population
density, and, like Buryats and Nenetses, serve as the titular group
for more than one nationality unit. They generally comprise a
small proportion of their units' population, and the Russians constitute a surprisingly high proportion.

The grossness of the non-East Slav category, however, conceals
the mixing of some nationalities. Since 1897 and in particular
since 1926, the Jews have been leaving the "Jewish Pale." The
Volga Germans and the Crimean Tatars, who were dispersed to
the East by the government during World War II, have not yet
been repatriated to their nationality areas.[15] Additional, rather
numerous groups that have experienced some dispersion include
the Mordvinians, Koreans (to various parts of the Far East,
Kazakhstan, and Uzbekistan), Gypsies, and, to some degree,
Armenians. However, since 1959 there has apparently been an
influx of Armenians to their home republic.[16]

This discussion has made it obvious that of the groups under
investigation, only the Russians are mixing. The other groups
appear to be concentrating. These trends are corroborated by
additional indices based upon Table 1. The dissimilarity index
(Table 6) derived from Lorenz curves supports these trends and
provides a good measure of mixing.[17] In 1897 it would have been
necessary to redistribute about 37 percent of the Russians in
order to distribute them equally, completely mixed, whereas in
1959 it would have required a redistribution of only 27 percent.
All of the other groups showed sharp concentrations; the non-
East Slavs and the Ukrainians have concentrated particularly
sharply since 1926.

MOR ⑥

Table 6.   Dissimilarity Index

	1897	1926	1959	Changes 1897–1959
Russians	.37	.29	.27	−10
Ukrainians	.57	.57	.65	+ 8
Belorussians	.78	.79	.81	+ 3
East Slavs	.14	.12	.15	+ 1
Non-East Slavs	.29	.29	.41	+12
Non-Russians	.28	.30	.34	+ 6

The redistribution of the Russians and the nationalities is shown in Table 7. This coefficient is derived simply by subtracting the proportion of a group that is in each region in 1897 from that in 1959, summing all positive (or negative) deviations, and dividing by 100. A value of zero signifies no redistribution, and a value of one means complete redistribution. Of course, redistribution is not the same as mixing. The coefficient of redistribution simply shows change in a variable over time. It does not indicate whether mixing or concentration occurred. Table 7 reveals expected patterns, except for the high value for Belorussia, which reflects the exodus of Belorussians from the West after the Baltic countries became independent. The chief reason behind the high values for the non-East Slavs shown in Tables 6 and 7 is found in the rate, higher than in Slavic areas, of natural increase effective since 1926 in most non-Slavic territory.

Table 7.   Coefficient of Redistribution

	1897–1959	1897–1926	1926–1959
Russians	.18	.06	.16
Ukrainians	.14	.09	.13
Belorussians	.18	.17	.08
East Slavs	.15	.07	.10
Non-East Slavs	.24	.07	.19
Non-Russians	.15	.06	.12

The coefficient of localization describes the distribution of a group in yet a different way; it is a measure of the relative regional concentration of a group compared to that of the total population (Table 8). The coefficient of localization is derived by subtracting the proportion of a group in each region from the proportion of the total population in each region, summing up all positive (or negative) deviations, and dividing by 100. Limits range from zero to one. If a group is distributed exactly like the total population, the value is zero. If all of a group were in a single region, the value would be one. The values obtained from this method of analysis nearly match those of the dissimilarity index, and essentially measure the same relationship. From both it can be seen that Russians are becoming more mixed, relative to the distribution of the total population, and Ukrainians, Belorussians, and non-East Slavs are becoming more concentrated. The distribution of the East Slavs comes very close to that of the total population, whereas that of the non-East Slavs does not.

Table 8.   Coefficient of Localization

	1897	1926	1959
Russians	.37	.36	.29
Ukrainians	.58	.57	.66
Belorussians	.78	.79	.81
East Slavs	.14	.13	.13
Non-East Slavs	.31	.35	.43
Non-Russians	.29	.33	.36

The Impact of Mixing

The effect of Russian mixing upon such socioeconomic variables as Russification, urbanization, and labor force becomes our next concern. This discussion will be confined to Russian mixing because Russians comprise the chief group mixing with nationalities. What might be the future pattern of mixing, why the Russians have mixed while the nationalities mostly have not, and whether nationality problems will or will not become more acute, from the geographic viewpoint, are other questions to be investigated.

The impact of Russian mixing poses a basic problem for understanding contemporary Soviet society and the social change which will occur in it during the near and distant future. However, it is also an extremely complex problem, because Russian mixing affects virtually every facet of non-Russian society. We lack data and first-hand experience concerning most problems. For these and other reasons, a complete discussion of this important subject clearly goes beyond the scope of this study. We will attempt, however, to establish the relationship between Russian mixing and a number of socioeconomic variables for which data are available.

The first question to be investigated is whether Russian mixing has resulted in or been accompanied by Russification? To facilitate our inquiry into the effect of mixing, Russification is operationally defined as the process through which a nationality adopts or begins to adopt Russian culture or certain of its aspects. It is further assumed that a non-Russian who adopts Russian as his native language has, despite the various distinctions that could be made, become Russified.

"Mixing" does not signify an even dispersion of Russians throughout a region harmoniously interacting with non-Russians. The Russians have clubbed together in the non-Russian areas. In 1959, 74 percent of the Russians outside the Russian SFSR lived in cities, where they comprised a significant minority if not a majority of the inhabitants. Most cities have become Russian cultural enclaves, and Russian is commonly the dominant language in them. Finally, it is not assumed that the mere presence of Russians in an administrative unit outside the Russian SFSR results in Russification. Their presence may be a necessary condition, but it is surely not a sufficient one.

To test the relationship, if any, between a Russian presence and the process of Russification, we have calculated the proportion of the total population that was Russian and the proportion of the non-Russians who spoke Russian as their native language for the 157 smallest administrative units from which data were available in 1959, as well as the nineteen economic regions and the fifteen union republics. We tested the statistical relationship between these two variables with rank correlation and obtained significant (at the 5 percent confidence level) positive correlations of .903, .863, and .638, respectively.

The Volgo-Vyatsk region ranks relatively high in proportion of Russians but low in Russification; the non-Russians there are chiefly non-Slavs. In the South and Belorussia, where the non-Russians are Slavs, the opposite pattern prevails. The deviation in the West is also high; again non-Slavs are involved. A high rate of Russification can be noted in the Russian core regions and low rates seen in Central Asia and the Transcaucasus. Table 5 presents data on Russification according to each nationality administrative unit. The rate is high in the Russian SFSR, where Russians predominate, and in the Karelian and Komi ASSRs, the Evrei and the Khakass AOs, and in many of the NOs. Clearly, Russian mixing with nationalities has intensified Russification processes.

It is also useful to determine whether Russian mixing in non-Russian areas is related to variables associated with modernization. The basic assumption is that the Russians are bearers of modernization in the USSR; thus, an increase in their percent of the total Russians living in a region should be accompanied by a corresponding increase in selected socioeconomic variables related to modernization. To test this notion, we have correlated the change occurring between 1897 and 1959 in the distribution of Russians with the change taking place in the distribution of a number of urban and work force variables for the nine economic regions located outside the Russian SFSR. These data have also been adjusted to make them as nearly comparable as possible. Russian mixing was significantly (at the 5 percent confidence level) and positively correlated with the distribution of the population in centers with 15,000 or more people and the population in centers numbering 15,000 to 99,999. This is to be expected, because most Russian migrants moved to the cities. However, Russian distribution did not correlate significantly with the population in centers of 100,000 or more inhabitants. This would seem to indicate that the Russians have been moving primarily to small cities. Perhaps this reflects the shortage of housing available in many non-Russian capitals and the widespread need in towns for service and administrative talents that could not easily be satisfied locally.

Changes in the percent of the total Soviet work force and the tertiary (service) work force were also significantly and positively related to Russian mixing. But the industrial and agricultural work force variables were not. It is not inconsistent that changes in the tertiary work force and small and medium urban centers were both significant variables, because small and medium cities act as service and administrative centers for surrounding agricultural areas. That the Russians are moving to areas where the total labor force has increased is not surprising, because Russian in-migrants have increased the labor force in non-Russian areas. Among all the variables which we have tried to make comparable, the work force variables are the least satisfactory. The industrial work force category includes handicrafts because, for 1897 data it was impossible to remove them with any precision. The inclusion of handicrafts inflated the figure for industrial labor force, particularly that of Czarist Central Asia, but also those in the Transcaucasus and the Jewish settlements in the Western Ukraine in 1897. In addition, data for 1897 and 1926 come from the censuses and represent the gainfully employed, whereas only average annual data are available for around 1959 (actually, 1961). The correlation between mixing and the industrial work force came close to being significant; Central Asia jutted sharply out of line. Perhaps with better data for a basis, this correlation would have been significant, as one might expect.

The dependency ratio (persons aged 0–19 and 60 or over) also significantly correlated with Russian mixing. This can be explained by the fact that many of the non-Russian areas enjoy high rates of natural increase, and areas of in-migration generally possess a younger population and a proportionally greater number of dependents. These relationships indicate that with the mixing of the Russians and the nationalities there has been a concomitant change in variables related to modernization.

Nationality mixing, of course, results from migration. To understand future patterns of mixing, we must consider future migratory patterns in the USSR. One authority advances the very simple, incisive view that migration in any geographic area, aside from the movement of political refugees, results from attempts to equalize economic density (the ratio between people and resources).[18] People move primarily in order to improve their living conditions. This can be accomplished in any given area by economic development, birth control, and migrations. Because economic development and birth control normally are very difficult to achieve, particularly in the short run, the main solution has been migration. Rather continuous migratory movements have characterized human history. It is apparent that fertility and economic development are closely related to migration. An analysis of the components of economic opportunity that relate to migration has shown that: "The availability of economic opportunities, in turn, is partly a function of the rate of growth of the economy, and partly a function of the rate of growth of the native work force." [19] These findings also emphasize that the rate of increase in labor productivity of the native workers constitutes an important determinant of the availability of economic opportunity. This tells us very simply that if an area has little or no economic development and a high rate of increase in its labor force, out-migration or a decline in living standards will occur. Within a country, regional differentials in the growth of the work force and in economic development generally result in an adjustment of the supply and demand of labor through migration. Because people move primarily for economic reasons, in order to understand these movements economic conditions in the area of origin and destination must be compared. Differences in language, culture, or distance may constitute intervening obstacles, but people will still attempt to improve their living conditions.

This simple theoretical structure provides useful insight into why the Irish and the Welsh move to England; the American Blacks to northern cities; southern Europeans to northern Europe; why the great overseas migrations occur, and the reasons for the massive rural migration to urban areas. In Czarist Russia and the USSR in the late nineteenth and the first part of the twentieth centuries, migration conformed to this pattern, as it does today.[20]

Government policy could affect migration and the mixing of nationalities. Though the government would like Russians to go forth and Russify, it does not mean that this will happen.[21] Soviet leaders also want to solve the problem caused by regional labor shortages through migration, especially to Siberia, and to stem the exodus from the land, to increase Slavic fertility, and to limit the growth of large cities. Actually, people migrate from southern Siberia and other areas with labor shortages more than they move into them, because real income has been less in the east. Rural depopulation proceeds apace. Slavic fertility continues to decline. Large cities grow and grow. Socioeconomic processes govern migration and fertility. "Jawboning" pressure tactics will not affect demographic behavior to an appreciable degree anywhere in the absence of social and economic change. Governments can appreciably affect demographic behavior only through applying effective, resolute action to change the social and economic structure or by employing the use of force. Forced migrations are not unknown in the USSR, but in the aggregate they have not played an important role in mixing populations. Most migration in the USSR is not centrally directed or subsidized.

The belief that there is a Soviet policy to disperse certain nationalities, or that population dispersion or exchange constitutes part of Soviet nationality policy, should be viewed in this light. Massive shifts were accomplished forcibly when the Volga Germans, the Crimean Tatars, and several other nationalities were compelled to migrate during World War II. If dispersion has been the Soviet policy for most nationalities, it has proved to be most unsuccessful, at least up to 1959. Moreover, the Soviet government should question whether dispersing or concentrating recalcitrant nationalities best minimizes the impact of their dissenting views throughout the USSR.[22]

The Russians have mixed with nationalities largely because traditional Russian areas have experienced the most rural out-migration. This has occurred since the nineteenth century, but particularly after the late 1920s, when rural depopulation began to accelerate. The Russian regions possessed a surplus agricultural population, experienced rapid natural increase until fairly

160 ROBERT A. LEWIS

recently, and had at their disposal relatively poor agricultural land resources. These factors resulted in low agricultural wages, which stimulated much out-migration. Between 1926 and 1959 the Ukraine underwent significantly less rural depopulation than Russian areas; and appreciable rural out-migration from Belorussia did not occur until at least World War II. Other regions have shown gains or only slight losses in rural population during this same period.

Between 1959 and 1970 the traditional Russian regions continued to suffer the greatest rural population declines, generally between 10 and 25 percent. Despite the substantial Russian rural out-migration continuing for more than a century, a great reservoir of potential rural out-migrants remains in traditional Russian areas. Relatively moderate rural losses have been registered in the Siberian, Western, Belorussian, Southwestern, and Donetsk-Dnepr regions since 1959. The other regions showed increases in their rural populations, the largest being 37 percent in Central Asia and 25 percent in Kazakhstan.

Between 1926 and 1959 urbanization increased the fastest in the Center, Donetsk-Dnepr, the Urals, Siberia, and the Far East. Still, significant urbanization was taking place in the non-Russian areas.[23] Since 1959, in fact, the greatest urbanization has occurred in non-Russian areas, particularly Central Asia, Kazakhstan, Belorussia, and Moldavia. In the 1960s industry has also developed the most in non-Russian areas. However, not all migrants have come from rural Russian areas. In 1963 about 52 percent of the urban migrants in the USSR originated from other cities,[24] very probably mainly from those in Russian areas.

Russians have thus sought to improve their living standards. First, they migrated primarily to cities in the European USSR, then to those in Siberia, and more recently very probably primarily to cities in non-Russian areas. Non-Russian urban centers have, up until fairly recently, grown less rapidly than those in Russian areas and the east. Most of the employment opportunities in these centers, in particular jobs requiring education or training, have been filled by Russians. There has been relatively little local rural-urban migration, particularly in non-Slavic areas where the indigenous population generally comprises a relatively small proportion of the urban population.

More Ukrainians have not left the Ukraine, most likely, because rural depopulation there has been less than in Russian areas. Slower Ukrainian outflow can be explained by their superior agricultural land resources, less of a surplus agricultural population, and, consequently, higher wages. In addition, the economy has developed appreciably in the Ukrainian republic, particularly in the Donetsk-Dnepr region. Despite considerable Russian in-migration, many jobs seem to have been available for Ukrainians. If a rural Ukrainian inside or outside the Ukraine planned to migrate to an urban area, he would probably choose Donetsk over Sverdlovsk for reasons connected with his nationality if not considerations relating to distance. This could account in part for the concentration of the Ukrainians in their home republic, although much linguistic Russification of those away from it must not be discounted. In Belorussia, depopulation of rural areas began relatively late. More recently it has been accompanied by significant industrialization and urbanization. This would tend to keep the rural out-migrants in Belorussia, particularly because Russian migration into the region has not been great.

Central Asia exemplifies current demographic patterns in non-Slavic areas of the USSR which should greatly affect future patterns of nationality mixing. The Kirgiz, Tajiks, Uzbeks, and Turkmens comprise only a small proportion of the urban population in their republics (less than one-third in 1959). In some cities their proportion has been declining. The Russians comprise the most numerous group living in these cities. There is very little local migration from countryside to town, and job opportunities in urban areas are being pre-empted by Russians and, to a lesser extent, other in-migrants. Consequently, the cities are culturally and linguistically Russian, and these rural areas are culturally and linguistically Turkic and Iranian. Natural increase of population in the rural areas is high. Crude birth rates in the Central Asian republics averaged between 30 and 40 per thousand of total population in the late 1960s; the higher the proportion of Russians in the republic, the lower the birth rate of that republic. In rural areas, the crude birth rate is the highest, probably over 40 per thousand, although there are no data available by nationality or covering rural areas. And it has not yet begun to decline, which is to be expected. Without change in the social structure or the socioeconomic change that normally occurs with urbanization, it is doubtful that rural Turkic and Iranian fertility will decline. Crude death rates are low, remaining generally between six and seven per thousand. Crude natural increase, therefore, comes to about 3 percent, except in the Kirgiz SSR, which has the highest proportion of Russians in Central Asia, where it is about 2.4 percent.[25] The population of Central Asia increased 44 percent between 1959 and 1970;[26] this rise included about half a million net in-migrants. Natural increase in the rural areas stands currently at no less than 3 percent annually, which means that the rural population doubles about every generation. Between 1959 and 1970 the rural population of Central Asia increased 37 percent. About a third of the rural population in 1959 belonged to the group between 0–9 years of age. This reflects a sharp drop in mortality rates for Central Asia since World War II. Almost 40 percent of the total population was fifteen years of age or below in 1959. Currently that group probably approaches 50 percent of the total. This age distribution resulting from the high rate of natural growth will increase the crude birth rates, decrease the crude death rates, and consequently increase the rate of crude natural increase even further.

Similar patterns are characteristic of many other non-Slavic areas in the USSR. Where the rural population is growing rapidly, there is little rural-urban migration, and the rural population is accumulating on the land. These, of course, are the problems of the underdeveloped world at large, and one would not expect to find them in a developed country like the USSR.

A prominent Soviet population specialist has claimed that in Central Asia these processes result from nationality factors. According to him, people move to Central Asia under economic pressure, but the local people do not move to the cities because they do not know Russian and the cities provide an alien cultural environment.[27] Unable to speak Russian, Central Asians have difficulty in being trained and communicating on the job. Only a small proportion of the factory and construction workers in the region are native to it, even though special efforts have been made to attract them. Some local people do not like the unpleasant conditions in factories and return to their villages. The same Soviet analyst thinks that although there has been a "coming together" (*sblizhenie*) of the people of the USSR, there will be no massive redistribution of population from such labor surplus regions as Central Asia, the Transcaucasus, and Moldavia to such labor deficit regions as Siberia and the Urals. This is so because nationality factors have not weakened sufficiently to permit it. However, he thinks that local rural-urban migration should be increased by decreasing the in-migration from other areas, and that both movements should be affected by economic incentives.

Conditions in Central Asia are not unique with respect to nationality processes and migration. People move to Central Asia primarily because of economic reasons. Locally, people will move to the urban centers when economic conditions dictate it. The chief problem to face would be the competition for and the availability of jobs if economic conditions promoted both migratory streams. The current rate of economic development in the cities could not simultaneously accommodate the current sizable migration from outside Central Asia and also the sizable increase of the indigenous work force of Central Asia which is expected in the 1970s.

If the economic crunch really occurred in Central Asia, there would be much more local rural-urban migration there than there is, regardless of nationality considerations. Linguistic and cultural barriers did not prevent Puerto Rican migration to New York, the Greek migration to Germany, nor the move by millions of European rural migrants to urban areas in the United States, where conditions in the factories were not very pleasant. Nationality and cultural factors might impede migration, but surely not stop it. Even though there is a sharp differential between real urban and rural incomes in various regions of the

USSR, in addition to many parts of Central Asia (and very probably in other non-Slavic areas), real urban-rural income differences are not yet great. This is because considerable rural development has occurred during the Soviet period and the impact of
the rapidly growing population on the work force has only recently begun to be felt. During a visit to the USSR I questioned
people about rural and urban incomes in the cotton areas of Central Asia (Tashkent, Bukhara, Samarkand, and Dushanbe). Repeatedly they answered that *kolkhoz* workers normally received
as much or more than comparable urban workers, and during the
cotton-picking season they were paid an additional salary. Several
times Russian urban workers complained about the fact that better housing was available on the *kolkhozes* than in towns. The
general conditions that I observed at the half-dozen *kolkhozes*
which I visited supported these contentions.

In Central Asia the large cohort aged 0–9 in 1959 will be entering the work force in the 1970s. It will greatly expand the
work force, particularly in rural areas. The rural economy may
be able to absorb some of this growth. But without continued
rapid rural development—which is limited by finite resources,
population control (very difficult to achieve because of social
conditions), or out-migration—there will be a decline in living
standards. Besides, any area that does not provide sufficient employment for its expanding work force and which experiences
declines in living standards can expect a growth of social pressure,
even in the USSR. In contrast to the under-developed world, however, Central Asia is part of a developed country which is currently experiencing labor shortages. Therefore, the surplus labor
in Central Asia will be able to migrate without undue restriction
to areas suffering labor shortages.

If these conditions continue to prevail during the 1970s, the
pressure of the growing work force will intensify and, at least by
the 1980s, there should be considerable out-migration from the
rural areas of Central Asia. If Russians continue to hold most, or
a significant proportion, of the jobs in the surrounding cities, rural
migrants will have to move to labor deficit areas elsewhere in the
USSR, such as Siberia or the Urals. However, out-migrants should

also come from other non-Slavic areas with conditions similar to Central Asia's. Nationality mixing in the USSR then would entail migration by many nationalities rather than primarily a settling of Russians in nationality areas. If the nationalities mix more, additional direct interaction will develop among the people of the Soviet Union. This will lead to further Russification, but not necessarily widespread loss of nationality identity. The trends evident in this process seem to be corroborated by experience elsewhere.[28] With nationalities and Russians competing for jobs and scarce resources, economic tension should grow. As the nationalities develop economically and educationally, they should make more demands upon the Soviet government. Under these circumstances Soviet nationality problems will almost certainly intensify and collectively become a dominant force shaping the future Soviet society.

NOTES

1. E. A. Wrigley, "Geography and Population," in R. J. Chorley and Peter Haggett (eds.), *Frontiers in Geographical Teaching* (London: Methuen and Co., Ltd., 1965).

2. *Pervaia vseobshchaia perepis' naseleniia Rossiiskoi Imperii 1897 g.* (St. Petersburg: Izdanie Tsentral'nago Statisticheskago Komiteta Ministerstva Vnutrennikh Diel, 1905), 89 vols.; *Vsesoiuznaia perepis' naseleniia 1926 goda* (Moscow: Izdanie Tsentral'nogo Statisticheskogo Upravleniia SSSR, 1929), 66 vols.; *Itogi vsesoiuznoi perepisi naseleniia 1959 goda* (Moscow: Gosstatizdat. Tsentral'noe Statisticheskoe Upravlenie SSSR, 1962–1963), 16 vols. The 1897 census was taken on February 9 (New Style); the 1926 census on December 17; and the 1959 on January 15.

3. A. A. Isupov, *Natsional'nyi sostav naseleniia SSSR* (Moscow: Izdatel'stvo "Statistika," 1961), pp. 30–31.

4. For a listing of the many East European censuses from which data for this study were obtained, see Robert A. Lewis and Richard H. Rowland, "Urbanization in Russia and the USSR: 1897–1966," *Annals of the Association of American Geographers* (December 1969), pp. 777, note 3.

5. For an interesting discussion of regionalization, see William Bunge, *Theoretical Geography* (Lund: C. W. K. Gleerup, Publishers, 1966), pp. 14–26, 95–100.

6. For a summary discussion of these procedures, see Robert A. Lewis and J. William Leasure, "Regional Population Changes in Russia and the USSR since 1851," *Slavic Review* (December 1966), pp. 663–68. A more detailed account appears in J. William Leasure and Robert A. Lewis, *Population Changes in Russia and the USSR: A Set of Comparable Territorial Units* (San Diego: San Diego State College Press, 1966).

7. For a detailed discussion of the comparable definitions pertaining to the different variables, see *Ibid*.

8. S. Bruk and V. Kozlov, "Voprosy o natsional'nosti i iazyke v predstoiashchei perepisi naseleniia," *Vestnik statistiki,* No. 3 (1968), pp. 32–37.

9. For a comparison of the questionnaires and instructions concerning the 1897 and 1926 censuses, see N. Ia. Vorob'ev, *Vsesoiuznaia perepis' naseleniia 1926 g.* (Moscow: Gosudarstvennoe Statisticheskoe Izdatel'stvo, 1957), pp. 83–104.

10. S. Bruk and V. Kozlov, p. 35.

11. J. William Leasure and Robert A. Lewis, "Internal Migration in the USSR: 1897–1926," *Demography,* Vol. 4, No. 2 (1967), p. 481.

12. Walter F. Wilcox, ed., *International Migrations,* Vol. II (New York: National Bureau of Economic Research, 1931), p. 523.

13. *Narodnoe khoziaistvo SSSR v 1967* (Moscow: Izdatel'stvo "Statistika," 1968), p. 191.

14. "Gody rosta. Soobshchenie TsSU SSSR o predvartitel'nykh itogakh vsesoiuznoi perepisi naseleniia 1970 goda," *Izvestiia* (April 19, 1970), p. 1.

15. S. I. Bruk and V. S. Apenchenko, eds. *Atlas narodov mira* (Moscow: Glavnoe Upravlenie Geodezii i Kartografii Gosudarstvennogo Geologicheskogo Komiteta SSSR, 1964), pp. 10–34. The editors have provided a most impressive source for further study of nationality distribution in the USSR and the world.

16. V. V. Pokshishevskii, "Migratsiia naseleniia v SSSR," *Priroda,* No. 9 (Sept., 1969), pp. 67–75.

17. A detailed explanation of this index and other indices in this paper can be found in Walter Isard, *Methods of Regional Analysis:*

An Introduction to Regional Science (Cambridge: The M.I.T. Press, 1960), pp. 249–70.

18. Eugene M. Kulischer, *Europe on the Move* (New York: Columbia University Press, 1948), p. 319.

19. A. J. Jaffe, *Amount and Structure of International Migrations: The Organizer's Report for Section 9.1* (London: The International Population Union, 1969), p. 7.

20. J. William Leasure and Robert A. Lewis, "Internal Migration in Russia in the Late Nineteenth Century," *Slavic Review,* Vol. XXVII, No. 3 (Sept., 1968), pp. 375–94; J. William Leasure and Robert A. Lewis, "Internal Migration in the USSR: 1897–1926," pp. 479–96; D. I. Valentei, *Teoriia i politika narodonaseleniia* (Moscow: "Vysshaia Shkola," 1967), pp. 126–43.

21. One of the more interesting statements about the government and assimilation is in M. Kh. Khakimov, "Some Problems of the Development of National Soviet Statehood during the Present Period," *Central Asian Review,* Vol. XII, No. 4 (1964), pp. 253–64.

22. For a summary statement about the work of the Swedish geographer Torsten Hägerstrand on this subject, see William Bunge, pp. 123–24.

23. Robert A. Lewis and Richard H. Rowland, pp. 776–96.

24. V. I. Perevedentsev, "Contemporary Migration in the USSR," *Soviet Geography: Review and Translation* (April 1969), p. 194.

25. *Narodnoe khoziaistvo SSSR v 1968 g.* (Moscow: Izdatel'stvo "Statistika," 1969), pp. 38–39.

26. "Gody rosta. Soobshchenie TsSU SSSR . . . ," p. 1.

27. V. I. Perevedentsev, "O vliianii etnicheskikh faktorov na territorial'noe pereraspredelenie naseleniia," *Izvestiia Akademii Nauk SSSR,* Seriia geograficheskaia, No. 4 (1965), pp. 31–39.

28. Charles Price, "The Study of Assimilation," in J. A. Jackson, ed., *Migration* (Cambridge: Cambridge University Press, 1969), pp. 186–88.

ALEXANDRE BENNIGSEN

ISLAMIC OR LOCAL CONSCIOUSNESS AMONG SOVIET NATIONALITIES?

The term "Muslim" carries no religious meaning in this study. We consider as Muslims those human groups which, before the October 1917 revolution, belonged to the Islamic cultural area, and which today conserve, more or less, the "Islamic way of life." About 75 percent of the Muslims in the Soviet Union belong to the Turkic linguistic family. The remaining 25 percent are equally divided between the Iranians and the Ibero-Caucasians of the North Caucasus. Geographically, the Muslims are divided between Central Asia and Kazakhstan (70 percent), middle Volga-Urals (15 percent), and North and East Caucasus (15 percent). Small Muslim groups exist in Western Siberia, in central Russia (the Kasimov Tatars in the Riazan region), in Belorussia and Lithuania (Lithuanian Tatars), and in all the main cities. The Muslim community of the Crimea has been deported to Central Asia.

The immense majority of Soviet Muslims belong to the Sunni rite of the Hanafite school (only the Dagestanians are of the Shafite school). The number of the *Imami Shii* (Twelvers) comes to about two million, including half of the Azeris, the Tats, the Karapapakhs of Armenia, the Ingiloys of Eastern Georgia, and some city dwellers in Central Asia (Bukhara, Samarkand, Tashkent) and in Transcaucasia; the *Ismaili Shii* (*Nizarits*) number about forty thousand in the Western Pamirs. The *Ahl-i Haqq* extremist Shii who deify Ali have some followers among the

Kurds (fewer than ten thousand?). The *Bahais* form some urban colonies in Astrakhan and Ashkhabad (fewer than five thousand?). Finally there are some fifteen thousand *Yezidis* ("Devil Worshipers") among the Kurds living around Mount Alagöz in Armenia.

Some Turkic groups such as the following do not belong to Islam: Chuvash[1] (1,469,766), Yakuts (236,655), Altays (45,-270), and Gagauz (123,821). The figures are according to the 1959 Soviet census, which revealed that there are some twenty-five to thirty million Muslims in the Soviet Union (see Table 9). The exact number is of course impossible to fix, and today their number must be much greater, perhaps forty million or even more. This important Muslim community, representing about 20 percent of the total population of the Soviet Union, is divided between thirty-eight different human groups, listed in the 1959 census. Some are nations (in Russian, *natsii*), others, subnationalities (in Russian, *narodnosti*), from the largest, the Uzbeks, who number over six million, to the smallest, the tiny subnationalities of Dagestan and the North Caucasus, numbering fewer than twenty-thousand persons. But all these "nations" and "subnationalities" have been created under the Soviet regime. Before the October 1917 revolution, with some very rare exceptions, the idea of belonging to a particular nation, to an Uzbek, Turkmen, or even a Tatar nation, simply did not exist in the consciousness either of the Muslim intelligentsia or of the public.

What we must try to investigate today is whether national consciousness among the Muslims of the Soviet Union is limited to their present nation—to a purely Uzbek national consciousness, or to a Chechen, or a Karakalpak national consciousness; or, whether their consciousness remains an "enlarged" one. Do they consider themselves as belonging to a larger unit, Turkistan, or Turkic race, or even to Islam in general? This problem is not merely academic. It has a very practical meaning. Remember some trends in the demographic evolution of the Soviet Union. If we consider the fertility rate or child-woman ratio (the proportion of children below ten years old to a thousand women between twenty and forty-nine years of age), we observe that it is

Table 9. Muslim People of the Soviet Union

I. TURKIC	Language	1939 Census	1959 Census	Status	Remarks
Uzbeks	W	4,844,000	6,004,000	nation	
Tatars	W	4,300,000	4,969,000	,,	
Kazakhs	W	3,099,000	3,581,000	,,	
Azeris	W	2,275,000	2,929,000	,,	
Turkmens	W	812,000	1,004,000	,,	
Bashkirs	W	843,000	983,000	,,	
Kirgiz	W	884,000	974,000	,,	
Karakalpaks	W	186,000	173,000	subnationality	Decrease due to assimilation by the Uzbeks & Kazakhs
Kumyks	W	95,000 (in 1926)	135,000	,,	
Uyghurs	W	109,000 (in 1926)	95,000	,,	Decrease due to assimilation by the Uzbeks
Karachays	W	76,000	81,000	,,	
Balkars	W	42,600	47,000	,,	
Nogays	W	36,000 (in 1926)	41,000	,,	
Turks	N	?	35,000	foreign minority	
			21,046,000		

II. IRANIAN	Language	1939 Census	1959 Census	Status	Remarks
Tajiks	W	1,229,000	1,397,000	nation	About 30% Muslims (Digors). About 20% are Yezidis; written language in Cyrillic script.
Ossetins	W	354,000	410,000	nation	
Kurds	W	46,000	59,000	foreign minority assimilated to a subnationality.	
Iranians	N	39,000	21,000	foreign minorities	Persian (Bahais or Shiites) colonies of Baku, Ashkhabad, Astrakhan and "Ironis" of Bukhara and Samarkand.
Tats	N	29,000 (1926)	11,000	ethnic group	The Muslim Tats; not to be confused with the Tat-speaking Dagestan Jews; assimilated by the Azeris.
Baluches	N	?	7,800	foreign minority	Assimilated by the Turkmens.
Afghans	N	?	1,900	foreign minority	Assimilated by the Tajiks.
			1,907,700		

Table continues

Table 9. (*continued*)

III. IBERO-CAUCASIAN	Language	1939 Census	1959 Census	Status	Remarks
Chechens	W	408,000	418,000	nation	Slow increase due to the deportation in 1944.
Karbardians	W	164,000	204,000	subnationality becoming a nation	
Ingushes	W	92,000	106,000	subnationality	Deported in 1944 with the Chechens.
Adygeis	W	88,000	88,000	,,	Same human group speaking the same language. Geographically and administratively divided.
	W				
Cherkess	W		30,000	,,	
Abkhaz	W	59,000 (1926)	74,000	,,	About 50% Muslims.
Abazins	W	14,000 (1926)	20,000	,,	
Dagestanians					
Avars	W	167,000 (1926)	268,000	,,	
Lezghins	W	134,000 (1926)	223,000	,,	
Dargins	W	126,000	158,000	,,	
Laks	W	40,000	64,000	,,	

	Language	1939 Census	1959 Census	Status	Remarks
Tabasarans	W	28,000	35,000	subnationality	
Aguls	N	7,500	8,000	ethnic group	Assimilated by the Lezghins and the Azeris.
Rutuls	N	13,000	7,000	"	"
Tsakhurs	N	3,300	6,000	"	"
Total Dagestan			1,701,000		
IV. OTHERS	Language	1939 Census	1959 Census	Status	Remarks
Dungans (Chinese Muslims)	W	4,600	21,000	foreign minority assimilated to a subnationality	Written language in Cyrillic script.
Arabs	N	22,000	8,000	ancient foreign minority	Assimilated by the Uzbeks.
Albanians	N	?	5,000	foreign minority	An unknown percentage of Muslims.

Key: W = written language
N = no written language

Source: "Naselenie," *Bolshaia sovetskaia entsiklopediia* Vol. Soiuz Sovetskikh Sotsialisticheskikh Respublik (Moscow: Gosudarstvennyi Nauchnyi Institut "Sovetskaia Entsiklopediia" OGIZ SSSR, 1947), pp. 50–70; *Itogi vsesoiuznoi perepisi naseleniia 1959 goda. SSSR* (Svodnyi tom). (Moscow: Gosstatizdat, 1962).
Remarks: Some Muslim groups not listed in the 1959 census: Talysh (about 80,000), Adzhars (about 100,000), Karapapakhs (8,000 ?), Ingiloys (Shiite Georgians), Hemshins (Muslim Armenians), and an unknown number of Muslim Finns (Maris, Mordvins, Udmurts) and Chuvash.

far from equal among various nationalities, and that the differences are enormous between different human groups in the Soviet Union. Russians have a very low ratio, one of the lowest in the world—exactly the same as the French, a ratio of 863 children 0–9 years of age per 1,000 women from twenty to forty-nine years old. Other Slavic groups have even lower ratios, such as the Ukrainians' of 710 per 1,000. The Belorussians' is hardly higher, 836 per 1,000. Remember that the child-woman ratio in the United States is 1,114:1,000. Compared to the low Slavic rates, all Soviet Muslim groups have rates which are among the highest in the world. In Central Asia the Turkmens have 1,809:1,000, the Uzbeks 1,878:1,000. The Kirgiz and the Kazakhs are even higher—1,885:1,000 and 1,896:1,000. And the Chechens of the Caucasus have the highest child-woman ratio in the world, 2,204:1,000.

This different evolution should lead in some twenty-five or thirty years to a curious result. If the trend continued, in the year 2000 the Soviet Union would probably have a Turkic and Muslim majority and a Russian and even a Slavic minority. So, it is vitally important to know whether this majority will be formed by some thirty different "nations" or by a closely unified community of more than one hundred million people. I do not pretend, of course, to be able to give an answer, whether positive or negative, to this major question, but simply to raise some points for discussion.

Let us first observe what the national consciousness consisted of in the general public and among the Muslim intelligentsia before the 1917 revolution. Then we shall analyze Soviet policy briefly in this field, and finally raise some points for discussion concerning the present evolution. The pre-revolutionary situation differed among the Muslim public or the intelligentsia. V. V. Barthold (1869–1930), speaking about the Turkistan Muslims, declared that when you ask a Turkistanian who he is, he will answer, first, that he is a Muslim; then, that he belongs to a particular clan or tribe if he is a nomad, or to a particular village or city if he is sedentary. In Central Asia the traditional distinction, still fully alive on the eve of the 1917 Revolution, was not linguistic (Turks versus Iranians), but between nomads and settled people. A pre-revolutionary Muslim, nomad or peasant, had absolutely no consciousness of belonging to a particular nation such as Turkmen, Uzbek, Kirgiz, Kazakh, or Karakalpak. The same may be said about the Volga Tatars or the Azeris. Even the names, "Azeri" or "Tatar," were not applied this way before the Revolution. The Volga Tatars called themselves "Turks," "Bulgars," or simply "Muslims"; the Azeris called themselves "Turks." So, for the public, the uniting bond was Islam.

Like all Islamic communities isolated among alien "infidels," the Muslims of Russia were deeply conscious of their religious affiliation, all the more so as the pressure of the Christian infidels became stronger. For this reason, in the Tatar area the religious consciousness was certainly stronger than in Azerbaijan or in Kazakhstan. A Muslim was not only a Muslim as distinct from a Christian, but he was also conscious of belonging to Islam as opposed to the Christians, in other words to the Russians. The feeling of religious brotherhood was certainly stronger among Russian Muslims than in the Muslim countries like the Ottoman Empire or Persia. This feeling of brotherhood existed even between the Sunni and the Shiia, especially in Transcaucasia. Before 1917 Muslim unity was definitely a reality. However, although religious consciousness constituted a bond of unity, it would be an exaggeration to conclude that the Muslims of Russia formed a homogeneous community—even from a purely religious point of view.

Before the revolution, for a very large proportion of Muslims, but mostly for the nomads of Central Asia and for some mountaineers of Caucasia, life was still ordered by the customary law, the *adat,* and not the Koranic law, the Shariat, and their religion was often a mixture of Islam and different pre-Islamic beliefs. So, it was difficult to consider the nomads to be on the same level as the strictly orthodox Uzbeks or Tatars.

Moreover, if Islam was a uniting bond, the social structure of different Muslim people was a strongly divisive factor. Muslim pre-Revolutionary society, generally based on the small patriarchal family, has retained many social traditions of the past, from the large joint family and from the clan system, in spite of the fact that large joint families had disappeared much earlier everywhere in the Russian Islamic world. These traditions, particularly the exogamic and, even more, the endogamic taboos, constituted direct obstacles to the formation of a national consciousness or even a simple sentiment of solidarity between different Muslim populations.

Among the nomads in Central Asia, especially, where the clans and tribes still existed, the consciousness and the loyalties scarcely went beyond a purely tribal stage. As an example, we cite the great tribal formations of Central Asia, like the Manghit, Qongrat, Nayman, and Kitay, which were to be found among different people, from the North Caucasus to the Urals and Central Asia. They formed part of the Kazakhs, Uzbeks, Karakalpaks, and even the Bashkirs and Nogays. Although separated by enormous distances and by great differences in dialects, members of these tribes considered themselves kinsmen, and their consciousness did not go farther than this purely tribal loyalty.

Some authors claim that a wider, national, consciousness was beginning to appear at the beginning of the twentieth century among the Kazakhs and the Turkmens, but it was still in a very embryonic stage. The feeling of belonging to a Kazakh or to a Turkmen nation was experienced only by a very restricted, modernist intelligentsia. So, before 1917 among the Muslim public there was not, and there could not be, a consciousness of belonging to a modern well-delineated nation. Their consciousness was pre-modern, of a purely religious type.

The ideal of adhering to a unique, pan-Turkic or pan-Muslim nation existed, however, among the pre-revolutionary Muslim intelligentsia. Russian pan-Turkism appeared in the late nineteenth century. It was born in Crimea, thanks to the effort of the great Crimean reformer, Ismail bey Gaspirali, and from there the movement spread to all Muslim Russia, to the Middle Volga, the Caucasus, and to Turkistan. The ideology of Gaspirali was summed up in his famous phrase *dilde, fikirde, ishte birlik*— "Union in language, thought and action." Its basis was a common modern school system and a common pan-Turkic language

—a simplified Istanbul Turkish, with the addition of some traditional Tatar words. This pan-Turkic language was supposed to be comprehensible to all Turks from the Bosphorus to Kashgar.

But Gaspirali's pan-Turkism was of a very peculiar type, being restricted to Muslims. It would be hard to find a single reference from before the Revolution to the brotherhood of all Turkic people, Muslims and non-Muslims—that is, of the Tatars, Uzbeks and the like with the Chuvash, Yakuts, or Gagauz. The "pan-Turanian" idea, the union of all Turks and even of all Uralic-Altaic people, was an invention of European Turkologists and was never accepted by the Muslim Turks themselves. On the contrary, "pan-Turkic" unity was broadly opened to non-Turkic Muslims, to the Iranian Tajiks, and to the North Caucasians. Indeed, in Russia, pan-Turkism and pan-Islamism were practically identical. There was never, in pre-revolutionary Russia, any conflict between pan-Turkism and pan-Islamism similar to the conflict which we found in the Ottoman Empire between pan-Turkism and pan-Islamism, or in the Arab lands between pan-Arabism and pan-Islamism. Such a conflict would have been unimaginable in Russia.

But the attempt by the Muslim intelligentsia to unify all Turkic Muslim people of Imperial Russia in one nation met with only limited, rather modest success. Indeed, this pan-Turkic idea, which was sponsored by the great Muslim union party, *Ittihad al-Muslimin,* could not be understood, and even less supported, by the public, and, from 1905 on, the unifying movement was challenged, in many territories, notably in Tatarstan, in Bashkiria, and in Transcaucasia, by regionalist ideologies opposed to pan-Turkic unity. When the October 1917 revolution broke out the fight between the unionists and the regionalists was still going on, and it was still impossible to decide which side had the best chance to win.

Something must be said also about the policy of Russian imperial authorities toward their Muslims' unity or disunity. The term "Muslims" was officially in use. In general, Russian authorities considered their Muslim community as a whole, and tried, with moderate success, to isolate different areas from one another, especially the technically less-developed areas from the more-developed area—that is, Turkistan and Kazakhstan from Tatar influence, the North Caucasus from Azeri influence, and all Russia from Turkish influence. They also tried to hamper the unification of the Muslim world by preserving social and cultural differences between different regions. This was a purely negative, defensive policy. One man, Nikolai Il'minskii, or rather a group of men, the Orthodox Missionaries of Kazan, specialists in anti-Muslim propaganda, understood the danger which the pan-Muslim movement represented for Russia, and they attempted to implement an active policy against it. Il'minskii and his colleagues tried to counterpoise the ideology of a modern nation to the ideology of Islam. They attempted to create a Christian Tatar nation and a Christian Kazakh nation in opposition to the Muslim *Umma* (people, community). This attempt was not very successful.

The problem of national consciousness changed radically during the Soviet regime. In contrast to the Czarist authorities, Soviet leaders, and first of all, Stalin, People's Commissar for Nationality Affairs, appreciated and feared the strength of the unifying movement among the Muslims, probably because his closest colleagues, in *Narkomnats,* were Muslim national communists, with strongly pronounced pan-Turkic ideas. Such was, in particular, Sultan Galiyev, with his project for a "Turanian Socialist Republic."

A detailed survey of Soviet Muslim policy would be outside our present research. Let me simply state what the goals of that policy were. The first aim was to divide the Muslim community as far as possible by separating the different parts of the *Umma* from one another. This policy had a manifold nature: administrative, political, and linguistic. The act of effecting administrative division into national units, not only in Central Asia but also in the Middle Volga and in the Caucasus, as well as the creation of new literary languages, had, for the most part, a purely artificial character. It did not respond to any real popular demand either by the Muslim intelligentsia (whether bourgeois or communist) or by the public. Numerous examples show the artificial character of national units created during the first years of the Soviet regime. One was the division of the Middle Volga Muslim group into two purely artificial nations, the Tatars and the Bashkirs, and the creation of two literary languages, Tatar and Bashkir. Even today, over fifty years after the creation of the Bashkir literary language (which is the official administrative language of the Bashkir Republic), only 60 percent of the Bashkirs designate Bashkir as their "first mother tongue," and 40 percent select Tatar. The same thing may be said about the division of the Chechens and the Ingush into two nations, or the creation of three different Cherkess (Circassian) languages—Adygei, Abazin, and Kabardin—in spite of the fact that these three languages represent only dialects of one and the same language. It would be difficult to discover in any Soviet publication of the 1920s a demand presented by the local intelligentsia to create a Chechen language different from the Ingush language. On the contrary, in that period Muslim intellectuals in the Caucasus, in Turkistan, or on the Middle Volga were fighting for unity.

The second aim of Soviet policy was the "drawing near" (in Russian, *sblizhenie*) of different Muslim groups to the Russians. It is obvious that this *sblizhenie* was a one-directional movement consisting of getting non-Russians nearer to the Russian people, "the elder brother," and accomplishing in its final stage the merging (*sliianie*) of a nationality into the Russian nation. There was never any question of encouraging *sblizhenie* or *sliianie* between different Muslim groups. The assimilation of the Bashkirs by the Tatars, *sblizhenie* between the Karakalpaks and the Uzbeks, or the assimilation of the Dargins by the Avars of Dagestan would certainly not have been considered as a progressive movement but as an act of local bourgeois nationalism.

The division in the 1920s of the previously undivided Soviet Muslim *Umma* into different nationality formations was purely artificial. But this does not mean that this arbitrary act decided from above produced no results. There is a parallel situation in the Arab world, which before World War I was even more closely united than the Turkic world in Russia. In 1918 the Arabs were also arbitrarily divided by the Western allies, France and Great

Britain. The frontiers drawn between different, newly created nations were also, at the beginning, purely artificial. But fifty years later these same barriers have grown into something real. Various Arab states have now achieved real existence through differentiated political and economic interests. One cannot say that the division of the Arab world into its present units will last forever, but it is evident that the frontiers of 1918 have become real obstacles to the unifying pan-Arabic movement. The same may be said of the Russian Muslims.

What do we know about the Soviet Muslims at the present time? There is only one certainty, and that is the power of national sentiment. But what kind of national sentiment—a local, restricted, purely Uzbek, Tatar or Karakalpak national sentiment? Or an extended, Turkistanian, pan-Turkic, or pan-Muslim sentiment? It is impossible to reply with assurance. We can only attempt to study the features pro and con of these two possibilities.

Since the October 1917 revolution two opposite trends have been at work within Soviet Islam. One is centrifugal; it is useless to deny it. The all-unifying languages which existed before the revolution, such as Arabic, Persian, Chaghatay, or the common Turkic language devised by Ismail Gaspirali for his newspaper *Terjuman* were proscribed by the authorities. The present separate Turkic languages tend to become more and more distant from one another, at least in their written form. The second piece of evidence for the centrifugal movement is the weakening (but not the disappearance) of religious sentiment. Finally, national republics, federative or autonomous, and even autonomous regions, have become realities, at least from a purely administrative point of view. Their existence is now necessary for the non-Russian bureaucratic and political cadres. As in the Arabic Middle East, the local, purely selfish interests of the leading social group, that is, the Party and Soviet bureaucrats, may be assimilated to local patriotism and finally lead to conflicting interests between different nationality units.

The opposite, centripetal trends are more difficult to survey. The Soviet system, by suppressing the nomads and by prohibiting all social traditions inherited from the past such as the endogamous and the exogamous taboos, and the leveling of all social differences, had destroyed all subnational, clannish, or tribal loyalties and consciousness. This certainly helped to bring different Muslim groups, formerly separated or even hostile one to another, closer together. But this evolution may facilitate either the emergence of a local national consciousness, or of a larger pan-Turkic consciousness. The second factor favoring centripetal evolution is the leveling brought about by all school and university programs. From the cultural point of view, the Muslim people, which, before the 1917 revolution, were very different from one another, are today close to the same educational level.

In addition there is the emergence of a very large non-Russian intelligentsia, much more numerous than the pre-revolutionary intelligentsia, with a strong desire to rediscover the national past of its people. Since World War II, and especially since Stalin's death in 1953, we can observe in all Muslim territories a passionate search, a real hunt for the national heritage, history, literature, and art; and of course this search leads to the rediscovery of a *common* Muslim past, of the common Arabo-Irano-Turkic traditional culture for the simple reason that there is no such thing as a purely Uzbek tradition, nor a purely Karakalpak culture, and that when a Karakalpak or an Uzbek intellectual tries to discover his origins he discovers a past common to all Turkic, or rather to all Muslim people on the territory of the Soviet Union. This is the most potent factor working for the rapprochement (*sblizhenie*) of all Soviet Muslim nations.

Which of the two trends, centrifugal or centripetal, will become the stronger? "God knows" (*Allah bilir*), as the Volga Tatars say. I personally believe that the centripetal drive will finally prevail. But to what kind of national consciousness will it lead? There are many possibilities. One is the resurgence of several regional groups, such as a Middle Volga Turkic group unifying the Tatars and the Bashkirs, or the appearance of a common Turkistanian "nation," extended also to the non-Turkic Tajiks. The second possibility, favored by some Turkic intellectuals indifferent to religious problems, may lead to an enlarged pan-Turkic group which would embrace even non-Muslim Turks like the Chuvash, Yakuts, and the Altays.

Finally, the present evolution may lead to the resurrection of a pan-Islamic consciousness. There are indications that even today, among the Turkistanians, Islam and nationality remain synonomous expressions. A recent article proved that a complete confusion between religious consciousness and national consciousness still exists among Kirgiz komsomol members.[2] In conclusion, "Allah and He alone" knows exactly what will happen to the Soviet Muslims, but in the not very distant future they probably will become one of the major human groups in the world.

NOTES

1. *Itogi vsesoiuznoi perepisi naseleniia 1959 goda. SSSR.* (Svodnyi tom) (Moscow: Gosstatizdat, 1962), pp. 184–86.

2. S. Dorzhenov, "Musulman li ia?" *Nauka i religiia,* No. 4 (1967), pp. 50–52.

VÁCLAV LAMSER

A SOCIOLOGICAL APPROACH TO
SOVIET NATIONALITY PROBLEMS

In considering the nature of the sociological approach to
"Soviet nationality problems," we immediately find that the first
word in that term is clear. *Soviet* is delineated by the territory of
the USSR. But the second word, *nationality,* deserves more attention. A nationality comprises a complex, changeable social
fact. In saying "complex" we assume several properties bound
into a unique, socially vital phenomenon. One nationality differs
from another as a complex whole. In this sense nationality is also
a changeable social fact spread all over the world.

Contemporary social sciences habitually approach a complex
social fact or problem from various standpoints. To some extent
this is necessary, because each social science demands its own
right to select an approach to social facts or problems. We wonder, however, whether several specialized approaches, even when
put together, can really grasp a social fact as a complex whole.
A nationality offers a good example of such a fact. Having this
in mind, we shall try to find a coordinating approach to it. We
presume to have found an appropriate access to it through sociology. But through what kind of sociology?

While advocating the sociological approach to nationality, we
admit that different types of sociology exist throughout the world.
In East Central Europe, for instance, there is a long tradition of
dealing with nationality problems. Being in contact with social
realities, East Central European sociology could not neglect
such an important social fact and problem as nationality. It would
be a luxury for small countries to lock sociology into a formal

theoretical framework, ignoring any contact with actual social facts and problems.

On the other hand, while formal sociological theories built upon concepts such as "system" and "social relationship" are taken into consideration, "groups," "groupings," "social units," and the like exist outside the approach to nationalities. Such "group" theories would fail if they were applied to a concrete nationality or to the configuration of nationalities which we specify in our title. Sociology in the United States divides the subject "nationality" between sociology and social or cultural anthropology, with a hesitant attitude toward the study of concrete, developed nationalities. This approach is not accepted universally in other countries.

There are other conceptions of sociology which do accept "the national society" as a matter of interest, however. They are able to deal directly with a nationality or with a concrete grouping of nationalities. Such a sociological framework provides a point of departure suitable for our analysis since the focus is put upon a concrete society. We shall proceed on these levels of analysis: Level 1: "the nationality." This is an abstract concept covering the whole field (all existing nationalities). In this sense it is a universal concept. Level 2: "the Soviet nationalities." This is a term designating a certain number of particular nationalities within the territory of the USSR. In comparison with Level 1, it is a less abstract concept representing an actual configuration of concrete nationalities. It is also less universal than "the nationality." Level 3: "a nationality" (in the USSR). This is a concrete, complex, and unique phenomenon.

Sociology of the type dealing with concepts on Level 1 (with "nationality") is abstract, universalistic, and might be specialized. If applied to conceptual Levels 2 and 3, it will be more concrete, less universal and comprehensive, and thus will coordinate other scholarly approaches to our subject. The current development of "area studies" raises at length the question of different types of sociology. We can reject some types as inappropriate to area studies. In general, however, we suppose sociology to be of use in area studies as a comprehensive social theory with coordinating and integrating functions in the approach to problems. Such a theory must be built upon a sufficiently substantive and methodological foundation. It is also applicable to new theory in international affairs.

The second methodological implication of our three Levels is found in the definition of "Soviet nationalities." We employ the definition used in official Soviet statistics as an operative definition. This is done without analyzing and evaluating this definition, whether it is true or not; otherwise, we could not use Soviet statistical data. This definition of "Soviet nationalities" covers 108 nationalities and ethnic groups (we omit Russians) listed in such official Soviet sources as the statistical yearbook and surveys of the Soviet economy. We shall refer to data from these sources throughout.[1]

The third suggestion arising from use of the three Levels lies in the choice of a relevant way to proceed on Levels 2 and 3. If we dealt merely with individual nationalities we could write many pages, but would never be able to look at the more universal phenomena and processes occurring on the Union-wide plane.

In analyzing the sociological definition of "nationality," we have to apply some special procedures. Definitions of "nation" or "nationality" are abundant. Leaving aside terminological differences between languages, and without recording the many definitions as such, we accept the analytic definition based on objective and subjective properties.

Synthetic definitions are mostly one-sided. Many such definitions have been criticized, because they cannot be applied to all nationalities. This is true if the definition refers only to a specific geographic and sociocultural situation. A more universal definition, which we need for analysis of the diverse Soviet nationalities, must be based upon a comparative method applicable to various nationalities. No definition other than an analytic one can be used.

Objective variables are represented in the columns of Table 10. Row A is devoted to statements about existing or nonexistent objective variables or variable-items (traits). Rows B and C include subjective variables, row D the action variable. The attri-

Table 10.   Analytic Definition of Nationality

	Common Territory a	Common Racial Origin b	Common Culture c	Common Polity d
Existence A	yes/no	clear/not clear	traits, e.g., language, way of life, institutions-organizations	traits, e.g., state govern-ment, parties, etc.
Conscious-ness of B	if it exists	yes/no	yes/no	if it exists
Desire for C	if it does not exist	not relevant	relevant for some items	if it does not exist
Efforts to achieve D	if it does not exist	not relevant	relevant for some items	if it does not exist

bute "common" implies a continuum from the "strong" occur-rence to the "weak" one, as follows—in column a: from compact territory to dispersed territory—in column b: clear racial origin-mixed (unclear) origin—in column c: only one language-bilingual (multilingual), similar-varied way of life, developed-undeveloped institutions and organizations—in column d: from sovereign state and political institutions to only limited local government.

Common history is not included, since objective and subjective variables have their past (longer or shorter) and present. The history of a nationality has been proceeding either simultaneously in all variables or unevenly, shifting from one variable to the other, sometimes from one variable-item (trait) to another. In fact, Table 10 is empty. It could be filled in with observed data and information referring to individual variables. The squares filled in would certainly be different for various nationalities.

The analytic definition (Table 10) offers a point of departure for considering what kinds of data and information are available to a researcher from outside and which information is within the reach of a participant observer such as a tourist or journalist. Our study is based upon several categories of information: (a) Data about the territory and the population. Statistical data are used only in relative numbers. Only preliminary data from the Soviet population census in 1970 are known (see the essay by Robert A. Lewis and the end sheets in this volume). Data from the census taken in 1959 are out of date. However, relative numbers or indices, even if deduced from older absolute numbers, do not change very much. (b) Information about the political institutions, to a limited extent. (c) Rather scarce information about nationality culture.

We shall use information obtained from direct participant observation as supporting data in the explanation. Such data relate mostly to behavior and to subjective variables. Casual observations in certain places may be superficial and puzzling. The available data and information are cross-tabulated here in order to produce a more sophisticated, deeper insight into the problems of Soviet nationalities. Nevertheless, this contribution no doubt consists more in building a conceptual framework applicable to a further study than in preparing an exhaustive analysis.

Probably the best way to deal with Soviet nationalities is to employ a typology as a point of departure for further explanation. Our typology is based upon the variables given in Table 10. If we presume all variables given in Table 10 to be present, we use the term "nationality." If some of them do not exist or are not developed (for example, common culture and common polity), we use a more modest term, "ethnic group." Because we are restricted by limitations in data and information, we can use neither all the variables nor one entire variable. We shall choose those criteria which we believe are important.

The first criterion to be used in constructing our typology is the size of a nationality. Size is expressed either through the extent of space settled by a nationality or in terms of the human quantity registered as belonging to a nationality. "Territorial extent" used as a unique measure of the size of nationality is misleading in connection with Soviet groups. There are many nationalities (or rather, ethnic groups) spread over immense territory. However, they do not possess very large numbers. Territorial extent has to be verified by checking the density of population. In this way, we can differentiate between compact or uncompact territories.

The second aspect in the question of size is the extent of "population belonging to a nationality." The key concept is "belonging." Available data suggest an operational definition which fits the official Soviet conception of nationality in general and a nationality in particular. This might contain biases. Nevertheless, the conventional 108 Soviet nationalities (excluding Russians) are represented in Table 11 according to their size.

Table 11. Size of Soviet Nationalities According to Population, 1959

Nationalities	i Large: More Than 10 Million	ii Medium: 1–10 Million	iii Small: 100,000– 1 Million	iv Very Small: Below 100,000
Slavic	1	2	1	2
Other European	—	5	4	5
Turkic	—	7	5	10
Finnic	—	3	4	4
Caucasian	—	2	6	10
Iranian	—	1	1	5
Paleo-Asiatic	—	—	—	8
Tungusic	—	—	—	6
Other Siberian	—	—	—	5
Mongol	—	—	2	1
Other Asiatic	—	—	1	7
TOTAL	1	20	24	63

Source: *Narodnoe khoziaistvo SSSR v 1965 godu.* Moscow: Gosudarstvennoe Statisticheskoe Izdatel'stvo, 1968.

The numerical proportion of small and very small nationalities to large and medium groups is about three to two (32:22). With the Russians it would be four to one (88:22). The percentage of population in the size categories works out as follows: one large nationality—17.7 percent (72.7 percent including the Russian); twenty medium nationalities—24.1 percent; twenty-four small nationalities—2.7 percent; and sixty-three very small nationalities—0.5 percent. The distribution in numbers of nationalities compared to the distribution in percentage of population shows small and very small nationalities to constitute such a small minority of the population that we have to assume that their proportion in the population cannot be substantially changed, even in the long run. Population size sets a precondition to the development of cultural and political institutions which need an ecological (territorial) basis, as do, for instance, larger or smaller towns. Nationalities or ethnic groups classified as "very small" possess almost no potential to develop towns and corresponding institutions. "Small" nationalities have but limited potential. (We shall meet this problem once more in later paragraphs dealing with the urbanization process.) We assume that the USSR recognizes these foreign policy constants in geopolitical terminology: the European continent, the Mediterranean, the Near and Middle East, Central and South Asia, China, the Far East, and the Polar regions. How might these constants be linked to the interests of corresponding Soviet nationalities? Distribution of the nationalities and Russians according to their political and cultural ties to larger (external) cultural and political areas could be stated approximately as follows (in percentages):

External Contact Areas	Percentage of Soviet Nationalities and Russians	
European continent		83 (28 excluding Russians)
Mediterranean	below	1
Near and Middle East		6
Central and South Asia		8½
China	below	1
Far East	below	1
Polar regions		1

The level of development is omitted from Table 10 intentionally. Development level refers to all objective variables of nationality, particularly to economic conditions, material standard of living, literacy, professional training, way of life, and to cultural and political institutions and activities. There is no doubt that the USSR is steadily developing. In the early 1920s, when systematic development under Soviet rule began, the economic level of nationalities was so unequal that in the following fifty years the Soviet leadership has not been able to achieve a unified, evenly developed society.

Our major concern focuses upon the fundamental processes of development and their potential impact upon nationalities. We shall propose three components to be considered in measuring the development level of Soviet nationalities. The following, derived from available data and information, are necessarily rather rough:

1) The proportion of the population employed in five societal sectors. This new approach, different from the usual three-sector economic scheme, includes both broader societal criteria and social activities typical of the more developed societies (sectors IV and V). The first sector is identical to the usual primary sector (agriculture, forestry, fishing, and mining). So is sector II (manufacturing, and industry). Sector III includes only material services (repairing, communal services, and the like). Sector IV refers to human services (education, teaching, health and social services). Information, knowledge, and communication (for example, data processing and scientific research) fall into Sector V.

The proportion of population employed in the five sectors conveys more than an index of industrialization. Such an index would not be adequate to measure differences between the economically most-developed nationalities like the Ukrainians and Estonians and the poorly developed. The breakdown of employment among sectors is but a comprehensive index of many other phenomena, such as institutions, organizations, and participation.

2) Urbanization is another component of development. We have to deal with it carefully, for some poorly developed nationalities enjoy a relatively high proportion of urban population. In contrast, some more-developed nationalities have a low urban proportion. Urbanization is influenced by climatic conditions and

related potentialities for agriculture. The southern zone of Siberia is, for instance, highly urbanized, whereas Belorussia and Moldavia encompass mostly rural areas.

Our index of urbanization is expressed by the proportion of population living in "towns," which are defined in Soviet statistics as communities having more than 2,500 inhabitants. This index is also rather rough. Soviet towns, particularly small ones, have a poor urban structure, meaning that they are deficient in urban centers, equipment, condition of buildings, ecological zoning, and the like.

3) The last component takes in cultural institutions and personalities—moving picture and drama theaters, film production, and concert halls, as well as figures like writers, composers, and artists. They support and vitalize the nationality culture. This component is difficult to measure. It can merely be estimated in an impressionistic way.

Besides the development process, we have to consider the location of selected nationalities, because we assume that the possibility of cross-cultural processes depends upon the location of people. The extent and position of Soviet territory on the earth's surface allow the Soviet government to control influence from the outside. The phenomenon of a closed society in all respects plays a substantial part in Soviet ideology, policies, culture, and consciousness of belonging to the Soviet whole. The Russians occupy the compactly settled core of Soviet territory and form some proportion of the population in peripheral territories. The nationalities, particularly those of medium and small size, occupy territories around the core. More than the inner nationalities they are located close to foreign political and cultural areas, and are vulnerable to external influence. Considering accessibility as a factor, we can classify four kinds of Soviet nationalities: (a) Inner nationalities exemplified by some Siberian nationalities or ethnic groups, enjoying compact historical settlement, and having no direct contact with foreign territories; (b) inner, dispersed nationalities, mostly very small ones; (c) peripheral, compact nationalities, like the Estonians and Georgians, with compact historical settlement and possessing at least their own cultural institutions; (d) peripheral foreign minorities, like Poles, Hungarians, and Japanese, whose political, cultural, and ethnic core is located in another, usually neighboring country. For this reason, they cannot be conceived as nationalities in a proper sense.

Having analyzed the criteria for our typology rather briefly we can proceed to construct the types. By combining four kinds of Soviet nationalities (a–d) with four sizes (mentioned in Table 11) we have sixteen types (i/a–iv/d). Some of them are not relevant (i/a; if we omit Russians, i/b, i/c, and i/d). Some are represented only by one nationality (i/c, ii/d) or by very few (iv/a). The further cross-tabulation of relevant types with development level shows a relatively high correlation between them. The interpretation rests in the size; nationalities which are large enough have a sufficient core and potential to be developed. If nationalities are too small they are exposed to a disintegrative process. In the interpretation, it is useful to examine political institutions of nationalities. We must limit ourselves to the political organization of the USSR, to the union republics, autonomous republics, autonomous *oblasts*, autonomous *krais*, and nationality *okrugs*. Comparing them to individual nationalities, and comparing population figures for territorial administrative units to the population according to nationalities, we can find out which nationalities possess no political institutions (in terms of administrative units) and which reach beyond or do not reach as far as the total population in a territorial administrative unit. If a nationality reaches beyond its territorial unit, there is a question where the members of it are located, whether in compact settlement in other territories or dispersed over several other territories. If a nationality does not come up to the population figure for its corresponding titular unit, other nationalities or Russians must obviously be present.

In this way, we derive the following types of nationalities according to political institutions: (a) without a corresponding titular political arrangement, such as Jews, Gypsies, some very small ethnic groups, and all foreign minorities (Poles being the only foreign minority reaching the category of medium size);

(b) nationalities having their own territorial administrative units, but reaching beyond them as well, the only nationality of medium size being the Tatar, others being small or very small; (c) nationalities not reaching the total population of their corresponding administrative units, this being true in all union republics (the percentage of the titular nationality usually runs between 60 and 80). Russians, and to some extent also Ukrainians, are spread all over the territory of the USSR. The Russians usually represent 10 to 20 percent of the republics' population. The spread of the nationalities depends upon their social mobility, particularly vertical mobility. These are apparently only individual cases.

Moving from political development of the USSR as a factor of crucial importance with respect to nationalities, we shall proceed to analyze two processes which characterize social development: social mobility and urbanization. The question to answer

Table 12. Structure of employment in the USSR (in early 1960s)

		Percentage		
	Sector	1929	1937	early 1960s
Ia	Agriculture, forestry			12.6 (excluding cooperative farmers)
Ib + II	Mining, manufacturing, construction	35.3	45.0	43.6
III	Material services			22.2
IV	Human services	10.3	13.1	13.4
V	Information, knowledge, etc.			3.2
	TOTAL			100.0

Source: *SSSR v tsifrakh. Kratkii statisticheskii sbornik.* Moscow: Izdatel'stvo "Statistika," 1968.

is how these processes affect Soviet nationalities. The process of
social mobility can be dealt with if we have an image of social
stratification in the USSR. Soviet statistics about class structure
are not very useful, because they reflect the official doctrine,
which portrays a socialist society composed merely of such components as workers, collective farmers (kolkhozniki), and employees. The category "employees" is particularly heterogeneous;
hence not susceptible to detailed analysis. Therefore, instead of
figures about class structure we shall use data about employed
population (Table 12). The percentage is arranged according to
employment sectors.

In order to compare the recent breakdown with the previous
structure we have shown data for 1929 and 1937 about the most
important sectors. From the data shown we can derive only
general assumptions regarding social mobility in the USSR.
They can be partially completed by information from direct
observation and research data. Since the end of the 1920s the
structure of the employed population in the USSR has shown a
surprisingly small change in sectors other than agriculture,
forestry, and fisheries (Ia). Of course, this does not mean that
there has been no social mobility. The statistical figures shown
could be misleading in this respect, because social mobility did
and does exist behind the relative numbers. Ever since the October, 1917, revolution the subsector of agriculture has been
the most important source for the labor force. Social mobility in
agriculture is entirely one-sided: from agriculture toward other
sectors or subsectors. Intragenerational mobility occurs mostly
from agriculture to mining or manufacturing, but sometimes also
to construction. Intergenerational mobility is more open, theoretically proceeding to all sectors; however, it is virtually limited
to mining plus sectors II and III. Social mobility to sector IV is
exceptional.

Economic activity in agriculture is connected with a specific
sociocultural environment which shapes a nationality. As we
have seen, the proportion of the population found in agriculture
or in rural areas provides no precise index of social development.
Nevertheless, when a large proportion of the rural population is

present in nationalities classified as "medium" and "small," it is seemingly a conservative factor in the true sense of the term. These nationalities conserve their traditional culture. At the same time, they are not well prepared to cope with problems generated by rapid social development. A simple example is the traditional folklore which the Soviet leadership likes to display abroad. Is folklore a feature of developed society or nationality? Certainly not.

In the early 1960s the mean for the rural population of the USSR was 51 percent, in 1970 44 percent.[2] Here are examples (compare Table 11) of the considerable number of "rural nationalities" (those having a percentage of farm population above the Soviet average):

Size i	Size ii	Size iii	Size iv
Ukrainians	Belorussians	Buryats	with some
	Lithuanians	Chechens	exceptions,
	Uzbeks	Kabardians	all of those
	Moldavians	Kalmyks	in this category

We have not given an exhaustive list of nationalities in the "rural" category because the most recent figures are not available. The examples shown above mostly reach so much higher than the Soviet average of rural population that we can assume they are still substantially unchanged. Furthermore, it is possible to cite a few examples of poorly developed nationalities which have a low proportion of rural population. They cannot, in principle, however, be considered "rural" nationalities: Komi, Chukchi, Khakass, and the like (mostly "very small," located in the subarctic zone).

Jobs included in Table 12's sectors II, III, IV, and V are concentrated primarily in towns and cities. Social mobility toward these sectors is therefore connected with urbanization. The mining industry (subsector Ib) is concentrated in some few geographic areas settled mostly by a mixture of nationalities. To many of them this becomes the first opportunity for exercising social mobility outward from agriculture (subsector Ia). Many

people live in a special kind of settlement, in so-called work-
men's communes (*rabochie poselki*). These are so far from being towns that they hardly qualify for inclusion in the process of
urbanization. Their economic activities do not correspond at all
to those of agricultural communes. They are small melting pots
of nationalities, but not very important in the larger picture.

Manufacturing enterprises have to be divided into two categories. First, there are specialized and for the most part highly
concentrated industrial plants like the automobile industry and
electrotechnical industry in the vicinity of such larger cities as
Moscow, Leningrad, Kiev, or Sverdlovsk. These industries require skilled and highly skilled workers. Social mobility leading
into these occupations is limited by migration to large cities. Such
movement is for the most part regulated. As a result the major
proportion of personnel is of Russian or Ukrainian origin. The
second category of enterprises produces consumer goods, and is
often dispersed throughout agricultural areas for economic reasons. Examples are the food industry, the cotton industry, and
tobacco manufacturing. Some can be found in the vicinity of
larger towns as well: dairies, bakeries, wholesale trade centers,
and the like. These industries use the local population for labor,
thus giving another opportunity for movement from agriculture
to different employment sectors.

Material services include a variety of subsidiary jobs, such as
catering and transport. They attract people from various nationalities, particularly into towns located in such sparsely populated
nonagricultural areas as parts of Siberia and the sub-arctic zone.
These jobs offer another opportunity for people to move from
their original settlements. Some material services, like repairing,
require more skilled workers and technicians than others. These
jobs are mostly occupied by people from larger, more developed
nationalities.

Human services in schools, medical care, and hospitals are to
a great extent locally bound. Personnel must speak the local language and be acquainted with the local government. Jobs in this
sector provide opportunities to selected members of the local

nationality. The number of opportunities depends upon the size of a nationality. The growth of opportunities is not parallel to the size of nationalities. The basic human services, in the primary school system, simple medical care, and so on, must be ever-present. They need but a limited population as potential receivers of services. On the other hand, highly specific human services, such as universities and specialized hospitals, demand a large potential constituency, and this magnitude can be achieved only in a large nationality. Specialized personnel must also be more qualified and trained than the semi-skilled. Nevertheless, human services comprise a sector with potential leadership positions in small and very small nationalities. These have been developing their own locally bound intelligentsia to an extent comparable with the size of the nationality.

Members of small or very small nationalities find some job opportunities both in material and human services. However, they must move to towns and cities where they will be dispersed among people of larger nationalities and, even more likely, among the Russians.

The top sector (V) of information, knowledge, and communication is the most universal one. The major proportion of personnel comes from Russia and the largest, most developed nationalities. Before speaking about nationalities, it must be remembered that the Russians fill a majority of such employment in the USSR. Whether this majority is proportional to its share of the total population is hard to say. The small and very small nationalities are scarcely represented. This is understandable, considering their population potential and, in some instances, the level of economic development. The proportion of sector V personnel from medium nationalities remains an open question.

On the whole, social mobility, which has been widening and accelerating in the USSR, is not developing evenly among all nationalities. Interfering in this process, in addition to the factors mentioned, are others. One is a consciousness of belonging to a unified nationality, an awareness spread mainly throughout medium and small, compact nationalities. This factor limits the migration and social mobility to opportunities within the area of the nationality itself, as in the Baltic republics. Dependence upon the socioeconomic development of one's own nationality might also limit vertical mobility to employment sectors II, III, IV, and V of Table 12. Other factors or circumstances coincide with urbanization. The rise of Soviet urbanization is demonstrated in Table 13.

Table 13.　Process of Urbanization in the USSR

Year	Percentage of Urban Population	
1913	17.6	(within present boundaries)
1926	17.9	
1939	32.6	
	31.6	(estimate for enlarged boundaries)
1959	48.9	
1970	56.0	

Source: *Narodnoe khoziaistvo SSSR v 1965 godu*, Moscow: Gosudar-stvennoe Statisticheskoe Izdatel'stvo, 1968, pp. 1–20; preliminary census data, "O predvaritel'nykh itogakh vsesoiuznoi perepisi naseleniia 1970 goda. Soobshchenie TsSU SSSR," *Pravda* (April 19, 1970), pp. 1–2.

With respect to the extent of Soviet territory and the uneven-ness of social mobility among nationalities, figures shown in Table 4 give but a rough orientation with no detailed figures shown for Soviet towns. Examining the figures, we can assume that urban growth refers to two kinds of areas: first, the metro-politan areas of the most important, developed cities (Moscow, Leningrad, Kiev, Tashkent, Baku, and Kharkov). Migration to

Source for Table 14 (below): "O predvaritel'nykh itogakh vsesoiuznoi perepisi naseleniia 1970 goda. Soobshchenie TsSU SSSR," *Pravda* (April 19, 1970), pp.1–2.

Key: SSR; SFSR = union republic
　　　ASSR　　= autonomous republic
　　　AO　　　= autonomous *oblast* (province)
　　　Kr　　　= autonomous *krai* (territory)
　　　NO　　　= nationality *okrug* (district)

Table 14. Urbanization in the USSR, According to Administrative Subdivisions (figures from the 1970 census)

		Level of Urbanization (percentage of urban dwellers)		
Very High: 65 and Above	High: 55.0–64.9	Medium: 40.0–54.9	Low: 25.0–39.9	Very Low: Below 24.9
Estonian SSR	(USSR)	Belorussian SSR	Kirgiz SSR	Nakhichevan ASSR
Karelian ASSR	Russian SFSR	Azerbaijan SSR	Moldavian SSR	Gorno-Altay AO
Khabarovsk Kr	Ukrainian SSR	Kazakh SSR	Tajik SSR	Gorno-Badakhshan AO
Primor Kr	Armenian SSR	Lithuanian SSR	Uzbek SSR	Komi-Permyak NO
Evrei AO	Latvian SSR	Turkmen SSR	Mordvin ASSR	Ust Orda Buryat NO
Arkhangel AO	Komi ASSR	Abkhaz ASSR	Chuvash ASSR	
Chukchi NO	Severo-Ossetin ASSR	Adzhar ASSR	Dagestan ASSR	
(Most Siberian oblasts)	Udmurt ASSR	Bashkir ASSR	Kalmyk ASSR	
	Yakut ASSR	Buryat ASSR	Karakalpak ASSR	
	Amur AO	Chechen-Ingush ASSR	Nagorno-Karabakh AO	
	Nenets AO	Kabardin-Balkar ASSR	Iugo-Ossetin AO	
	Astrakhan AO	Mari ASSR	Evenki NO	
	Aga Buryat AO	Tatar ASSR	Koryak NO	
	Khanty-Mansi NO	Tuvin ASSR		
	Taimyr NO	Altay Kr		
	(European industrial oblasts)	Krasnodar Kr		
	(Few Siberian oblasts)	Adygi AO		
		Yamalo-Nenets NO		
		(European agroindustrial oblasts)		

these areas is controlled, limited largely to skilled personnel and to people in high positions. Second, there are areas under a policy of preferred development, mostly for such economic reasons as the presence of mining industries and machine production industries. The rapidly growing towns have been attracting people from nationalities situated nearby. This is occurring in the Urals, and in West and East Siberian, Central Asian, and Caucasus areas.

In order to complete the survey of urbanization among the nationalities, we have organized the list of Soviet administrative subdivisions into five ranges of density in Table 14.

The table corroborates what we have said about the effect of an agricultural environment and climatic conditions upon social mobility and migration. It also reveals the settlement policy of the Soviet government in newly developing areas. In considering "nationality" mobility, we have to examine the relationship between social mobility and migration. From this viewpoint there are three types of social mobility, both horizontal and vertical, active in the USSR:

1) Social mobility occurs within the attraction area of a town in a sparsely populated territory. Such an area may be very large, particularly in Siberia and Central Asia. Small and very small nationalities or ethnic groups, which are affected by this type of migration, have been dispersing into the town population. Migrating members of a nationality have thus been losing their original setting and their sociocultural background as well. People have been absorbed into the new environment when they were alone or in a tiny minority. Table 14 refers to regions experiencing rapid urbanization affecting nationalities which live in the vicinity. For many reasons such urbanization provides the only solution for nationalities living under hard climatic conditions. There, economic development is conceivable but industrialization concentrated.

2) Social mobility is kept within the boundaries of a *compact* nationality. We emphasize the attribute "compact," because dispersed nationalities fall under the previously mentioned type of

social mobility and migration. Compact nationalities must be large enough and must have developed all five sectors, or at least four sectors (without a considerable sector V) of employment (Table 12), in order to give opportunities for social mobility. If that is not so, social mobility is limited to sectors I, II, and III. Those who decide to move or who are selected for vertical mobility (for schools, military careers, party bureaucracy, and the like) have to abandon their nationality setting and prepare to merge into the new sociocultural environment. Knowledge of the proportion of people which stays in the nationality setting and that which leaves it could serve as a measure of nationality self-awareness. From personal impressions, we assume this type of social mobility to have been occurring in Estonia, Latvia, and the Transcaucasian republics. On the other hand, the predominantly agricultural nationalities are handicapped in exercising this type of social mobility because they lack appropriate institutions or organizations and, consequently, proper jobs for the purpose.

3) Besides the extent of industrialization and urbanization, the size of nationality becomes to a great degree an important factor in social mobility. Both the territory and the quantity of population represent a potential necessary for building up institutional organizations like universities, research institutes, high school systems, cultural organizations, and banking, as well as political institutions other than the government. Considering the typology of Soviet nationalities, we can surmise which nationalities have a broad potential, which ones have but a narrow potential, and, finally, which ones have almost no potential (mostly "small" nationalities and all "very small" nationalities).

There is actually but one nationality, along with the Russian group, having a broad potential, and, on a Union-wide scale, almost unlimited social mobility and migration. Ukrainians are spread all over the territory of the USSR, as are Russians (the latter, however, to a much greater degree). These two represent as well the third type of social mobility and migration.

The nationality potential becomes most evident in cities and large towns, because specialized institutions and higher-level organizations such as schools, theaters, moving picture production, scientific institutes, higher organizational levels of political party, and labor unions are concentrated there. Developing its own peculiar life, a nationality needs at least large towns. For urbanization, the present situation and the possible future development are shown to some extent in Table 14. Statistical data, however, gloss over the urban structure, particularly the extent of town centers where institutions customarily are located. Under urban conditions prevalent in the Ukrainian SSR, only towns with over 100,000 inhabitants can be considered appropriate to a more developed nationality life. In Siberia, the Urals, and Central Asia the requirement is still higher. There, towns must concentrate at least 300,000 inhabitants within them.

The size of towns supplies but a rough indication of nationality life. One other indicator is suggested by positions in institutional organizations (economic, political, and cultural), because they relate to power and influence. When we speak of these matters we touch on the political aspect of nationality problems. Soviet nationality policy is guided by official doctrine. After the October, 1917, revolution, and in theory even before, nationality policy oscillated between proletarian internationalism and socialist patriotism. Nationalism was soon rejected as a symptom of bourgeois thought, behavior, and policy. The definition of "nationalism" was very flexible. In practical terms its meaning was determined by the power centers. Soviet patriotism was and is opposed to the "nationalism" of individual nationalities. Nationality problems within the USSR cannot be separated from the totality of policies effectuated on the principle of "proletarian internationalism and socialist patriotism." In this manner, Soviet nationality policy serves as a link in the chain of internal and foreign policies. Domestic nationality policy reacts to foreign stimuli sensitively, and, conversely, Soviet foreign policy cannot neglect the nationality problems within the territory of the USSR. Nationality policy is conceived within a broader Soviet context which is presumed to have five zones as follows:

ZONES OF SOVIET POLICIES

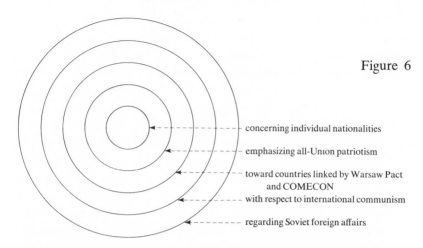

Figure 6

concerning individual nationalities

emphasizing all-Union patriotism

toward countries linked by Warsaw Pact
and COMECON

with respect to international communism

regarding Soviet foreign affairs

All five zones are united by the common party leadership in Moscow. Party policies and state policies blend into a whole; and party bodies play a decisive role among the individual nationalities. "Local interests" are subordinated to broader interests.

Up to 1968, Soviet nationality policies oscillated between Union-wide interests and those of individual nationalities. Union-wide interests were at least proportional to the size of the nationalities. Since the Soviet intervention in Czechoslovakia of August 1968, Soviet nationality affairs have started becoming a part of a larger policy extended to the Warsaw Pact countries. This new trend in Soviet policy has been confirmed by the Soviet-Czechoslovak agreement of May 9, 1970.

The Soviet leadership has constantly emphasized the unity of the international communist and workers' movement as well as the unity of "the socialist camp" (which is more directly within reach of the Moscow leadership). Conspicuous recently, this broader emphasis overshadows domestic Soviet nationality policy. Nationality policy is effectuated rather in territorial administrative units than upon the basis of proper nationalities. In an imaginary triangle—party, state, nationality—the first two are quite obviously preferred. In discussing the official policy or policies, the question remains: to what extent do official policies coincide with actual social and cultural processes in the individual nationalities, or, are they far removed from those processes? At present, it is too early to evaluate the latest Soviet policy. Even it, to be sure, does not function in an international vacuum, but is subject to certain outside influences which merit scrutiny.

"External" influence is of course that which comes from outside the USSR. But, from a nationality's viewpoint, "external" influence also implies an effect exerted by one nationality upon another within the USSR. This second type is not our concern, here, though it touches upon the relationship existing between Russians as well as Ukrainians, the largest nationality, and nationalities of medium, small, and very small size. There appear to be two main sources of external influence, that from the socialist countries, and influence from the rest of the world. These two sources are distinguished here, because they correspond to distinct policies toward foreign countries carried out by the Soviet party leadership and government. This takes into consideration both interstate movement and other restrictive or facilitating practices in the USSR.

Let us exclude formal contacts, which occur mostly in elite groupings like the party apparatus, the diplomatic corps, and in rigidly selected clusters of economic and technical personnel. The positions of people who are in steady contact with the outside world are so exceptional that these men and women are, by the nature of things, separated from other people. Their capacity to transmit such external influence is therefore limited to small social circles. Of course, this depends upon their receptivity to external influence. Barriers against the possibility of face-to-face contacts with outsiders and receiving foreign mass media of communication are not only of an objective nature. Subjective blocks are complex phenomena which can perhaps be understood after a deep inquiry into the ideological and cultural background of the people. In any case, routes from the elite groupings with contacts to the external world lead mostly into large cities such as Moscow, Leningrad, Kiev, Tashkent, and a few others, but have a very limited impact upon wider geographic areas. In fact, the channels of such international communication are very complicated, and opinion formation under such circumstances is hardly understandable to a foreign observer.

We can be much more interested in the "informal" contacts in which a growing number of people in the USSR have been participating. Presumably they are "informal," for these encounters describe no official pattern and no explicit official aims similar to those of, for example, diplomacy. Two kinds of these informal contacts, direct and indirect, may be found. In order to prepare a framework for further analysis we shall attempt to classify both direct and indirect contacts.

Direct contacts are those in which people are personally involved. These are contacts of Soviet citizens with the outside world with an immediate experience of the place, or they may be contacts with foreigners who come to the USSR and are met by some Soviet citizens on various occasions. *Indirect contacts* are those which are more or less mediated by other people or by the mass media. The mediating of communication includes one or more mediators. Mediating brings about a reshaping of experience, gives impressions and information—it is called, in the theory of communication, "semantic noise." The resulting output might be inaccurate, perhaps not valid; nevertheless, it is an important factor in shaping Soviet public opinion as well as the public opinion of the nationalities. Official propaganda has to counter-balance this influence as it is exerted. The more inaccurate the outside effort, the easier the work of official propaganda. Both inaccuracy of messages and insensitiveness of foreign media to Soviet sociocultural conditions are the most questionable devices for positively influencing Soviet individuals.

In classifying the usual direct and indirect contacts we have also suggested the barriers which people encounter in their striving for and/or in effectuating of contacts with foreigners. The obstacles are numerous. Contacts are also watched carefully by Soviet authorities. Leaving aside frontier security, let us turn our attention to other control mechanisms which affect both direct and indirect contacts.

Tourism in both directions is controlled. Soviet tourists intending to visit communist countries are selected through administrative and economic screening. Prices of foreign travel are high. Those Soviet citizens who intend to go to other countries are carefully selected. Traveling abroad, tourists have a partially organized program, and also are somewhat free to see what they want.

Foreign tourists coming to the USSR usually have an itinerary prepared by an official Soviet travel agency which includes some towns and other interesting places in the USSR as well as some activities. Foreign tourists are free for a limited time and they can see what they want; however, ordinarily they cannot leave the cities. The number of Soviet tourists going to other communist countries has been growing. Nevertheless, it touches a relatively limited proportion of the Soviet population, mostly that of urban origin coming from materially better-situated strata. The organized exchange of workers or cooperative farmers gives an opportunity for outside contact as well. The number of people involved is, however, also relatively small. Access to non-communist countries is very limited, for the time being. Thus, it is not too significant, quantitatively, as a source of external influence.

People coming into the USSR are routed to relatively few places. They leave wide territories of the USSR untouched. Soviet citizens who meet them live mostly in large towns or visit a few recreation areas. We can assume that these places crystallize and disseminate some external influence. Access to foreign mass media is also controlled. Availability of foreign press and literature is limited to official and scientific institutions, more exactly, to some positions within these institutions. Although foreign scientific literature has been imported into the USSR in growing volume, only a limited number of copies circulate, so that only scientists and other prominent people can read them immediately, others having to wait for a long time until their turn comes.

Radio broadcasting from outside the communist countries has but a limited range, mainly in the marginal territories of the USSR. More important it has but limited influence in Estonia,

Karelia, Latvia, Armenia and some other Transcaucasian areas. Western radio broadcasting stations are audible in many parts of the USSR if they are not jammed. People listen to the programs, but what proportion can hardly be estimated. Chinese radio broadcasting runs day and night, reaching the Asian part of the USSR. Its influence is negligible. Telecasts emanating from outside neighboring countries have almost no impact upon the Soviet population. The only exception is provided by Finnish television, which exerts some influence in Estonia.

Possibilities open to mass media from the communist countries are much greater in the USSR. Access to their press and literature is but slightly limited. East Central European radio broadcasting is audible in the western parts of the USSR. In addition, programs are officially exchanged between the two areas both in radio and TV. In summary, the influence of different kinds of foreign mass media of communication seems to fall into the following order of importance: (1) Books, mostly specialized literature; (2) radio broadcasting on current issues; (3) magazines; (4) newspapers; (5) television broadcasting. There are many similarities and differences between the mass media of the other communist countries and those of the USSR. The function of East European mass media in the USSR cannot be underestimated. In many respects these media introduce something new, stirring the quiet surface. The process is relatively fast in fashions, superficial features of people's behavior (mostly the urban population), and in the human thought concerning current issues. It is very slow in the diffusion of some cultural traits, even though it is not received by all nationalities and population categories in the same way.

Our analysis of contacts, channels of communication, and the diffusion process cannot neglect the capacity and/or the willingness of Soviet citizens to receive foreign communications. This capacity and willingness put together make up the crucial receptivity. The capacity to receive external influence is determined by language skill and by some experience with foreign cultures. This capacity is certainly not the same in all nationalities and social strata (or population categories), is no doubt higher in compact peripheral nationalities. Unquestionably higher among young graduates than in the older generation, it is very high throughout those foreign minorities or nationalities like the Poles, Armenians, Azerbaijanians, and Estonians, who have identical or similar counterparts outside the USSR.

Willingness to receive in this way is a deep-rooted psychic phenomenon shaped by many factors. Roughly speaking, it depends upon the size of the nationality. This supplies, however, but a prerequisite for developing other factors in the political culture and in the common culture of a nationality. Large nationalities are more likely self-involved, having a feeling of messianism; small nationalities are probably self-involved for a defensive purpose. Willingness to receive new thoughts and impressions cannot be explained in mechanical terms. For instance, it cannot always be said that the more self-involved a nationality is the less willing it is to receive foreign influence. The relationship is more complicated. The modern history of the Russians themselves has demonstrated that self-involvement and receptivity must be looked upon in relation to various strata and population categories. The nature and intensity of self-involvement predetermine the images held of foreign nations and cultures. The matter requires much further study, however.

We must beware of entertaining superficial, old-fashioned opinions assessing external influence upon the USSR in terms of western culture and the process of westernization. External influence must be conceived in terms of several cultural areas, both European and Asiatic. To examine external influence we must not neglect the fact that a great part of the USSR is and was for a long time made up of cultural areas of its own. The cultural autonomy of large and some medium nationalities has been strengthened in recent decades. This has an impact upon the images such people hold of foreign nations and cultures.

In general it can be concluded that the nationality problems of the USSR are to be looked upon from the perspective of their sociocultural development. We have considered but two major processes, industrialization and urbanization, leaving unstudied other subtle developments. The impact of development processes is favorable in some instances and unfavorable in others toward the future autonomous existence of nationalities. The development process will be especially advantageous to large nationalities like the Ukrainians. Their size represents a larger potential for evolving diversified institutions, social stratification, and for both horizontal and vertical mobility. We can assume that these nationalities will maintain their key positions notwithstanding application of a milder or tougher nationality policy of the Soviet regime.

By contrast, the very small nationalities have no possibility for future development within their own nationality framework. They will be obliged to merge into a broader, more or less homogeneous environment. Medium and small nationalities lying between the above-mentioned categories actually have two possibilities. They will either keep step with sociocultural development or they will be more and more conservative, lagging behind. More urbanized nationalities have a better chance in this respect than those mostly rural and agricultural. Some medium nationalities hold a critical position in the USSR, since they are distinct in many properties and they have been developing their own culture, institutions, and way of life for centuries. They will not merge into a larger whole easily. The less-developed, medium, and small nationalities with traditional cultures and ways of life will be able to keep their nationality only on condition that they can develop their own modern framework; otherwise, they will be obliged to merge into a larger entity.

External influence upon the young, well-educated generation is growing stronger in spite of the more or less tough isolationist official policy. But external influence will not unambiguously favor growing nationality self-involvement. Among more-developed nationalities, at least, outside influence will promote universal elements, traits, and patterns in culture as well as in political life. In scrutinizing the question of external influence, we cannot underestimate the function of East Central European countries like Czechoslovakia and Hungary in the historical and geopolitical mission of bringing western and eastern spheres of the European continent together.

NOTES

1. *Narodnoe khoziaistvo SSSR v 1965 godu* (Moscow: Gosudarstvennoe Statistichiskoe Izdatel'stvo, 1968); *SSSR v tsifrakh. Kratkii statisticheskii sbornik* (Moscow: Izdatel'stvo "Statistika," 1968); A. P. Kudriashov, *Sovremennaia nauchno-tekhnicheskaia revoliutsiia i ee osobennosti* (Moscow: Izdatel'stvo "Mysl'," 1965).

2. "O predvaritel'nykh itogakh vsesoiuznoi perepisi naseleniia 1970 goda. Soobshchenie TsSU SSSR," *Pravda* (April 19, 1970), pp. 1–2.

PAULA G. RUBEL

ETHNIC IDENTITY AMONG
THE SOVIET NATIONALITIES

The persistence of different ethnic groups within nation-states is an acknowledged fact. Recognition of this general phenomenon may serve us well in an examination of the specific nationality problems in the USSR. It will also inject an element of realism into the flights of social and political theorizing frequently launched by social scientists without reference to contributions in this field offered by anthropology. To demonstrate the potential of this discipline for nationality study we shall consider certain concepts, developed by anthropologists, relating to the subject of ethnic identity, the kinds of conceptual models utilized to study it, and the applicability of these models to the situation of Soviet nationalities.

Anthropology has by no means yet acquired a "unified field theory" regarding ethnic identity. Furthermore, what is really happening to nationalities inside the Soviet Union is difficult to determine. Without first-hand field material gathered in an undoctrinaire fashion, no firm conclusions can be reached concerning the problem of ethnicity in the USSR. Present-day Soviet social science remains too rigid to elicit the sorts of field material with which to approach our problem quite satisfactorily. Perhaps Soviet scholars themselves may not understand the value, to their own country's policymakers, of moving beyond such a doctrinaire framework of ethnic study.

Therefore, in order to cast some light upon a murky scene we shall first integrate concepts about ethnic identity taken from selected empirical research concerning various societies, into a tentative analytical framework designed to be applied to the Soviet situation. Then we shall draw upon our own experience and that of others, acquired from studying certain Soviet and non-Soviet nationalities, in order to suggest the appropriateness of this framework to a consideration of problems in the USSR.

The anthropological approach to studying ethnicity has been characterized, in general, by several different methodological components. The comparative, or cross-cultural, method will play a significant part in the following analysis. Although in the West we do not find cases completely analogous to the Soviet nationality complex, insights into it may be obtained by considering variables functioning in sociocultural situations somewhat similar to those of the Soviet Union. A second, central feature of this approach places emphasis upon the processual stream of events and a developmental framework in which sociocultural phenomena are seen to constitute a dynamic, interrelated process or evolving system, not simply a succession of separate, static structural states. This accent upon the processual, the developmental, the diachronic assumes importance if the goal of our investigation is to find a causal explanation of what originates, sustains, or weakens ethnic identification.

In the ongoing sequence of events, the past always exerts some influence upon the present. Frequently, elements of the past may play an ideological role in the present as both myth and as symbol of reality. This is particularly true with respect to the symbolic content of ethnic identity. This proposed analytical framework can be applied to the study of the Soviet situation where the events of the past, the 1917 Revolution and the like, continue to be part of the changing contemporary scene.

The process of sociocultural development, whether characterized by continuity or by change, involves making decisions about what courses of action are to be selected from among several choices or options. The range of these options varies in each context, within particular cultures, from a single choice enforced by external authority, or a single choice enforced by an absence of a cultural alternative, to the presence of many choices. Decision making as a group phenomenon brings into play leadership and followership and will be seen, below, to relate to the role of what we have called "intermediaries." The degree to which followers adhere to particular choices of their leaders depends upon mechanisms of social control.

Another anthropological technique which will be employed in this inquiry relates to building models consisting of such sociocultural variables as rule of descent (e.g., patrilineal inheritance), land tenure (e.g., communal holding), and rule of marriage (e.g., exogamy). The procedure in constructing a model begins with an examination of the selected variables in a series of societies in order to observe the particular patterns of their interrelationship through time in each society and to reveal the determinate relationships among the variables. Such causal interrelations are those in which at least two sociocultural variables influence each other or one or more act upon others directly or indirectly.

To illustrate, if we select variables A (rule of descent), B (land tenure), and C (rule of marriage) for consideration, we may then proceed to examine these variables in operation through time in societies I (Kalmyk), II (Uzbek), and III (Chukchi). These variables may have particular ranges or a certain number of permutations. Such ranges and permutations vary, depending upon the nature of the particular variable. The objective is to determine which permutations of the three selected variables interrelate in each society and how this interrelation changes through time. The model then developed becomes a statement which replicates the determinate relations, describing the patterns of interconnection on an abstract level between the variables which comprise the model. It is our aim to use insights gained from studying comparative material to develop a theoretical framework for analyzing problems of ethnic identity. Such models may then allow us to predict the course of development of ethnic groups and the process of interethnic relations in other societies. We hope, despite severe limitations in data and the absence of first-hand material gathered in the USSR with a non-Soviet frame of reference, to suggest the ways in which this framework might be utilized in order to illuminate the dynamic role which ethnicity or ethnic identity as well as nationality or nationalism, have played and will continue to play in Soviet nationality affairs. We hope that our model may be suggestive and provide an impetus for full-scale exploration of the way in which the character of ethnic identity may shift, over time, in response to variations in societal features which comprise related variables of our model.

Some of the analytical tools which anthropology provides for the study of ethnic identity include, first, what may be called whole societal models. The model of the plural society, though used in anthropology, was first defined by a political scientist, on the basis of his experience in the colonial Far East.[1] He defined a plural society as one which includes groups which maintain separate religions, languages, ideologies, and ways of life. Different segments (groups) of the plural societal community live separately, even though parts of the same political unit. He also saw a division of labor along such group lines. Thus, the market place becomes another locus of interrelationship. This was a vague and somewhat general definition of a plural society. Somewhat later an anthropologist re-examined this concept in the Caribbean environment and elaborated upon it.[2] He sought to catch the essence of a particular ethnographic situation which did not fit the usual homogeneous societal concept. In re-examining the concept of the plural society, he distinguished between what he called social and cultural, social being defined as the patterns of interrelationship, and cultural being the content, the value, the meaning, the semantic context. He believed that institutions consisted of both groupings and norms of behavior, and recognized that the definition of society was central to a consideration of the concept of a "plural society." He defined a society's limits on the basis of territorial distinctness, and more crucially, political control—that is, there is a government as a locus of power. On the basis of these definitions, he set up a tripartite typology. Homogeneous societies he defined as those consisting of social groups with a single set of institutions involving interdependence of action, ideas, values, patterns of social relationship, and political distinctness. These are usually very simple types of societies, but they may be more complex, so long as they fit his definition by possessing a single set of institutions.

The second category comprised societies characterized by social and cultural pluralism. In these instances the social and cultural are not conterminous. There is a formal diversity in the basic system of institutions. Kinship, education, religion, property and economy, and recreation are handled in different institutional contexts for the different sociocultural segments (groups). Institutional roles in the different sociocultural segments of the population are defined differently. In order to regulate behavior between these different segments there had to be a monopoly of power by one segment. There is in this particular type of society more reliance upon regulation than on common motivation. Integrative and organizational problems always arise in this kind of society. The cultural segments are usually hierarchically arranged. In addition to one segment's having a monopoly of power, there might be a hierarchical arrangement of the others combined in the plural society.

The last of these three anthropological categories consisted of societies exhibiting cultural heterogeneity.[3] These were not societies showing diversity in formal institutions, but rather ones possessing a single basic institutional system in a number of styles, or a basic system with a number of institutional variants. These, for example, were ethnic groups who shared the same basic institutions, but presented different, distinctive life styles. Because the concept of the "plural society" was examined by an anthropologist within the Caribbean area, the racial factor also entered into the picture. Some of the cultural segments of the population might at times be racially distinguished. He also suggested a connection between the socially and culturally plural society and population migration. His paper prompted comment by a conference discussant, who noted the possibility of arranging a kind of sequence employing the Caribbean societies so that cultural pluralism might be considered a way station to cultural heterogeneity.[4]

What are the problems raised by the concept of the "plural

society"? First, the concept consists of statements about a series of static structural states defined by sets of sociocultural attributes. This formulation would tend to exclude most actual cases if one held hard and fast to the definition by attributes. In terms of our political scientist's original conceptualization, field reports emanating from the Caribbean and southeast Asia note relationships, other than political, between cultural segments. Such groups meet in the market place, for example. Other kinds of interstitial relationships functioning between cultural segments were also documented. A model could be built to encompass the anthropologist's structures of homogeneous, heterogeneous, and plural societies,[5] placing them in a processual developmental frame. Referring to the above discussion of model building, such an analytical framework would consist of a set of characteristics whose particular ranges of variation and determinate interrelationships have been ascertained by examining a number of societies. It is then possible to generate a series of forms (constructs) representing the societal structures, or what one may call the possible "way stations" on the road to homogeneity or assimilation. Empirical examples which one might examine would correspond to these permutations of the variables.

The next whole society concept which we shall examine with specific regard to its suitability for studying the Soviet situation is an approach developed by the anthropologist Robert Redfield, according to whom nation states encompass Great and Little Traditions.[6] The Great Tradition is represented by the elite tradition, the esoteric knowledge possessed by the elite, and the like. The Little Tradition refers to the concepts, the values, and the cultural material of the little folk. These conceptualizations have been utilized in an analysis of materials drawn from the Soviet Union.[7] The authors of that analysis see what they call a two-story culture in Soviet Central Asia. Each level is characterized by different values. The lower is the Little Tradition, which they call private culture. Here, traditional values have remained intact because they are ceremonially reinforced. The upper story, the Great Tradition, they call public culture. This consists of Russian traits.

However, this particular application of the "whole society" concept is too simplistic and limited, for it neglects the elements of the earlier Great Tradition of the area—the Islamic tradition. This tradition may continue to be maintained on both levels. The local elite seemed, in this formulation, to constitute the top floor. However, the Russian cultural component, which is also operative in Soviet Central Asia, seems to be ignored. These "whole society" models—the most generalizing of frameworks—constitute but one type of analytical approach which anthropology offers for the examination of what might be called multiethnic societies.

Research, empirical investigation, and analysis have also been pursued in connection with different, but more specific, parts of the proposed analytical framework, portions of which have been subsumed under other rubrics but which bear a central relationship to the general problem being considered. Many studies have been concerned with the question of acculturation (culture change as the result of contact between two cultures) and assimilation of one sociocultural group into another—heterogeneity becoming homogeneity and with its obverse, the maintenance of difference—heterogeneity and pluralism being maintained. One also finds situations in which development goes in the opposite direction—that is, toward the creation of ethnic groups. The maintenance of sociocultural differences relates to maintenance of ethnic identity. This of course is the logical concept with which to begin a more detailed investigation.

Ethnic identity has been defined in various ways. The important elements or criteria include the presence of mechanisms by which individuals recognize members of their own or another social group and by which they recognize persons who do or do not share a culture or symbol system. The shared belief system is a crucial aspect of ethnic identity encompassing shared meanings, a belief in uniqueness and recognition of the uniqueness of certain symbols. These elements which individuals recognize to be unique to their group may not in fact be unique. The symbols and traits used to signify uniqueness are frequently borrowed from other groups, though the meanings invested in them may be unique. Research on the Soviet Chukchi, a small northern Siberian group, indicates that throughout three hundred years of change many of the elements which the Chukchi have continued to identify as Chukchi and which to them signify (symbolize) their group, their identity, and their culture were actually borrowed from other cultural groups.[8] Among the Kalmyk Mongols this was also found to be so.[9] Frequently, elements borrowed from Russian culture, and from Yugoslavian and Bulgarian cultures —all of these cultures with which the Kalmyks had made contact—became part of Kalmyk tradition and were used by Kalmyks as signifiers of Kalmyk cultural identity. Looking at such a group from a historical standpoint, one frequently finds that the body of traits which signifies this group change as time goes on. Over a period of two or three hundred years the cultural elements within that body of tradition may become greatly altered. A belief in uniqueness may also encompass a belief in superiority. Another equally important factor in ethnic identity is the nature of social interaction.

Cross-cultural comparison shows that groups vary in terms of the intensity of these two criteria—the shared belief system and social participation—and these criteria vary independently. From a study of Todos Santos people in Mexico emerged a fourfold typology based upon the intersection of these two variables:[10]

1) Groups that exhibit a high degree of shared belief and a high level of social participation, and sometimes even making of items (traits) of the cultural system sacred. Religion incorporates many cultural items. This tends to assist in the preservation of ethnicity. The Old Believers, a Russian fundamentalist sect, exemplify this type of group. Many of their cultural elements became items imbued with religious feeling. This aided in the perpetuation of the culture of the Old Believers. The Hutterites in the United States supply another such example.[11]

2) Groups that exhibit a high proportion of shared beliefs, but low social participation represent a type of combination, frequently found, in which social stratification is present. In them,

different socioeconomic groups may not interact with one another, yet share many common traits.

3) Groups exhibiting low sharing of cultural traits, but a high degree of social participation. In this instance, we have an example of ethnic identity's being maintained by social interaction between members of the group. For example, Blacks seem currently to fit this pattern. We are now seeing cultural content increasingly being used to signify American Black identity. We are, thus, observing the growth and strengthening of ethnic identity and group cohesion in the case of Blacks.

4) The intersection of low social participation and low sharing of beliefs would not sustain the existence of an ethnic group.

Another important anthropological concept related to studying ethnic identity is the recognition of distinctions between in-group and out-group. This recognition may be accomplished in a variety of ways. The presence of a structure of status categories may differentiate the two groups. The presence of certain kinds of boundary-maintenance mechanisms also serves to preserve distinctions. These include endogamy (marrying only within the group); the presence of distinctive features such as language or other traits which are recognized by both insiders and outsiders as being distinctive; the presence of separatist religious structure and a body of esoteric knowledge; conformity to certain behavioral patterns of the in-group; externally perceptible characteristics including different physical features. Minimally, there must be some means present by which the out-group can recognize the in-group and members of the in-group can recognize one another. The question of a need for the required ecological (territorial) basis in order to maintain the sociocultural integration of ethnic groups is also relevant. Must there necessarily be some kind of territorial dimension for an ethnic group? Work on American Jews shows that this is not necessarily the case.[12] The presence of common traditions, common identity, a single value system and some ethnic institutions, synogogues and organizations has served to maintain ethnic identity for the Jews without adding a territorial dimension or a single locale. The Kalmyks provide another case in point.[13] They live interspersed among other individuals, not being territorially delimited yet maintaining a high intensity of social interaction within their own Kalmyk group and a low degree of social interaction with outsiders. Whether or not the degree of in-group ethnocentrism correlates with out-group hostility is also another important factor to consider.[14]

Acculturation may be seen as a process leading ultimately to the complete assimilation of one sociocultural group into another. Various "points" or intermediate stages along the way, as well as complete assimilation, have been recognized in anthropological work. Several of these "points," which represent different combinations of variables, have been recognized empirically. Assimilation, at one end of the continuum, has been defined as the process by which persons originally possessing culturally heterogeneous frames of reference converge toward a common frame of reference as a result of interaction.[15] The term "monistic assimilation" refers to a situation where a positive value is ascribed to a host culture and a negative value to one's own culture, the host's replacing one's own.[16] This constellation of variables represents what occurs when immigration takes place. It is also applicable where two groups come into contact and one group completely adopts the institutions, the value systems, and the way of life of the other. There is a second kind of assimilation, characterized by interpenetration and fusion, in which persons and groups acquire the memories, sentiments, and attitudes of other persons and groups by sharing experiences. Both are incorporated into a new common, cultural life. Progressive disappearance of barriers and the erosion of the norms of social distance then follow. The Soviet "assimilationists' " view, which will be discussed further below, encompasses this second type of assimilation.

A third type—pluralistic assimilation or pluralistic accommodation—has also been isolated by scholars. It is characterized by the continuation of two groups as part of the same community. They preserve differences, each retaining part of its own culture, and between them only a partial, shared frame of reference exists. Differences between the groups are perpetuated, the groups being accepted by each other as enduring entities. This kind of partial assimilation may be seen as similar, analytically, to cultural hetterogeneity or pluralism, since by definition groups may be equal or unequal.[17] Assimilation is the end point of several kinds of processes. Furthermore, the process may be only partially completed.

Investigations have isolated particular features exhibited by ethnic groups, features which appear to correlate with rapidity of acculturation. For example, in work with Hungarian immigrants to the United States it was found that social mobility related to acculturation, which is more rapid for upwardly mobile groups than groups not so mobile. Lessening social distance between immigrant and host also correlates with increasing acculturation, as does the speed of internalizing change.[18]

The converse—maintenance of separation, ethnic persistence, and even ethnic group-creation—has also been the subject of research. Apparently, the greater the difference in the attributes —language, race, and religion, or culture traits—the easier the maintenance of separate identities between two cultures coming together. If two closely related groups come together, they appear to merge quite easily. Soviet ethnographers, for example, document cases in which some very small Georgian groups have merged into larger Georgian entities.[19] Dagestan is very frequently given as an example of a place where this kind of agglomeration has taken place.

There are certain sociocultural attributes which, if maintained, impede acculturation and support the maintenance of ethnic identity and ethnic group solidarity. These include endogamy, an ideology of common descent, and institutional completeness. The latter refers to the situation where a large number of ethnic institutions, such as newspapers, welfare societies, and social clubs, are present and serve to support a rich social life.[20] The greater the degree of ethnic institutionalization or the more institutional completeness present, the stronger the maintenance of ethnic identity. Research has also shown that institutional completeness correlates with a large number of social ties within the group and fewer outside of the group.[21] However, ethnic institutions may at times shift function and become a route of transition between the ethnic group and its host society. Negative valuation of any ethnic group by outsiders also buttresses the feeling of ethnic identity.

Examination of the character and attributes of ethnic groups which have persisted is also relevant to our analytical framework for consideration of nationality problems in the USSR. Ethnic identity and ethnic group organization apparently persist despite the fact that there may be changes in many cultural features. One group may take over the language of another group, participate in its economic institutions, adopt dress or diet, be incorporated into the political, economic and educational institutions of that other group, and yet still maintain its original identity. Beliefs, values, goals, and meanings, those traits which make up what is called ideology, appear to be more durable than material traits such as dress or house type. Social and cultural structures and patterns often persist though cultural content may change. Study of the Kalmyks provides numerous instances of this.[22] Persistence of ceremonial patterns and change in culture content at marriage is exemplified when the bride, formerly expected to ride on a horse of a certain color from the home of her parents to the home of the groom, now rides in a car whose color is chosen astrologically. Religious institutions also serve as the foci of preserving ethnicity. Groups based in part on religious beliefs apparently possess a greater potential for survival than groups that have no common religious base.

Often an essential religious festival plays an important role. This is also exemplified, by the Kalmyk experience, in the important role played by the Buddhist New Year (a month-long celebration that involves ceremonial visiting of all kin). Kalmyk informants who had lived in the Soviet Union until World War II have reported that even during the 1930s, after collectivization, Kalmyks were still participating in the Buddhist ceremonial, though they followed a very abbreviated version of it. They exchanged gifts of limited value, and recirculated items so that everyone had enough presents to give. The pattern, however, was there; the ceremonial was still operating. Data on the Iroquois and other groups reveal parallels to this case, showing that these ceremonies apparently reinforce ethnicity.[23]

They involve symbols of group identity and contact with the past; and serve to reinforce the symbol system of the group. These ceremonies also involve patterns of in-group social interaction, either in the context of an informal, interpersonal network, or within formal institutions, and they add additional reinforcement to identification. Immigration and settlement as a group, or what is known as "chain group settlement," on the other hand, impedes merging.[24] When individuals come into contact with another culture, as individuals, the likelihood of such persons' maintaining their former ethnic identity is lessened.

Ethnic group formation is another type of process. Ideology often provides the catalyst when ethnic groups are formed. Segregation, endogamy, and shared in-group characteristics which may develop as the result of participation in a certain religion then add strong support to this kind of ethnic group formation. The American Hutterites and Russian Old Believers exemplify this process of ethnic group formation. The combination of features of ethnic identity which have been retained, plus new features, may transform a group into an ethnic group which is really a new social entity.[25] The Irish as an ethnic group in the United States are not the Irish of Ireland but a different group. They exhibit a culture which is a combination of Irish traits and other traits which have together formed a new kind of identity—the Irish-American.

Ethnic groups have also been considered as "minority groups." The analytical concept "minority group" is not defined numerically but in terms of disability resulting from prejudice, discrimination, segregation, or persecution at the hands of the majority. Members of a minority group may or may not comprise a numerical minority. In this line of thinking the "majority" is categorized as the people in control, politically and economically. Disabilities experienced by a minority frequently relate to shared characteristics which serve to differentiate them from the majority: differences in physical features, race, language, and religion. Attributes which have been ascribed to minorities, so defined, resemble those presented for the ethnic group. They include self-consciousness and membership by virtue of birth and endogamy.

However, analytical consideration of minorities involves emphasis upon conflict and power relationships. Economic power, based upon the control of resources resting in the hands of one group, is seen by some as important in minority group formation and perpetuation. The definition of the minority in terms of position in the social structure, and the lack of political power, as opposed to those who do have political power, is also important. The Soviet nationalities supply an example in this instance. The degree to which ethnic groups and nationalities (nationalities are administratively recognized ethnic groups) are minorities in this usage must be determined empirically, though some investigators see all ethnic groups as minorities by this definition.[26] The definition they adhere to, however, implies that, by removing the disabilities, assimilation will result. This is a question which must be investigated empirically. Their definition also ignores the perpetuation of the group by virtue of mechanisms internal to the ingroup structure and its operation. Factors both internal and external must be considered.

This survey of the different aspects of anthropological theory relating to the proposed framework has illustrated several points concerning group identity. The different perspectives from which the problem can be viewed, and the complex types of constellations of features found empirically, reinforces our view that any simple structural typology is inadequate. We have isolated the features or variables relevant to the proposed model. These include the following sets of sociocultural characteristics: first, the nature of formal institutions, status categories, role definition, ideology, social interaction patterns, and marriage practices; second, the nature of group existence and identity and the nature of boundary maintenance mechanisms; third (perhaps the most important for our consideration of the Soviet case), the nature of the political power structure, the role of "native elites" and intermediaries, relations within the power structure between the groups identified, the presence or absence of subjugation and discrimination, and the political ideology of the power structure.

The Soviet Union is ostensibly a multinational state. Remarks about one specific example selected from the numerous possibilities—the Kalmyk Mongols—and some generalizations about nationalities in Central Asia will help to suggest the utility of the analytical framework which has been proposed above. The model may be examined in two temporal domains. It involves three sections in interaction. The first temporal domain embraces the pre-1917 period, when Russian culture and the Russian political structure were interacting with the ethnic groups or non-Russian political states. In the period after the 1917 revolution, the Russian cultural sector remains partially distinct from Soviet culture and the Soviet political power structure, and these in turn interrelate with the third sector comprised by the ethnic group or (non-Russian) nationality.

Beginning with the pre-revolutionary period in Russia, we see the frontier gradually moving east and south during the sixteenth to nineteenth centuries. This expansion resulted in contacts between the Russians, with their autocractic political system, and a variety of non-Russian ethnic groups or indigenous states. These encounters, though similar for most groups, differed in detail in each case, according to the time of occurrence, the locale, and the level of complexity of the culture being encountered by the Russians. It is obvious that the encounter with the Chukchi and the Yakut differed from encounters with the khanates of Khiva or Bukhara. Results of each encounter varied.[27]

The Kalmyk Mongols may be used to illustrate the process involved. They began to move west from Dzungaria at the beginning of the seventeenth century and by 1609 they were located in the area around the Caspian Sea. Actual correspondence between the Kalmyk khan of that time and the czar demonstrates that at this point Kalmyks were dealing with the Russian political leadership on an equal basis as separate political entities. As the Russian incursion into the area became more extensive, czarist pressure grew stronger, and the balance in the political situation quickly shifted in favor of Moscow. By the eighteenth century, after the very powerful khan, Ayuka, died, the situation changed to such an extent that the Kalmyks felt they were about to be engulfed by the Russians. In 1776 a large body of Kalmyks moved east again, their intention being to return to their original homeland in Dzungaria. Only a very small number survived this terrible migration eastward. Those Kalmyks who did not move east remained in the vicinity of the Caspian Sea.

Gradually, after 1776, we see the increasing encroachment of the Russian administrative structure and, beginning at the top, the reworking by the Russians of the indigenous political structure. The Russians periodically reorganized the Kalmyk political structure and promulgated new law codes. Though the political officials remained Kalmyk, except at the very top—the khan's position being eliminated—the nature of the political structure and the manner of its articulation with the Russian political structure continued to change in the direction of closer incorporation into the Russian structure. Despite these alterations in the political sphere during the nineteenth century, the life of the Kalmyks remained relatively unchanged. There were contacts with the Russians in the market place, and increased land pressure through colonization from Russia, but the Kalmyks continued to pursue nomadic pastoralism as a basis of subsistence and were not made sedentary, despite decimation of their herds. The basic economic and sociocultural patterns persisted. For example, the institution of marriage seen in 1776, and again at various points in the 1800s up to 1895 for which ethnographic accounts are available, retains the same basic patterns of the ceremonial, even in small details. It is clear that our processual framework with its interrelated variables is appropriate here. Up to this point, political variables manifested in the form of the stronger Russian political structure were in the process of supplanting the Kalmyk political structure. Related land pressure and interaction in the market place also had begun to have their effect upon the economic structure. However, for the time being other institutions remained relatively unimpaired.

Some Kalmyks moved to the Don River area at the beginning of the nineteenth century. Contact with the Russians became more intensified. Their political structure, in the Don region, was reworked much more extensively than before. The two Kalmyk populations—in the Caspian and Don areas—began to differ. For example, there is a noticeable dialectal divergence between the language spoken by those Kalmyks descended from the people who lived on the Don and Kalmyks who are progeny of the people around Astrakhan. Though the general structure of Kalmyk culture remained the same, by the beginning of the twentieth century Kalmyks in the Don area could be found living in sod houses, in the summertime moving into tents in the back yard, and sometimes moving quite a distance away with their herds. Some of these Kalmyks practiced farming, while others rented their land to Russians, who farmed it with the Kalmyks assisting in the harvesting. It is clear that factors had been introduced which moved the Kalmyk system toward greater economic interaction with the Russians. Shifts in cultural patterns also were becoming evident.

The turn of the twentieth century also marked an increase in numbers of the Kalmyk elite who obtained a Russian education. During this period, something likened to a revitalization movement also developed.[28] This represented a conscious attempt on the part of members of the indigenous intelligentsia—the elite —in the face of increased shifts in cultural pattern from Kalmyk to Russian, to combine those Russian cultural items (traits) which they felt to be of value with the best Kalmyk cultural items, which they thought should be maintained. The amalgam was to serve consciously as a vehicle for the maintenance of Kalmyk identity. Concurrent with this renewal in the area of secular culture, a religious revitalization commenced, as well.[29]   The Kalmyks profess Lamaist Buddhism. At this time they began to reactivate and strengthen their connections with Tibet, to revitalize their religious practices, to set up religious schools, and to reorganize the clergy.

Turning from Kalmyk affairs to what happened in Central Asia before 1917, we find that following the Russian expansion leading to the takeover of the area in the nineteenth century, a colonial type of administration was established. Directed change did not become a central aspect of czarist policy. The interest of the Russians, by and large, lay primarily in exploiting the

extractive industries. The beginning of this period was characterized by indirect rule through local Asian political leaders.
Little changed in the way of life. However, the standard of living rose. Education became increasingly available, producing
an intelligentsia which resembled that of the Kalmyks. These were
people interested in cultural change but not interested in doing
away with their traditional culture or identity.

The beginning of the twentieth century marked the commence-
ment of a czarist resettlement program bringing large numbers
of Russians into the Central Asian area. By this time some local
people, the Kazakhs, for example, had begun to work the mines
for Russian and European companies and some people began
to become more sedentary. The cities in Central Asia, particularly, showed the results of culture change. But in places like
Tashkent, new populations were accommodated by the development of segregated "quarters" rather than through an amalgama-
tion of populations. In both of these examples—the Kalmyk and
Central Asian—traditional cultural elements began to be replaced by Russian elements in subsistence and to some extent in
other spheres. Furthermore, in both instances, though there was
a gradual erosion of political power beginning at the top, group
identity and the "traditional social structure" remained relatively
secure. The Kalmyk, and Turkic, and Iranian groups in Central
Asia remained separate ethnic entities, and in some cases in
Central Asia they also remained separate though subordinated
political entities. They were treated as separate groups by others
and by the Russian government.

Moving to the post-1917 period, it is notable that there has not
been a single consistent communist policy toward nationalities,
but a great deal of variation in it through time and even within
one time period. This vacillation in political philosophy, and in
specific policy regarding nationalities, constitutes an important
variable in determining the nature of ethnic groups in the post-
revolutionary period. Sovietization, which it is here conceptually
advantageous to separate from Russification, encompasses the
Communist Party philosophy and its implementation through
the political structure of the state. Thus, what is determined to

be Soviet sociocultural content is decided by the Soviet political structure. Following a very brief period of self-determination for non-Russian groups after 1917, political consolidation occurred and new governmental policy took shape. This displayed conscious attempts on the part of the political power organization to effect sweeping change and to introduce Soviet sociocultural content in place of traditional (local) sociocultural content.

Economically, one of the main aims was to speed industrialization. This required in many cases the training of indigenous workers or the bringing in of Russian personnel to nationality regions. In agriculture, after a brief period of land reallocation, collectivization and a drive toward mechanization occurred. The land-holding system was in this way drastically changed. Affecting the pastoral groups was a drive toward making them sedentary. This in turn was coupled with the attempt to develop Sovietized pastoral collectives. Another factor, not peculiar to Sovietization, was the continued colonization by Russians in nationality areas. The Slavs remained separate from the local population, by and large. In time this, of course, began to shift the balance of population in certain Soviet republics and had an obvious effect upon the political structure by reducing indigenous control over political life of the nationalities.

Looking at Soviet society, it is apparent that the leadership tried to revolutionize the "traditional" social structure, but frequently met with failure in their endeavors. Such were the attempts to shift to a territorial basis of social organization from a kin basis, wherever the social structure based on kinship had survived into the modern era. When difficulties were encountered by the regime, the kin principle was often, to some extent, allowed to persist. For example, collectives have been organized along kin lines.[30] Frequently this clustering of kin was something which happened after the social reorganization. A Kalmyk informant has described to the author the way in which one individual would move to a collective and would then be followed there by all his relatives. Thus, collectives might, in effect, become clusters of kin groups as the result of the manipulation, by the people, of both the choices and options available to them.

In Central Asia there were also attempts on the part of the Soviet government to make fundamental changes in the traditional social structure and to undermine it by changing the legal status of women.[31] By the official promulgation of decrees and constitutional guarantees, women, who had previously been second-class citizens, received the right to initiate divorce proceedings, to receive equal inheritance, to bear witness equally in court. They acquired the right to full-fledged emancipation in public life, including education, professional training, and participation in all pursuits on an equal footing with men. Difficulties which this program for change encountered have been well documented.[32]

Intermarriage between the nationalities and the Russians seldom occurred. On the basis of information received from a Central Asian informant, it has been noted repeatedly that even when Russians and representatives of nationalities settle side by side, they do not interrelate with one another and do not usually intermarry.[33]

The extension of educational opportunities became a mechanism by which attempts were made to develop a local trained cadre loyal to the Soviet political system. Though various difficulties and some opposition were encountered by the authorities, local elites, nevertheless, did develop. The principle guiding the leadership at first was to destroy local customs by presenting an alternative and by infiltrating new ideas rather than actually suppressing existing patterns.

The Soviet ideological "platform" on nationalities over the years has been like an intricate Chinese puzzle, involuted and doctrinaire. There are two basically ambivalent positions, one, nationality development and the prolonged existence of nationalities, and the second—opposed to the first—the coming together or the assimilation and merging of nationalities. The official attitude toward nationality problems is often vaguely stated, and there are signs that conflict and debate continue among Soviet policymakers on this point. In their writings, the proponents of these two central positions have adopted certain points of view concerning the definition of nationality, its relation to prenational ethnic forms as the attributes of nationalities, and the presence or absence of common psychological makeup. The opinions obviously relate to their general position on ethnic continuity.

It is interesting to observe that a number of leading Soviet ethnographers in 1961 took a position which would appear to place them among the assimilationists. They saw current developments in the USSR as proceeding in two directions, one continuing the consolidation and development of socialist nationalities. The other they described as a general process of intensified coming-together among socialist nationalities on the basis of development of brotherly cooperation and friendly international ties in the fields of economic, cultural, and intellectual life. This second process is said to be accompanied by the establishment of "forms of culture and everyday life common to the USSR as a homogeneous culture." [34] It is still a question whether such a culture can develop without coercion, even if consciously and exclusively supported by a strongly committed Soviet state structure. The article by Soviet ethnographers goes on to describe the development of nationalities as the result of consolidation of small groups, "the transition to higher state forms, gradual assimilation," and "the increasingly monolithic character of these nations." [35] Historical or ethnographic areas are envisioned where "valuable habits of labor" have been developed in response to an environment which includes cultural items of practical value: clothing, types of houses, and objects of this kind. This characterizes a regional level of cultural difference. In addition, and more important, is the formation of Union-wide traditions and cultural forms, including Marxist-Leninist philosophy and other such culture traits and social patterns.

Taking this as the general background for consideration of two detailed examples in the post-1917 period, we shall begin with the Kalmyks in the Don area. They were at first very anti-communist, and many of them fled the region after the 1917 revolution. Those who remained were installed in what became, in 1920, the Kalmyk Autonomous Oblast, in 1936 transformed into the Kalmyk Autonomous Soviet Socialist Republic. By 1929 Sovietization had reached the phase of collectivization, accompanied with the state government's attempts to collectivize the Kalmyks forcibly. Many strongly resisted such collectivization. Today they frequently refer to this period as the "hungry days." To make soup, they often had to put on the fire a kettle containing only water and a piece of leather. Their herds confiscated, most finally were starved into accepting collectivization. Those who remained recalcitrant were shipped eastward. Collectivization was then implemented in the Don region. During this same period, great efforts were made to stamp out Lamaist Buddhism among the Kalmyks. Officials closed all the Lamaist Buddhist temples and monasteries. Despite this pressure, informants have indicated that some religious practices continued on a private basis. Those not members of the clergy who remembered details of ceremonies assisted in performing attenuated versions of these ceremonies. Occasionally, priests who had gone into hiding also led services. The celebration of Tsagan-Sar, the Buddhist New Year, was the most important of the occasions which continued to be celebrated by the Kalmyks.

The Soviet regime did support Kalmyk language study in primary schools. Furthermore, the government during this period selectively preserved other "signs of Kalmyk identity." One gesture was the holding of a national celebration in the Kalmyk Republic in the 1930s on the occasion of the five-hundredth anniversary of the Dzungar Epic, the Kalmyk heroic epic.

During World War II, the Kalmyks, accused of collaborating with the Germans, were shipped out almost *en masse* to Siberia. They became nonpersons and their Republic was abolished. Not until 1957–1958 were they repatriated, some returning to a Kalmyk "homeland" peopled with Ukrainians and Russians. Thus, the Kalmyks now form a numerical minority of the population in their traditional area. In spite of this, information about the Kalmyks in the USSR today indicates that some of their traditions have been maintained.[36] Further data about current kinship and marriage practices reveal some striking similarities between Kalmyk marriage procedures and those observed among Kalmyks now living in the United States.[37] There is a surprising perpetuation of many elements from the earlier social structure both in the United States and in the USSR, despite the existence of different circumstances involving change. In both cases the preservation of cultural items is selective. Kalmyk language continues to be taught in the primary schools of the reconstituted Kalmyk Autonomous SSR, and newspapers and journals are published in Kalmyk.

In Central Asia, after the 1917 revolution broke out in European Russia, there were attempts to effect political self-determination. Their prompt failure ushered in a period of Soviet consolidation during which life remained fairly normal. After 1928 began the drive toward collectivization. Mass Russian colonization in Central Asia resumed and continued intermittently during the next decade. An official anti-Islamic movement was also launched. Ethnographic information for past and present eras, summarized from pre-revolutionary and Soviet sources,[38] shows considerable contrast in the degree of detail and coverage offered for different ethnic groups and periods. Among Central Asian ethnic groups, variations in the kinds of shifts that take place as well as in the nature of the persistence and continuity of traits typify the present character of the nomadic pattern, settlement form, and house type. We find a combination of new and old, and people "cling tenaciously to those items which do not interfere with material progress," [39] or can be modified to serve it. Syntheses between traditional and Soviet forms can be found in type of clothing, in diet, and other things. Central Asian elites have been referred to, for example, as "Soviet bais," a combination of "Soviet" with the local term for leader,[40] because these members of the indigenous elite function as intermediaries and continue to focus upon their traditional culture. Such action contributes to the maintenance of traits which sustain ethnic identity. Simultaneously, they hold positions in the Soviet system.

The government's antireligious drive produced interesting effects. Mosques, madrassahs, and other religious structures in general were closed wholesale throughout the entire area. The number of religious personnel was greatly decreased. Frequency of ceremonies and prayer recitations performed was also reduced. Islamic structure after 1917, unlike the pre-revolutionary period, seems to be greatly weakened. However, pre-Islamic elements and aspects of ceremonies in the form of the local traditions remained, and continue to serve as means of ethnic identity. These had survived the Islamic overlay, particularly among the Kazakhs, and were allowed to continue. Local customs, like paying bride price, definitely went against Soviet efforts to try and effect change in the social structure. Though such practices were officially suppressed, ethnic identity and separateness is still maintained. Russians and Central Asians live in separate villages and in separate quarters of each city. This pattern presumes a low rate of interaction between groups.[41] Groups are still endogamous for the most part. Despite the loss of many features of religion, there is still a body of pre-Islamic custom and way of life. Boundaries between groups are maintained. Nevertheless, it is interesting to note that members of the Institute of Ethnography in Moscow have cited some six hundred recorded intermarriages in Tashkent to prove that Central Asians are no longer endogamous.[42]

My very brief visit in 1968 to a collective farm located about 25 kilometers outside Tashkent revealed something about the nature of ethnic maintenance. This small farm specialized in grape growing. Members spoke only Uzbek. They ate Uzbek food. Most wore the Uzbek skullcap, but other clothes were not traditional.

Previously, minute tribal divisions had been seen as a barrier to nationality unity.[43] Destruction of such compartmentalization implemented a lower level of nationalism, and was encouraged from above by the Soviet government in order to circumvent the development of pan-Turanism, which the regime saw as a potential rival to its power. This is the nationalism which the Soviet assimilationist seeks to eliminate by the development of a Union-wide culture showing only regional variance. Cultural differentiation of the regions rests upon adaptation of traits to the environment and is related to subsistence patterns. Expressions of nationality, developed earlier, rested, in the Kalmyk and Central Asian cases, upon selectivity of cultural elements by the groups, with various features being utilized as signifiers of ethnic, that is nationality, identity. The local elite, which forms a connecting link between traditional and "Soviet" culture as intermediaries, though Soviet educated, still looks to its ethnic group. Thus, Kazakhbaev, Secretary of the Kirgiz Communist Party Central Committee, notes that the authorities do not interfere in matters of local custom, this in order to avoid stirring up negative public opinion.[44] Social control obviously still supports the local Central Asian structure. The intelligentsia are said to participate in such customs, for they consider that this is "the law of our nation."

It may be concluded from our analyses that a key factor in determining which direction the Soviet Union will go with regard to its nationalities (toward assimilation or away from it) is the manner in which the ideological schisms, still apparently present in Soviet political policymaking on the question of the future of nationalities, will be bridged. The schism between assimilationists and the moderates (those tolerant of variation) seems to be operative still. It underlies the vagueness of current official policy on ethnic identity. Ideological factors central to political policy determine the manner in which ethnic identity or national feeling will be characterized or symbolized if such policy is adhered to. The assimilationists support the notion that a homogeneous Soviet culture will eventually come into being with the merging of an ethnically diverse population. Published sources suggest that they apparently have not directly faced the question of how the ethnic identity and nationality allegiance of individuals may be established or changed. When the Soviet assimilationists mention a need for struggle and coerciveness, their belief probably results from the conviction that compulsion may ultimately supply the only means for accomplishing their end. But available cross-cultural data do not support the contention that coercion is a successful means of forcing such change. Compulsion, in fact, may produce the opposite effect, strengthening and reinforcing nationality and ethnic identity.

Another avenue of approach to change, one more remote but not outside the limit of possibility, is the enculturation (rearing) of a new Soviet generation of non-Russians beginning in the nursery and continuing within a complex of institutions which is completely Soviet, probably strongly Russian, in character. This kind of Soviet cultural development has been discussed inside the USSR during the 1960s as well as in studies about other countries.[45] A resort to varying the population within each collective, moving people around and intermingling populations, might also bring about the ethnic intermixture apparently desired by Soviet authorities. However, the example of the Kalmyks raises doubts. When they returned from Siberia in 1957–1958 to live as a numerical minority among other groups, the Kalmyks maintained their separateness. This seems to indicate that such mechanical mixing does not always succeed in bringing about loss of ethnic identity and a consequent merging. Yet, another possibility exists, and a shift of allegiance by the indigenous elite—the intermediaries—from a local frame of reference to a Union-wide one might be accomplished by giving them more of a stake in political control and decisionmaking while preserving their leadership role with local followers.

The Soviet decision to suppress religion seemed, for the regime, a correct choice in terms of conclusions drawn from our cross-cultural framework. The move enjoyed greater success in accomplishing a shift to secular Soviet traditions in some areas than in others. Throughout Central Asia, pre-Islamic institutions which, because they were local custom, were not suppressed showed strength and integratedness, and easily provided a continuing focus for ethnicity. For the Russians themselves, that part of the Orthodox religion which was centered in the home has, very likely, also been preserved along with other aspects of the religion, despite the debilitation of the formal religious structure outside the household.

Another key factor influencing Soviet nationalities toward or away from assimilation and merging derives from the cross-cultural data. It shows that there is a kind of inertia and conservatism about ethnicity and nationality identity. The moderate, tolerant Soviet policy position on nationalities relates to this phenomenon. Such policy is a further development of earlier decisions to maintain discrete nationalities, gradually reshaping them by encouraging mobility and growing industrialization. This procedure accords with the realities of the situation. It is also in line with the kinds of economic or social, even political, adjustments which groups can make without a loss of identity.

This survey of cross-cultural material has produced a series of variables related to the problem of assessing nationality identification. An examination of Soviet material, in terms of these variables, has shown in the case of the Soviet Union that the power structure plays a key role, with special emphasis being placed upon political ideology. Because of the nature of the Soviet bureaucratic structure, there is usually a gap, varying in size, between political philosophy and the political actualities of the system. The uncertainty of the current official position makes this all the more true. We feel that the local elites may play a pivotal role in determining the future course of nationality events, given the alternatives within the political philosophy. The nature of group existence and components of institutionalization, meaning, symbols, and interaction patterns, as they interrelate with the other variables, also will play significant roles in determining the outcome.

The anthropological models presented here are relatively simplistic in comparison with the actuality of the Soviet Union, whose numerous nationalities impinge on each other as well as upon the Soviet political structure. Reputable Western scholars engaging in such investigations frequently produce very different analyses of what is happening in the USSR. Some take a position that Sovietization is rapidly occurring;[46] others maintain that beneath the layer of surface assimilation virile nationalism seethes.[47] Although I have recently visited the Soviet Union, I have not been permitted to conduct field work there. Consequently, it is impossible to take a final position on the subject.

A tourist passing through the Tashkent area might, however, support the position that multinationality retains its vital energy in the culture of the people of the USSR.

NOTES

1. I. S. Furnivall, *Colonial Policy and Practices: A Comparative Study of Burma and Netherlands India* (London: Cambridge University Press, 1948).

2. M. G. Smith, "Social and Cultural Pluralism," *Social and Cultural Pluralism in the Caribbean* (Annals of the New York Academy of Sciences, Vol. 83) (1960), pp. 763–77.

3. *Ibid.*

4. Charles Wagley [Discussant, M. G. Smith, "Social and Cultural Pluralism"] *Social and Cultural Pluralism in the Caribbean* (Annals of the New York Academy of Sciences, Vol. 83, Art. 5) (1960), pp. 777–80.

5. Furnivall, *Ibid.;* Smith, *Ibid.*

6. Robert Redfield; Milton Singer, "The Cultural Role of Cities," *Economic Development and Culture Change* (Chicago: University of Chicago Press, 1954), pp. 53–73.

7. Stephen Dunn; Ethel Dunn, "Soviet Regime and Native Culture in Central Asia and Kazakhstan: The Major Peoples," *Current Anthropology,* No. 8 (1967), pp. 147–208.

8. Dorothy Libby, "Three Hundred Years of Chuckchi Ethnic Identity," *Man and Culture* (Philadelphia: University of Pennsylvania Press, 1960), pp. 208–304.

9. Paula Rubel, *The Kalmyk Mongols: A Study in Continuity and Change* (Bloomington: Indiana University Press, 1967).

10. W. Ross Crumrine, "The House Cross of the Mayo Indians of Sonora Mexico," *Anthropological Papers of University of Arizona,* No. 8 (1964), pp. 1–57.

11. I. W. Eaton, "Controlled Acculturation: a Survival Technique of Hutterites," *American Sociological Review,* No. 17 (1952), pp. 331–40.

12. A. Etzioni, "The Ghetto: A Re-evaluation," *Social Forces,* No. 37 (1959), pp. 255–62.

13. Rubel, *Ibid.*

14. Donald T. Campbell; Robert A. LeVine, "A Proposal for Co-operative Cross-Cultural Research on Ethnocentrism," *Journal of Conflict Resolution* V, No. 1 (1961), pp. 82–108.

15. R. Taft, "Shared Frame of Reference Concept Applied to Assimilation of Immigrants," *Human Relations* No. 6 (1953), pp. 45–55.

16. *Ibid.*

17. Smith, *Ibid.*

18. S. A. Weinstock, "Some Factors that Retard or Accelerate the Rate of Acculturation with Specific Reference to Hungarian Immigrants," *Human Relations* No. 17 (1964), pp. 321–40.

19. V. K. Gardanov; B. O. Dolgikh; T. A. Zhdanko, "Osnovnye napravleniia etnicheskikh protsessov u narodov SSSR," *Sovetskaia etnografiia* No. 4 (1961), pp. 9–29. Translation in *Soviet Anthropology and Archeology* No. 1 (Summer, 1962), pp. 3–18.

20. Raymond Breton, "Institutional Completeness of Ethnic Communities and the Personal Relations of Immigrants," *American Journal of Sociology* No. 70 (1964), pp. 193–205.

21. *Ibid.*

22. Rubel, *Ibid.*

23. Anne Shimony, *Conservatism Among the Iroquois at the 6 Nations Reserve* (New Haven: Yale University Publications in Anthropology No. 65, 1961); J. H. Howard, "Cultural Persistence and Cultural Change as Reflected in Oklahoma-Seneca-Cayuga Ceremonialism," *Plains Anthropologist* No. 6 (1961), pp. 21–36.

24. C. A. Price, "Immigration and Group Settlement," *The Cultural Integration of Immigrants* (Paris: UNESCO, 1959), pp. 267–88.

25. Nathan Glazer; Daniel P. Moynihan, *Beyond the Melting Pot* (Cambridge: Harvard University Press, 1963).

26. Charles Wagley; Marvin Harris, *Minorities in the New World* (New York: Columbia University Press, 1958).

27. Edward Allworth, "Encounter," *Central Asia: A Century of Russian Rule* (New York: Columbia University Press, 1967), pp. 7–35, 37–53.

28. Fred Adelman, *Kalmyk Cultural Renewal* (Ann Arbor: University Microfilms, 1960).

29. *Ibid.*

30. Personal Communication to the author from Fred Adelman; Dunn and Dunn, p. 155.

31. Gregory J. Massell, "Law as an Instrument of Revolutionary Change in a Traditional Milieu: the Case of Soviet Central Asia," *Law and Society Review* Vol. II, No. 2 (1968), pp. 179–228.

32. *Ibid.,* pp. 200–201.

33. Richard Pipes, "The Soviet Impact on Central Asia," *Problems of Communism* No. 2 (1957), p. 30.

34. Gardanov, Dolgikh, and Zhdanko, *Ibid.,* p. 25.

35. *Ibid.,* p. 10 ff.

36. Personal Communication to the author from V. Viktorova.

37. *Ibid.*

38. Elizabeth Bacon, *Central Asians under Russian Rule* (Ithaca: Cornell University Press, 1966); Dunn and Dunn, *ibid.;* Lawrence Krader, *Peoples of Central Asia* (Bloomington: Indiana University Publications; Uralic and Altaic Series Vol. 26, 2d ed., 1966).

39. Richard Pipes, "Muslims of Soviet Central Asia: Trends and Prospects," *Middle East Journal* IX (1955), p. 155.

40. Dunn and Dunn, No. 8, p. 168.

41. Pipes, *ibid.,* IX, p. 30.

42. Dunn and Dunn, No. 8, p. 194.

43. Pipes, "The Soviet Impact on Central Asia," p. 26.

44. Gardanov, Dolgikh and Zhdanko, No. 4, p. 20.

45. *Ibid.,* pp. 25–28; Bruno Bettelheim, *The Children of the Dream* (New York: Macmillan, 1969).

46. Frederick Barghoorn, *Soviet Russian Nationalism* (New York: Oxford University Press, 1956).

47. Pipes, "The Soviet Impact on Central Asia," *Ibid.*

EDWARD ALLWORTH

MATERIALS FOR SOVIET NATIONALITY STUDY: THE PROBLEM OF BIBLIOGRAPHY

In Soviet studies, finding bibliography especially pertinent to the Union-wide nationality question and specific problems as such—quite aside from locating materials about individual nationalities—presents special difficulties. Published bibliographies of this character may be considered inadequate to their task, whether as an aid to reading and research or as scholarship in itself. Seldom consulted, they can hardly guide the growing, serious interest and future development in the study of Soviet nationality problems.

Results of this bibliographical neglect become strikingly apparent from the realization that no comprehensive, systematic list of printed books, articles and maps (bibliography)[1] regarding Soviet nationality problems has ever been published in the USSR. At the same time, a survey of the principal registers of publishing, *Book Annals* (Knizhnaia letopis', 1907–1970, with gaps), and *Annals of Journal Articles* (Letopis' zhurnal'nykh statei, and its predecessors, 1926–1970) will reveal that thousands of publications, suitable for systematic classification and listing, about nationality problems have been issued since 1907 in the area encompassed by the USSR. Most recently, bibliographical evi-

---

[1] "Bibliography," *ALA Glossaries* (Chicago: American Library Association, 1943), p. 11, describes a bibliography as "A list of books, maps, etc., differing from a catalogue and not being necessarily a list of materials in a collection, a library, or a group of libraries."

dence has been showing that the nearly unabating flow of such writings has approximated at least seventy-five books, pamphlets, and articles a year, on the average, in Russian alone. Additional works respecting the larger nationality problems frequently appear in Ukrainian, Uzbek, and other languages of the USSR.

Considering the importance of the nationality subject, it is therefore startling, in a land of extraordinarily productive bibliographers like the USSR, to discover an oversight of such magnitude in the preparation of research aids. This lapse can be explained only by some serious hindrance to fulfillment of a suitable bibliographical effort. Indirectly, of course, an inhibiting effect upon the publishing of any bibliography may be exerted by technical and economic, scholarly or political factors. Because so many volumes of useful bibliography in other fields regularly appear in the USSR, and specialists in the nationality subject are numerous, the limitation placed upon bibliography concerning nationality problems seems to be neither technical and economic nor scholarly. If such a bibliographical work has officially been given low priority, the action seems inconsistent with the massive outpouring of publications about the subject which are permitted to appear in other forms. Downgrading bibliographical work on the broad problems does not signify an absence of Party interest.

Political caution implicit in the lack of appropriate, exhaustive bibliographies providing an overview of the whole question of nationality problems in the USSR seems to reflect a great reluctance on the part of the Soviet leadership to face these potentially divisive issues openly again. Khrushchev's destruction of the dead Stalin's claim to infallibility in the nationality field left no prominent authority to replace the former dictator. In the vacuum, theoreticians find themselves balked by a conceptual block which may reflect uncertainty or disagreement over how best, from the Party viewpoint, to conceive of Soviet nationality problems in these changing times. Regardless of such indecision, most likely nationality problems comprise political property over which control has been monopolized by the Party secretariat.

Today, bibliographies and other Soviet books about nationality frequently emanate from the publishing houses of research libraries, the Ministry of Culture, or others outside the Party press. This abdication of open responsibility may express the Party's distaste at this time for strongly committing itself to almost any position other than the flexible "Leninist" line regarding nationality problems. The issuing of a major bibliography about such general problems has apparently not been publicly barred by the authorities. Quite obviously, neither have they ordered its preparation and publication. The very slightness in the stature of authorized lists which have occasionally emerged paradoxically adds considerable weight to all these suppositions.

If the background to the long delay in issuing adequate research aids for the field remains a mystery, neither is the direct cause of the obvious nationality gap in Soviet bibliography so easy to determine. It is understandable that informed Soviet bibliographers use circumspection concerning a subject long guarded possessively by politicians. Outright proscriptions against completing any major bibliography in the field may not have been issued, but explicit deterrents against compilation of rigorously inclusive lists in bibliographical research have appeared. A device which may serve to warn innovative Soviet bibliographers away from scholarly objectivity, if not participation in nationality research, could be something like the "Regulations about Retrospective General Bibliography of Printed Work Published in the Union and Autonomous Republics of the USSR during the pre-Revolutionary Period," issued in 1965–1966 by the Committee on the Press attached to the USSR Council of Ministers and Ministry of Culture. In addition to the prescriptive features of these Regulations—calling for bibliography to reflect achievements in nationality culture—the prohibitions are broad. In following them, a bibliographer is obliged to censor writings he believes the authorities may consider reactionary, religious, mystical, vulgar, or devoid of scholarly or practical worth.[2] To gauge what the contemporary regime may construe to be overly

[2] "Polozhenie o retrospektivnoi obshchei bibliografii proizvedenii pechati, izdannykh v soiuznykh i avtonomnykh respublikakh SSSR za dorevoliutsionnyi period," *Sovetskaia bibliografiia* No. 1 (95) (1966), pp. 4, 61–62.

conservative or totally worthless might become an unusually demanding responsibility. Bibliographers probably have little incentive to attempt it in a controversial field.

Experienced bibliographers cannot have overlooked or forgotten the even more pointed instructions issued to the profession in the 1930s, when "vigilance" became a watchword in research libraries as well as the overtly political arena. Those were the years when balanced bibliographies officially ceased to be acceptable to the Soviet authorities. The policy emerged in familiar Soviet fashion. Without warning, bibliographers who had disregarded the importance of political nuances in their previous research were, after the fact, accused of various faults. One critic charged bibliographers with being " 'objective' toward Trotsky, an enemy of the people," when they included his published writings in their lists. Another Party spokesman attacked objective, apolitical bibliography for putting itself "at the service of scholastic pseudo-science and bibliographical formalism." [3] And so it went. Extensive bibliographies valuable for research into certain nationality and other problems, like A. V. Mez'er's *Dictionary Index to the Field of Books* (1931–1934),[4] suffered from political denunciations so severe that reference to them became unacceptable.

By depriving scholars access to balanced lists of works, the politicizing of Soviet bibliography caused a great loss to scholarship in this and perhaps every field it touched. Little consolation may be taken from the knowledge that in making bibliography responsive to Party direction Soviet communists inadvertently created for us another barometer of ideological and political weather. Bibliographies can now be expected to reflect the range of acceptability allowed to writings within a particular field like

[3] "Vyshe bol'shevistskuiu bditel'nost' na bibliograficheskom fronte," *Sovetskaia bibliografiia* II (14) (1936), pp. 9–10; V. Lutskii, "Sbornik Akademii Nauk po bibliografii Vostoka, *Bibliografiia Vostoka*, vyp. 1 (1932) . . . ," *Sovetskaia bibliografiia* No. 1 (5) (1934), p. 150.

[4] A. V. Mez'er, *Slovarnyi ukazatel' po knigovedeniiu* (Moscow-Leningrad: Gosudarstvennoe Sotsial'no-Ekonomicheskoe Izdatel'stvo, 1931–1934).

nationality problems at a given period. Soviet bibliographies, unlike most Western counterparts, thus provide at a glance fairly permanent evidence concerning official attitudes prevalent at a certain past time, information which is not always easily garnered from less compact, condensed sources. Thus does the official nature of Soviet bibliographies make them documents of sorts. Bibliographies as a whole have been employed in yet another manner for research into the development of Soviet nationality language or other problems connected with publishing, for example.[5] In the Soviet case, when the bibliography is used as evidence it turns out to provide essentially negative findings —revealing to the experienced researcher the omissions—mainly what or who has been stricken from the accepted lists. Thus, the continued absence from bibliographies of Leon Trotsky, that articulate, leading actor upon the Soviet political stage, simply confirms the persistence of Stalinism in today's Soviet bibliography as well as politics.

Retrospective subject bibliographies in the field of nationality problems have also generally skipped over hundreds of significant published works, many of general importance, attributable to men who suffered under Stalin. Some of those especially vital to the development of thought at the center as well as on the periphery in regard to nationality were Aqimet Baytursin-uli, Aliqan Bokeyqan-uli (Bukeikhanov), S. M. Dimanshtein, Abdalrauf Fitrat, Sultan Galiev, Atajan Hashimov, Mehmed Emin Resul-Zade, and Georgii Safarov. Two significant studies contributed by Safarov were *The Nationality Question and the Proletariat* (1922) and his "The Nationality Question in the Post-October Period," (1922).[6] Dimanshtein's "Ten Years of the Party's

[5] Edward Allworth, "La rivalité entre le Russe et les Langues orientales dans les Territoires asiatiques de l'U.R.S.S.," *Cahiers du Monde russe et soviétique* Vol. VII, No. 4 (1966), pp. 531–63; Louise Noëlle Malclès, *Bibliography*, trans. Theodore C. Hines (New York: The Scarecrow Press, Inc., 1961), p. 8.

[6] Georgii Safarov, *Natsional'nyi vopros i proletariat* (Petrograd: Gosudarstvennoe Izdatel'stvo, 1922); Georgii Safarov, "Natsional'nyi vopros v posleoktiabr'skii period," *Za 5 let* (Moscow: Izdatel'stvo "Krasnaia

and Soviet Government's Nationality Policy" (1927) and many others qualify for inclusion in a comprehensive listing. Abdalrauf Fitrat's Uzbek-language "A Nation Lacking Nobility and Steadfasteness Has No Right to Exist" (1915) likewise belongs to this class of works,[7] and is the more valuable in our study for rendering a view of "nationality" from the perspective of Samarkand. Intentional exclusions of this sort leave blanks both in bibliographies about the general question and in systematic lists singling out individual nationalities or their republics.

About the different nationalities or regions, Soviet publishers have printed a stupendous array of bibliographies over the years. Examples of this diversity can be found in the earlier, and particularly well-prepared regional lists. One, providing Russian-language entries about Central Asia, is "For the Tenth Anniversary of the Partition of Central Asia According to Nationality" (1934). The second selection presents only nationality-language entries from the Soviet northland: *Directory to Writings Published in the Languages of the Northern People, 1931–1934* (1935).[8] Areal bibliographies like this pair, along with those devoted to separate nationalities, constitute an impressive apparatus of scholarship assisting the pursuit of information about practical consequences of developments and action affecting areas and nationalities in the USSR.

Rewarding as study of regional bibliographies may be, such lists hardly meet the needs of researchers seeking direct access to Union-wide nationality issues and problems. Nor do they solve the theoretical nationality problems which ideology and Russian dominance in the USSR pose. Soviet bibliographers have thus prepared lists of bibliographies about areas, and have

Nov' " Glavpolitprosvet, 1922), pp. 78–119; S. M. Dimanshtein, "10 let natsional'noi politiki partii i sovvlasti," *Novyi Vostok* No. 19 (1927), pp. i–xxii.

[7] Abdalrauf Fitrat, "Himmat wa säbati bolmagan millatning haqq-i hayati yoqdur," *Ayinä* No. 7 (Jan. 14, 1915), pp. 162–65.

[8] "K desiatiletiiu natsional'nogo razmezhevaniia Srednei Azii," *Vestnik Kommunisticheskoi Akademii* No. 5/6 (1934), pp. 138–49; *Ukazatel' literatury izdannoi na iazykakh narodov severa v 1931–1934 gg.* (Leningrad: Izdatel'stvo Instituta Narodov Severa TsIK SSSR, 1935), 31 pp.

also provided extensive bibliographies about writing and research concerning local matters published within the confines of such disciplines as anthropology, history, or literature. One of the richest of these compilations telling a great deal about different nationalities is *Materials for a Bibliography about the History of the Peoples of the USSR, 16th–17th Centuries* (1933). Sergei A. Tokarev contributed another of these bibliographies, in ethnology and with geographical overtones, appended to his *Ethnology of the Peoples of the USSR* (1958). A third of this sort, selected from among many possibilities because of its special interest for the study of Soviet nationality problems, was compiled by B. S. Khorev and is entitled: "Soviet Writings about Population Geography as well as Associated Disciplines (1955–1961)" (1962).[9]

Still lacking, remain bibliographies organized along academic disciplinary lines which illuminate the general nationality problems, as opposed to local details. Missing, besides this kind of systematic list, and the sort of bibliography which should contain references to the banned works contributed by Fitrat, Safarov, and their colleagues, are substantial, multidisciplinary, rationalized bibliographic treatments of general nationality theory or practice. As a result, we are left with no satisfactory basic compilation or combination of them to recommend with confidence for standard reference in this field.

Ideally, a reliable primary research bibliography would, if not exhaustive, make known at the outset its limits and arrangement in content and chronology, its own sources (publications searched), and the method of selection employed. There is also

[9] S. V. Tokarev, *Etnografiia narodov SSSR. Istoricheskie osnovy byta i kul'tury* (Moscow: Izdatel'stvo Moskovskogo Universiteta, 1958), bibliography pp. 568–80; S. V. Voznesenskii, *Materialy dlia bibliografii po istorii narodov SSSR XVI–XVII vv.* (Leningrad: Izdatel'stvo Akademii Nauk; Vol. 7 *Trudy* Istoriko-Arkheologicheskogo Instituta, 1933), 353 pp.; B. S. Khorev (comp.), "Sovetskaia literatura po geografii naseleniia i smezhnym distsiplinam (1955–1961 gg.)," *Materialy I mezhduvedomstvennogo soveshchaniia po geografii naseleniia (ianvar'-fevral' 1962 g.)* (Moscow-Leningrad: Geograficheskoe Obshchestvo Soiuza SSR, Obzor Issledovanii po Geografii Naseleniia v SSSR, vyp. VI, 1962), pp. 28–114.

genuine advantage to be gained in considering references evaluated by an experienced scholar working in his own specialization. Of course, his is necessarily a rather intuitive method, carefully selective but often not best suited to the preparation of extensive, up-to-date subject bibliographies. In any case, the record as yet reveals no mature Western author who concentrates primarily or exclusively upon this bibliographical sphere; consequently, a specialized, systematic list of materials covering our general field is yet to become available in print. "Books found" at random and listed without benefit of long experience in the field can scarcely constitute a reliable guide to writings, although a list of rare "books found" and identified with certain library collections (a "union list," according to librarians) may represent a directory of titles one step higher in complexity than the list with subject leanings assembled purely at random. In this connection, Soviet bibliographies, unlike some Western lists, rarely offer information about where the books and articles they present may be consulted. Like Western authors, Soviet scholars also often attach what appear to be "found" reference lists to their printed studies. This may testify to a certain lack of system in the basic research for the book itself.

Except for very general materials, entries in the well-planned bibliography about Soviet nationality problems would be organized into parallel, discrete classifications, perhaps under disciplines, or, more useful yet, refined subordinate subjects, with due attention to the importance of chronology and the principal developments in the substantive field. Systematic listings of works about Soviet nationality problems in general should include publications in the various Soviet languages representing the relevant documentary and statistical sources, works of the important authors and criticisms of their writings, essays by lesser but original commentators and thinkers in the field, and histories or analyses of the development of nationality problems.

For most research purposes, there is little value in dividing entries simply into types of publication (documents, textbooks, journal articles, and the like), because those headings fail to convey the substance of the categories. Finally, if an extensive, separate bibliography is indexed and organized so that it can be approached from two directions—through discipline as well as refined specific subject—it will offer both Western and Soviet scholars a basic starting point for either disciplinary or true interdisciplinary inquiries into Soviet nationality problems. At this stage of progress in our study of the Soviet nationality field, there is probably no established list of gross (disciplinary) and precise subjects acceptable to all disciplines or scholars.

The categories given in annotations to T. N. Kopreev's work, below, with its flamboyant approach, "[Category] 4, Communist and Workers' Parties of the Capitalist Countries in the Avant Guard of the Struggle of People for National Independence and Democratic Freedoms," promise scant hope for permanent agreement concerning a subject classification system among world scholars. Existing Soviet bibliographies in the general nationality field may be criticized for their lack of both disciplinary and recognizable subordinate subject divisions, and on many other counts. Nevertheless, they seem to follow certain practices or rules, though specific subject categories vary widely among those lists devoted to the Soviet nationality field. Disadvantages of their organization are obvious in such instances as the separating of the Marx-Lenin-Stalin canon, as a category, from various subject classifications into which most such writings might be distributed. "Documents," too, customarily stand apart for no substantive reason. Remaining works nearly always find a place under ideological catchwords contemporary to the time of compilation which serve as bibliographical categories. Headings like the specimen from Kopreev's list, or from bibliographies which employ categories like "The Friendship of People(s)," or "Building Communism" ordinarily impose too loose a framework upon the compilation to discipline sufficiently either its content or bibliographical methodology.

Exceptions to this pattern rarely occur, coming to light in instances when the Soviet bibliographer, by design or necessity, broadens the scope of a compilation and in addition encompasses a larger less selective number of entries than has been usual. Meaningful subclassifications seem logically to evolve out of a greater variety of published titles. A recent and unusual medium-length bibliography about the nationality question provides an interesting demonstration of this development. In the Soviet bibliography, L. I. Frolova's *Nationality Relations in the USSR . . .* (1966) (see annotated list of bibliographies, below), all the bibliographical material purports to be organized under two grand headings, (A) "The Marxist-Leninist Theory and Program on the Nationality Question" and (B) "The Building of Communism and the Further Drawing-Together [*sblizhenie*], Mutual Enrichment and Unity of Socialist Nations [*natsii*]." In actuality, title A. splits further into three categories: (1) Marx, Engels, and Lenin about the Nationality Question; (2) Materials from the CPSU (Communist Party of the Soviet Union) and the Soviet Government; (3) Laws of Development Pertaining to the Rise and Development of Nations [*natsii*] and Subnationalities [*narodnosti*] of the New Type. These, like those which follow, six major plus five subclasses, could perhaps better dispense with the two large, stock headings A. and B. and stand alone.

The second major class, category B., subdivides far beyond category A. (numbers have been changed hereafter to make them run consecutively): (4) General; (5) Economic Development of the Soviet Socialist Nations and their Collaboration in Creating the Material-Technical Base for Communism; (6) The Political Base for the Flourishing and Drawing-Together of Socialist Nations—*a.* The Development of Soviet National(ity) Statehood; *b.* Strengthening the Social Homogeneity of the Socialist Nations; (7) Altering the Spiritual Makeup of Socialist Nations—*a.* The Comprehensive Development and Drawing-Together of the Socialist Nations' Cultures; *b.* New National(ity) Traditions; *c.* The Free Development of Nationality Languages; (8) Bringing up the Toilers in a Spirit of Internationalism and Socialist Patriotism; (9) The Triumph of Leninist Nationality Policy. Friendship Among the Various People of the USSR.

Readers will recognize the majority of these to be code words carrying particular messages about the accepted Soviet viewpoint toward nationality problems in 1966. Because of their ideological burden, this set of subclassifications, excepting numbers 1, 2, and 4, appears unlikely to serve, in its present form, as a standard aid to Western scholars organizing material for research into such problems. The principal difference between our outline, to be proposed below, and the scheme employed in roughly comparable Soviet bibliographies seems to lie in the fact that our suggested list tries to cover the entire subject spectrum, bringing out nationality distinctions of all kinds in a neutral fashion. Soviet subject categories in this field sometimes appear deliberately to avoid distinguishing the features of such problems. And they give trouble by offering a contrasting combination of author groups, simple headings covering types of publications, and subject categories—in this way destroying an opportunity for achieving a consistent, parallel approach throughout. In spite of this criticism, Frolova's method has particular merit for the Western scholar who desires to analyze exactly what the Soviet authors and speakers are attempting to obscure or convey, in their own terms.

The categories we offer, minus that ideological overlay, in the following proposal can be seen to approximate several sections employed in her *Nationality Relations in the USSR*. . . . Certain common ground in the field must exist, therefore. Upon it the beginning of a comparable East-West approach could be launched. To enhance the possibility that such a meeting place may be discovered, this tentative set of categories (Table 15) for bibliographical research into Soviet nationality problems is offered.

Titles of published articles, documents, chapters, and books which make up the hypothetical bibliography may be subclassified within categories. Heading number IX could effectively serve with further divisions such as (A) Relations between Russia and a nationality; (B) Relations between two or more nationalities; (C) Relations among Soviet nationalities and foreign nationalities. The present sequence of ten headings is subject to considerable further refinement of this sort, so long as the number of subcategories does not become so great that as a system the plan loses coherence and its original meaning. That concept, it can be seen, provides a place for recording materials about

Table 15. Soviet Nationality Problems—A Bibliography. Subject
Categories for Entries

GENERAL: Unclassifiable media, archives, bibliography.

  I. The idea or concept of Soviet nationality, as such; theories about
     nationality development.
 II. Personal, individual nationality and citizenship; biography of the
     identifiable member of a nationality group; "nationality man"
     contrasted with "Soviet man."
III. Identification with locale, city, region, and terrain; attitudes to-
     ward existing or past nationality administrative unit (SSR, ASSR,
     AO, NO, etc.); nationality distribution patterns and trends in
     population and inhabited territory.
 IV. Linguistic, racial, ethnological identifications; problems of dis-
     crimination especially related to these identifications.
  V. Social-cultural (excluding artistic or economic) behavior, proc-
     esses, structure, and institutions characteristic of a nationality as
     a group.
 VI. Genres and styles of esthetic expression and subjects or themes
     unique to or characteristic of a nationality, in literature, music,
     and other arts.
VII. Patterns and activity of employment, production methods, and
     products peculiar to or characteristic of a nationality or area.
VIII. Particularism and localism in government, party, laws, and ad-
     ministration, at the SSR or lower level.
 IX. Relations between one Soviet nationality and another nationality
     or nationalities (domestic or foreign), or with the Russians; actions
     taken by central USSR government and Party especially aimed at
     or affecting a certain nationality or some Soviet nationalities, but
     not Russians; or, if touching Russians, not in the manner charac-
     teristic for the nationalities.
  X. Official Union-wide policy concerning nationality, as such, and
     commentaries on the policy; laws and decisions regarding na-
     tionality.

nationality and, to some extent, regarding individual nationalities. But for nationalities the data compiled are required to reinforce consideration of the central nationality question rather
than all details about every nationality—clearly an impossible
function for one bibliography.

The censorship restrictions which guide Soviet work in this field have placed emphasis in general Soviet nationality bibliography, since the early 1930s, upon the presentation of highly selective short lists of "suggested readings." These characteristically repeat a selection of writings, authored by the pillars of "Marxism-Leninism," in combination with the latest speeches or newspaper articles of Party leaders contemporary to the publication. Bibilographies compiled in this fashion retain some historical interest mainly, as was said, because they corroborate and register trends of political acceptability in the printed work about a field. One widely circulated example of this genre is the work by S. V. Kazakov, *Leninist Nationality Policy. Suggested Readings* (1956).[10] It may be termed a landmark and apparently one of the most recent separate published bibliographies in this field. The pamphlet documents, by its very issuance, the dramatic turn taken in Soviet nationality affairs with the muting of pervasive Stalinism in 1956. Nikita Khrushchev's speech to the XXth Congress of the CPSU (Communist Party of the Soviet Union) helped to slough off the burden of Stalin's dead hand from bibliography as well as politics, Soviet nationality policy, and theory. With his small bibliography Kazakov made a remarkable contribution with what might seem to have been a very modest effort. He helped to jar thinking and writing about Soviet nationality policy in the USSR from the rigidities of the Stalinist past. Following Khrushchev's lead, Kazakov noted in his introduction that the recent Congress "had armed the Party for liquidating traces of the [Stalin] cult of personality in all spheres of ideological work, including the sphere of the nationality question as well." (See Bibliography of Bibliographies, below.)

Eradicating such survivals from bibliographical works meant supplanting Stalin's writings with Lenin's and emphasizing the pre-eminence of Lenin among Marxist theoreticians concerned with the nationality question. Accordingly, twenty-three such entries by Lenin appear in a basic list devoted to theory and the

[10] S. V. Kazakov, *Leninskaia natsional'naia politika. Rekomendatel'nyi ukazatel' literatury* (Moscow: Ministerstvo Kul'tury RSFSR, Gosudarstvennaia ordena Lenina Biblioteka SSSR imeni V. I. Lenina, 1956).

Party program regarding the nationality question. In the same section are found just one title by Stalin plus two works of Marx and Engels. From the early post-October 1917 period are selected ten writings by Lenin against three by Stalin, and some from the pens of Mikhail Kalinin and others. Beyond this point in the entire bibliography, Stalin's name does not appear. Lenin is represented by numerous additional entries, followed by those of Khrushchev, Klimentii E. Voroshilov, Georgi K. Zhukov, Lazar M. Kaganovich, Otto V. Kuusinen, Georgi M. Malenkov, Anastas I. Mikoian, Vyacheslav M. Molotov, Mikhail A. Suslov, D. T. Shepilov, Chou En-lai, Liu Shao Chi, and others. Resolutions, editions of the Soviet constitution, and joint communiques with foreign countries fill out the listing.

Liberally annotated, this bibliography's entries are divided into sections devoted to these themes: Marxist-Leninist Theory and the Program regarding the Nationality Question; The 1917 Revolution and Resolution of the Nationality Question in the USSR; Further Development of the Economy and Culture of the Union Republics in the Sixth 5-Year Plan; Foreign Policy of the USSR—A Policy of Peace and Friendship between All Peoples; Decisions of the XXth CPSU Congress; Principles of Proletarian Internationalism—the Bases of the Mutual Relations of the Nationalities in the Peoples' Democracies.

There are indications that publication of this list, innocuous as it may appear, required fortitude on the part of some anti-Stalinist Soviet political leaders. Compilation of the work was completed, wrote Kazakov, by mid-July, 1956, thus preventing the inclusion of a standard numbered reference to the printed stenographic report for the XXth Congress, also potentially a controversial publication, which came out with the date 1956. Nevertheless, the bibliographical booklet was not released for printing until December 23, 1957. Although it retained the publication date 1956 on its title page, the work no doubt appeared in early 1958 though registered in the *Bibliography of Soviet Bibliographies* for 1957, rather than its imprint year 1956. Since Khrushchev's fall in 1964 Kazakov's bibliography, already severely dated, has become politically obsolete.

Outside the USSR, particularly in America and western Europe, the supply and quality of bibliography remains extremely limited with respect to the many Soviet nationality problems. In the West difficulties are not the same as those in the USSR, of course. Certainly, no political limitations or prescriptions direct the work in this field. All the same, such bibliography remains a relatively under-developed field. Appropriate library holdings are scattered and incomplete. Broad interest in Soviet nationality problems has begun to develop only within recent years, although individual scholars worked in the field earlier. Few patterns in the development of our bibliography can be discerned unless it may be seen that Americans and Europeans have assembled bibliographies, often with great care, in most cases merely to serve their own specialized writings. This style of research has produced isolated lists of works pertaining to a number of rather narrow subjects, usually in literature or history. In general scholarship here, Soviet nationality problems, as such, have been left by and large to political scientists. The over-all result to date, in bibliographical terms, can at best be described as haphazard, and most individual efforts as less than systematic, though sometimes lengthy and therefore profitable to scan.

Despite all these serious limitations, Soviet and Western bibliography dealing with the field of Soviet nationality problems has its uses. Lacking planned, comprehensive bibliographies, the best lists available seem to be thorough chronological surveys such as the specimen compiled by L. I. Frolova covering Russian-language work issued between 1964–1966, and described both above and below. In any case, existing compilations have to be taken into account if an effective approach to preparing a fresh systematic list of published work in this field is to be undertaken. To demonstrate possibilities in exploiting the old as well as developing something new, and to supply a selected reading list from experienced scholars regarding a broad range of Soviet nationality problems, three lists of references are offered here: (1) The first, perhaps the only bibliography of bibliographies printed in the field of general Soviet nationality problems, presents published Soviet and Western bibliographies; (2) the second represents our continuation of Frolova's effort described above and included in list No. 1. It provides coverage of Soviet periodical publishing in this field from 1967 through 1969; (3) the last group of titles is composed of selected readings relevant to each of the discussions about nationality problems given in this book. The list of readings, suggested by authors of the various chapters, is characterized mainly by the abundance of works in Western languages and the accessibility of such entries in American research libraries.

1. BIBLIOGRAPHY OF BIBLIOGRAPHIES ABOUT GENERAL SOVIET NATIONALITY PROBLEMS

Soviet Bibliographies

BAGLIKOV, B.   LENINSKIE PROIZVEDENIIA PO NATSIONAL'NOMU VOPROSU. MOSCOW: GOSUDARSTVENNOE IZDATEL'STVO POLITICHESKOI LITERATURY, 1962. 110000 copies, 64 pp. (Bibliog. p. 63), Russian language, 22 titles.

BATYROV, SHADZHA B.   FORMIROVANIE I RAZVITIE SOTSIALISTICHESKIKH NATSII V SSSR. MOSCOW: IZDATEL'STVO AKADEMII NAUK SSSR, 1962. 3500 copies, 368 pp. (Bibliog. pp. 361–68), Russian language, 5 lists.

"BIBLIOGRAFIIA INOSTRANNOI LITERATURY PO NATSIONAL'NOMU [I KOLONIAL'NOMU] VOPROSU," REVOLIUTSIIA I NATSIONAL'NOSTI, nos. 5, 8 (1932). (Bibliog. No. 5, pp. 118–24; No. 8, pp. 119–23), European languages.

"BIBLIOGRAFIIA INOSTRANNOI LITERATURY PO NATSIONAL'NOMU VOPROSU," REVOLIUTSIIA I NATSIONAL'NOSTI, NO. 6 (1932). (Bibliog. pp. 96–99), European languages.

BURMISTROVA, T. IU.   OBZOR SOVETSKOI LITERATURY O SOTSIALISTICHESKOM INTERNATSIONALIZME. MATERIALY VSESOIUZNOI KONFERENTSII "TEORETICHESKIE VOPROSY SOTS. INTERNATSIONALIZMA." MOSCOW: "ZNANIE," 1968. 500 copies, 25 pp.

DRABKINA, E. L.   NATSIONAL'NYI I KOLONIAL'NYI VOPROS V TSARSKOI ROSSII. MOSCOW: IZDATEL'STVO KOMMUNISTICHESKOI AKADEMII, 1930. 5000 copies, 189 pp.

FROLOVA, L. I.(COMP.).   NATSIONAL'NYE OTNOSHENIIA V SSSR NA SOVREMENNOM ETAPE. KNIGI I STAT'I IZ ZHURNALOV I SBORNIKOV ZA 1964–1966 GG. MOSCOW: MINISTERSTVO KUL'TURY SSSR. GOSUDARSTVENNAIA ORDENA LENINA BIBLIOTEKA IMENI V. I. LENINA, 1966. 850 copies, 46 pp., Russian language, 229 titles.

GROSHEV, I. I.   ISTORICHES KII OPYT KPSS PO OSUSHESTVLENIIU LENINSKOI NATSIONAL'NOI POLITIKI. MOSCOW: IZDATEL'STVO "MYSL," 1967. 10300 copies, 420 pp. (Bibliog. pp. 403–18), Russian language.

I. L.   "OBZOR POSLEVOENNOI BURZHUAZNOI LITERATURY PO VOPROSU O 'SUSHCHNOSTI' NATSII," REVOLIUTSIIA I NATSIONAL'NOSTI, No. 7 (1930). (Bibliog. pp. 120–23), Russian and European languages.

KAZAKOV, SERGEI VASIL'EVICH.   LENINSKAIA NATSIONAL'NAIA POLITIKA; REKOMENDATEL'NYI UKAZATEL' LITERATURY. MOSCOW: MINISTERSTVO KUL'TURY RSFSR; GOS. ORDENA LENINA BIBLIOTEKA IMENI V. I. LENINA, 1956. 20000 copies, 43 pp., Russian language, 130 titles.

KAZAKOV, S. V.   VELIKAIA DRUZHBA NARODOV SSSR. KRATKII
REKOMENDATEL'NYI OBZOR LITERATURY. MOSCOW: GOS. B-KA SSSR
IM. LENINA, 1951. 20000 copies, 68 pp., 82 titles.

KOPREEV, T. N. (COMP.)   MARKSIZM-LENINIZM O NATSIONAL'NO
KOLONIAL'NOM VOPROSE. UKAZATEL' LITERATURY. LENINGRAD:
GOSUDARSTVENNAIA ORDENA TRUDOVOI KRASNOI ZNAMENI PUBLICHNAIA
BIBLIOTEKA IM. M. E. SALTYKOV-SHCHEDRINA, 1953 (end of year).
20000 copies, 48 pp., 125 titles.

KUDRIAVTSEV, N. F. (COMP.).   RAZVITIE NATSIONAL'NYKH OTNOSHENII
V SSSR V PERIOD RAZVERNUTOGO STROITEL'STVA KOMMUNISTICHESKOGO
OBSHCHESTVA. MOSCOW: GOS. B-KA SSSR IM. LENINA, 1961. 6
Leaves, Russian language, 49 titles.

LEVIN, S. E.   O RABOTE I. V. STALINA "MARKSIZM I NATSIONAL'NYI
VOPROS." REKOMENDATEL'NYI SPISOK LITERATURY K 10–1 LEKTSII
TSIKLA "PROZVEDENII KLASSIKOV MARKSIZM-LENINIZM." MOSCOW:
VSESOIUZNOE OBSHCHESTVO PO RASPROSTRANENIIU POLIT. I NAUCH.
ZNANII, 1949 (2d., revised ed.), 1952 (3d ed.). 1500 copies (3d ed.),
4 pp., 19 titles.

LEVIN, S. E.   O RABOTE I. V. STALINA "NATSIONAL'NYI VOPROS I LENINIZM."
REKOMENDATEL'NYI SPISOK LITERATURY K LEKTSII. MOSCOW:
VSESOIUZNOE OBSHCHESTVO PO RASPROSTRANENIIU POLIT. I NAUCH.
ZNANII, 1949. 4 pp., 19 titles.

LIBOVA, F. M.; [P. SHATS].   "NATSIONAL'NYI VOPROS I NATSIONAL'NAIA
POLITIKA," REVOLIUTSIIA I NATSIONAL'NOSTI, no. 2 (1935), nos. 1
2 (1936). (Bibliog., no. 2 [1935] pp. 92–97; no. 1 [1936] pp. 94–97;
no. 2 [1936] pp. 83–85.

MARKSIZM I NATSIONAL'NAIA PROBLEMA. SBORNIK PERVYI.
[EKATERINOSLAV]: GOSUDARSTVENNOE IZDATEL'STVO UKRAINY, 1923.
5000 copies, 278 pp., (Bibliog. pp. 275–78), Russian and European
languages.

MATERIALY VSESOIUZNOGO KOORDINATSIONNOGO SOVESHCHANIIA PO
PROBLEME "RAZVITIE NATSIONAL'NYKH OTNOSHENII V USLOVIIAKH
PEREKHODA OT SOTSIALIZMA K KOMMUNIZMU." MOSCOW: 1963. Parts
I, II, (Bibliog. Part I pp. 124–34; Part 2 pp. 67–71, 355 titles.

"NATSIONAL'NO-TERRITORIAL'NOE RAZMEZHEVANIE SOIUZA SSR,"
REVOLIUTSIIA I NATSIONAL'NOSTI, no. 1 (1935), (Bibliog. pp. 88–97),
Russian language.

"NATSIONAL'NYI I NATSIONAL'NO-KOLONIAL'NYI VOPROS," BOL'SHAIA
SOVETSKAIA ENTSIKLOPEDIIA, vol. 41 (MOSCOW), 1939, pp. 381–97.
(Bibliog. pp. 396–97), Russian language.

NECHAEV, V.   NATSIONAL'NYI VOPROS V TREKH PROGRAMMAKH
KOMMUNISTICHESKOI PARTII. TULA: PRIOKSKOE KNIZHNOE IZDATEL'STVO,
1966. 3000 copies, 164 pp. (Bibliog. pp. 160–63), Russian language.

"SPISOK NOVYKH KNIG I STATEI PO VOPROSAM NATSIONAL'NOI I
KOLONIAL'NOI POLITIKI I NATS. REV. DVIZHENIIA NA VOSTOKE,"
REVOLIUTSIIA I NATSIONAL'NOSTEI, NO. 2 (1933). (Bibliog. pp.
100–104), Russian language.

STENCHUK, BOGDAN. CHTO I KAK OTSTAIVAET I. DZIUBA (ESCHE RAZ
O KNIGE "INTERNATSIONALIZM CHI RUSIFIKATSIIA") KIEV: OBSHCHESTVO
KUL'TURNYKH SVIAZEI S UKRAINTSAMI ZA RUBEZHOM, 1970. 196 pp.,
(Bibliog. pp. 171–96), book in English, bibliog. titles in Soviet
languages.

TEIMUROV, KH.; M. MIRZOEV. CHTO CHITAT' O DRUZHBE NARODOV SSSR.
BAKU: RESPUBL. PUBLICHNAIA BIBLIOTEKA IM. AKHUNDOVA, 1949. 88
pp., 39 titles.

UKAZATEL' STATEI I MATERIALOV POMESHCHENNYKH V "ZHIZNI
NATSIONAL'NOSTEI" ZA 1918–1922 GG. MOSCOW: NARODNYI KOMISSARIAT
PO DELAM NATSIONAL'NOSTEI, 1922. 104 pp., Russian language.
(See also " 'ZHIZN' NATS.' . . . " below)

"UKAZATEL' TSITIRUEMYKH LITERATURNYKH ISTOCHNIKOV," I. STALIN,
MARKSIZM I NATSIONAL'NO-KOLONIAL'NYI VOPROS. MOSCOW: PARTIINOE
IZDATEL'STVO/PARTIZDAT TSK VKP(B), 1934 (also in 1937 and 1938
eds.). 50000 copies, 232 pp. (Bibliog. pp. 228–30), Russian,
Czech, and European languages.

UL'IANOV, G. K. OBZOR LITERATURY PO VOPROSAM KUL'TURY I
PROSVESHCHENIIA NARODOV SSSR. MOSCOW-LENINGRAD: NARODNYI
KOMISSARIAT PROVESHCHENIIA RSFSR, GOSIZDAT, 1930. 247 pp.
(Bibliog. pp. 26–28, 146–52), Russian language.

VAKHIDOV, M. "K VOPROSU IZMENENIIA NATSIONAL'NOGO
PSIKHOLOGICHESKOGO SKLADA NARODOV (NA PRIMERE UZB. NARODA),"
NAUCHNYE TRUDY (TASHK, UN-T) NO. 327 (TASHKENT 1968). (Bibliog.
pp. 3–19), Russian language, 11 titles.

VALEEV, M. EDINOI SEM'EI ZAVETNOI TSELI. DEIATEL'NOST' KPSS PO
DAL'NEISHEMU SBLIZHENIIU NARODOV SSSR V BOR'BE ZA POBEDU
KOMMUNIZMA. MOSCOW: IZDATEL'STVO POLITICHESKOI LITERATURY,
1963. 45000 copies, 183 pp. (Bibliog. pp. 178–83), 70 titles.

" 'ZHIZN' NATS.' EZHEMESIACHNYI ZHURNAL PO VOPROSAM POLITIKI,
EKONOMIKI I KUL'TURY NATSIONAL'NOSTEI RSFSR . . . . SODERZHANIE
NO. 1, 2, 3, 4, 5 ZHURN. 'ZHIZN' NATSIONAL'NOSTEI' [1923–24],"
ZHIZN' NATSIONAL'NOSTEI NO. 1 (6) (1924), pp. 191–196.

Western Bibliographies

BOERSNER, DEMETRIO. THE BOLSHEVIKS AND THE NATIONAL AND
COLONIAL QUESTION (1917–1928). GENEVA: LIBRARIE E. DROZ., 1957.
285 pp. (Bibliog. pp. 277–85), European (including English)
languages, 5 lists.

CONQUEST, ROBERT, ed.   SOVIET NATIONALITIES POLICY IN PRACTICE.
LONDON: THE BODLEY HEAD, SOVIET STUDIES SERIES, 1967. 160 pp.
(Bibliog. pp. 152–60), Russian, European languages.

DAVIS, HORACE B.   NATIONALISM AND SOCIALISM. MARXIST AND LABOR
THEORIES OF NATIONALISM TO 1917. NEW YORK AND LONDON:
MONTHLY REVIEW PRESS, 1967. 258 pp. (Bibliog. pp. 237–43),
European languages, 4 lists.

LOW, ALFRED D.   LENIN ON THE QUESTION OF NATIONALITY. NEW YORK:
BOOKMAN ASSOCIATES, 1958. 193 pp. (Bibliog. pp. 177–90), Russian
and European languages, 7 lists.

MEISSNER, BORIS.   SOWJETUNION UND SELBSTBESTIMMUNGSRECHT.
COLOGNE: VERLAG WISSENSCHAFT UND POLITIK KÖLN, 1962. 464 pp.
(Bibliog. pp. 131–46), Russian and European languages.

PIPES, RICHARD.   THE FORMATION OF THE SOVIET UNION; COMMUNISM
AND NATIONALISM, 1917–1923. CAMBRIDGE: HARVARD UNIVERSITY
PRESS, [1954] 1964 (Revised ed.). 365 pp. (Bibliog. pp. 305–
28), Russian and European languages, 6 lists.

TILLET, LOWELL.   THE GREAT FRIENDSHIP. SOVIET HISTORIANS ON THE
NON-RUSSIAN NATIONALITIES. CHAPEL HILL: THE UNIVERSITY OF
NORTH CAROLINA PRESS, 1969. 468 pp. (Bibliog. pp. 425–59), Russian
and European languages, 4 lists.

2. RECENT SOVIET WRITINGS ABOUT NATIONALITY PROBLEMS

For those conducting research into contemporary developments, the following bibliography of 123 Russian-language titles, compiled by John Hanselman, will provide substantial material. The list should be regarded as a sequel to the bibliography prepared by L. I. Frolova, described in the Bibliography of Bibliographies immediately preceding this section. Journal articles shown here, the titles for which have been drawn exhaustively from the Moscow central register, *Annals of Journal Articles* (Letopis' zhurnal'nykh statei) covering the three publishing years 1967–1969, are augmented by a selection of book titles, for the same years, taken from *Book Annals* (Knizhnaia letopis'). Article entries in this list are arranged according to the system of classification employed in the Russian *Annals of Journal Articles*. Categories I through XIII in nos. 1–52 (1967), 1–52 (1968), 1–52 (1969), and 1–20 (1970) of the periodicals were searched. The headings, with additional subdivisions as shown in part by the list itself, comprise the first set of categories employed in the "Outline of Classifications for Writings," *Letopis' zhurnal'nykh statei* No. 1 (1970), pp. 219–22: I. Marxism-Leninism; II. Communist Party of the Soviet Union; III. Komsomol. Soviet youth; IV. Social sciences as a whole; V. Philosophy. Social-Political teachings; VI. History; VII. Political economy. History of economic teachings; VIII. International relations. Worldwide economy; IX. Communist development in the USSR; X. Planning. Statistics. Accounting. Organization and management of production; XI. Finance; XII. Labor in the USSR; XIII. State and Law.

I.1. Works by the pillars of Marxism-Leninism.
OGANIAN, A. G. "V. I. LENIN O SBLIZHENII NATSII PRI SOTSIALIZME," DOKLADY MIISP (MOSK. IN-T INZHENEROV S.-KH. PROIZVODSTVA), T. 3, VYP. 6 (1967), pp. 111–20.
TADEVOSIAN, E. V. "LENINSKIE PRINTSIPY I FORMY RESHENIIA NATSIONAL'NOGO VOPROSA," VOPROSY FILOSOFII, NO. 12 (1967), pp. 15–25.

I.2. Writings about the pillars of Marxism-Leninism. Works about Marxism-Leninism.

BAGDASH, KH.   "LENINIZM O NATSIONAL'NOM VOPROSE I PROLETARSKOM
INTERNATSIONALIZME. (STAT'IA GENERAL'NOGO SEKR. TSK SIRIISKOI
KOMPARTII)," KOMMUNIST, NO. 8 (1969), pp. 14–24.

KIRICHENKO, M. G.   "RAZVITIE KOMMUNISTICHESKOI PARTIEI LENINSKIKH
IDEI O SOVETSKOI NATSIONAL'NOI GOSUDARSTVENNOSTI," SOVETSKOE
GOSUDARSTVO I PRAVO, NO. 2 (1968), pp. 12–22.

KURITSYN, V. M.   "V. I. LENIN I STANOVLENIE EDINOI ZAKONNOSTI V
SOVETSKOM SOIUZNOM MNOGONATSIONAL'NOM GOSUDARSTVE,"
SOVETSKOE GOSUDARSTVO I PRAVO, NO. 1 (1969), pp. 19–28.

"LENIN I MNOGONATSIONAL'NAIA KUL'TURA," RUSSKII IAZYK V
NATSIONAL'NOI SHKOLE, NO. 2 (1967), pp. 3–6.

"LENINSKAIA NATSIONAL'NAIA POLITIKA I BOR'BA PARTII ZA EE
OSUSHCHESTVLENIE (METOD. MATERIALY K POLIT. ZANIATIIAM PO TEME
LENINSKAIA NATSIONAL'NAIA POLITIKA I BOR'BA PARTII ZA EE
OSUSHCHESTVLENIE. NERUSHIMAIA DRUZHBA NARODOV SSSR—ZALOG
USPEKHOV KOMMUNISTICHEKOGO STROITEL'STVA)," KOMMUNIST
VOORUZH. SIL, NO. 1 (1969), pp. 73–80.

MORDINOV, A. E.   "V. I. LENIN O SUSHCHNOSTI NATSIONAL'NYKH
OTNOSHENII PRI SOTSIALIZME," POLIARNAIA ZVEZDA, NO. 4 (1969),
pp. 91–101.

NIIAZOV, P. M.   "NATSIONAL'NYI VOPROS V TRUDAKH K. MARKSA I F.
ENGEL'SA," OBSHCHESTV. NAUKI V UZBEKISTANE, NO. 4 (1969),
pp. 21–25.

SERGEEV, I.   "OSNOVA LENINSKOI NATSIONAL'NOI PROGRAMMY. K
55-LETIIU RABOTY V. I. LENINA 'O PRAVE NATSII NA SAMOOPREDELENIE',"
KOMMUNIST BELORUSSII, NO. 4 (1969), pp. 36–39.

VOROB'EV, V. F.   "V. I. LENIN O NATSIONAL'NOM I INTERNATSIONAL'NOM
V KHUDOZHESTVENNOM TVORCHESTVE," VOPROSY RUSSKOI
LITERATURY, VYP. 1 (1967), pp. 11–21.

ZAITSEVA, E. A.   "IZDANIE LENINSKIKH RABOT PO NATSIONAL'NOMU
VOPROSU ZA GODY SOVETSKOI VLASTI. BIBLIOGR. OBZOR," ISTORIIA SSSR,
NO. 2 (1969), pp. 180–190.

II.1. General questions concerning the Party. Party program. Party statutes.

GROSHEV, I. I.   "LENINSKAIA NATSIONAL'NAIA POLITIKA KPSS I EE ROL' V
POSTROENII SOTSIALIZMA I KOMMUNIZMA. KONSUL'TATSIIA," VOPROSY
ISTORII KPSS, NO. 12 (1968), pp. 92–102.

LAKHTIKOV, M.   "LENINSKAIA NATSIONAL'NAIA POLITIKA I BOR'BA KPSS
ZA EE OSUSHCHESTVLENIE," KOMMUNIST VOORUZHENNYKH SIL, NO. 10
(1967), pp. 71–77.

OGANIAN, A. G. "KURS PARTII—NA DAL'NEISHII PODEM EDINOI
MNOGONATSIONAL'NOI KUL'TURY NARODOV SSSR," DOKLADY MIISP
(MOSK. IN-T INZHENEROV S.-KH. PROIZVODSTVA), T. 3, VYP. 6 (1966),
pp. 103–10.
TSAMERIAN, I. P. "MEZHDUNARODNOE ZNACHENIE OPYTA KPSS PO
RESHENIIU NATSIONAL'NOGO VOPROSA V SSSR," VOPROSY ISTORII KPSS,
NO. 9 (1968), pp. 41–55.

II.3. Ideological effort.
AKHUNZIANOV, T. "NATSIONAL'NAIA POLITIKA KPSS I PARTIINAIA
PROPAGANDA. (PO OPYTU PART. ORGANIZATSII BASHK. ASSR)," POLIT.
SAMOOBRAZOVANIE, NO. 12 (1967), pp. 93–97.
BODIUL, I. "SBLIZHENIE SOTSIALISTICHESKIKH NATSII I VOPROSY
INTERNATSIONAL'NOGO VOSPITANIIA SOVETSKIKH LIUDEI," KOMMUNIST
MOLDAVII, NO. 8 (1968), pp. 33–49.

II.4. Party history.
ESMENEEV, S. D. "LENINSKAIA PROGRAMMA PARTII PO NATSIONAL'NOMU
VOPROSU. KONSUL'TATSIIA," VOPROSY ISTORII KPSS, NO. 1 (1968),
pp. 98–108.
KUULI, O. "NATSIONAL'NAIA POLITIKA KOMPARTII ESTONII V 30-GODAKH,"
KOMMUNIST ESTONII, NO. 6 (1967), pp. 30–36.

*V.1. General questions of philosophy and social-political teach-
ings. Marxist-Leninist philosophy. Scientific communism.*
AGAEV, A. G. "NATSIIA, EE SUSHCHNOST' I SAMOSOZNANIE," VOPROSY
ISTORII, NO. 7 (1967), pp. 87–104.
ANANCHENKO, N. P. "OT NATSII K INTERNATSIONAL'NOI OBSHCHOSTI
LIUDEI," VOPROSY ISTORII, NO. 3 (1967), pp. 82–96.
BARSYKOV, A. A. "K VOPROSU O DIALEKTIKE RAZVITIIA NATSIONAL'NYKH
OTNOSHENII V USLOVIIAKH STROITEL'STVA KOMMUNIZMA," SBORNIK
NAUCH. RABOT ASPIRANTOV (KABARD.-BALKAR UN-T), VYP. 2 (1968),
pp. 56–65.
BULATOV, M. R. "O KHARAKTERE DVUKH TENDENTSII V NATSIONAL'NOM
VOPROSE V USLOVIIAKH SOTSIALIZMA I RAZVERNUTOGO
KOMMUNISTICHESKOGO STROITEL'STVA," TRUDY KAZAN. S.-KH. IN-TA,
VYP. 53 (1967), pp. 5–11.
BULATOV, M. R. "OSOBENNOSTI DEISTVIIA DVUKH TENDENTSII V
NATSIONAL'NOM VOPROSE V PROTSESSE SKLADYVANIIA I RAZVITIIA
MEZHNATSIONAL'NOI OBSHCHNOSTI SOVETSKOGO NARODA," TRUDY KAZAN.
S. KH. IN-TA, VYP. 53 (1967), pp. 12–21.
BUTENKO, A. "INTERNATSIONAL'NOE I NATSIONAL'NOE V MIRE
SOTSIALIZMA," NOVOE VREMIA, NO. 41 (1969), pp. 2–5.

CHIKLIAUKOV, I. P. "STROITEL'STVO KOMMUNIZMA I FORMIROVANIE
MARKSISTSKO-LENINSKOGO MIROVOZRENIIA V NATSIONAL'NOM VOPROSE,"
SBORNIK TRUDOV UL'IAN. POLITEKHN. IN-TA, T. 6, VYP. 1 (1968), pp.
73–87.

DROZDOV, I. F. "IAVLIAIUTSIA LI TRADITSII PRIZNAKOM NATSII?" VOPROSY
ISTORII, NO. 3 (1968), pp. 83–91.

DZHUNUSOV, M. S. "TEORIIA I PRAKTIKA RAZVITIIA SOTSIALISTCHESKIKH
NATSIONAL'NYKH OTNOSHENII," VOPROSY FILOSOFII, NO. 9 (1967),
pp. 26–36.

EFIMOV, A. V. "O NAPRAVLENIIAKH V IZUCHENII NATSII," NOVAIA I
NOVEISHAIA ISTORIIA, NO. 4 (1967), pp. 31–42.

FILATOV, V. N. "O STRUKTURE NATSIONAL'NOGO SAMOSOZNANIIA,"
IZVESTIIA AN KIRG. SSR, NO. 6 (1968), pp. 84–86.

GORIACHEVA, A. I. "IAVLIAETSIA LI PSIKHICHESKII SKLAD PRIZNAKOM
NATSII?" VOPROSY ISTORII, NO. 8 (1967), pp. 91–104.

IMANKHULOV, B. "NATSIONAL'NYI VOPROS I SOVREMENNOST',"
PARTIINAIA ZHIZN' KAZAKHSTANA, NO. 8 (1969), pp. 41–46.

ISAEV, M. I. "NATSIIA I IAZYK," VOPROSY ISTORII, NO. 2 (1968), pp.
99–112.

KALTAKHCHIAN, S. T. "PIAT'DESIAT LET ISTORICHESKOI PROVERKI
MARKSISTSKO-LENINSKOGO UCHENIIA O NATSII," NAUCHNYE DOKLADY
VYSSHEI SHKOLY. FILOSOF. NAUKI, NO. 5 (1967), pp. 23–33.

KALTAKHCHIAN, S. T.; Z. M. KHOLONINA. "DISKUSSIIA O NATSII I
GOSUDARSTVE," VOPROSY ISTORII, NO. 5 (1967), pp. 187–93.

KARTASHOVA, N. S. "O PROTSESSE SBLIZHENIIA I SLIIANIIA NATSII,"
UCHENYE ZAPISKI (MOSK. PED. IN-T), NO. 290 (1968), pp. 276–82.

KOZLOV, V. I. "NEKOTORYE PROBLEMY TEORII NATSII," VOPROSY
ISTORII, NO. 1 (1967), pp. 88–99.

KULICHENKO, M. I. "IUBILEINAIA LITERATURA O MESTE I ROLI
NATSIONAL'NOGO VOPROSA V OKTIABR'SKOI REVOLIUTSII (ISTORIOGR.
OBZOR)," VOPROSY ISTORII KPSS, NO. 3 (1969), pp. 107–19.

LOPATKINA, V. S. "K VOPROSU O DVUKH ISTORICHESKIKH TENDENTSIIAKH
V RAZVITII NATSIONAL'NYKH OTNOSHENII PRI KAPITALIZME I
SOTSIALIZME," UCHENYE ZAPISKI (SARAT. IURID. IN-T), VYP. 15
(1967), pp. 43–59.

"NAROD—RESHAIUSHCHAIA SILA ISTORICHESKOGO RAZVITIIA," KOMMUNIST
UZBEKISTANA, NO. 8 (1968), pp. 72–79.

NUROVA, S. S. "NARODNOST' KAK FORMA ISTORICHESKOI OBSHCHNOSTI
LIUDEI," SBORNIK RABOT ASPIRANTOV (KIRG. UN-T), VYP. 3 (1967), pp.
116–29.

ROGACHEV, P. M.; M. A. SVERDLIN. "O PREOBLADAIUSHCHEI TENDENTSII
RAZVITIIA NATSII V SOVETSKOI OBSHCHNOSTI," VOPROSY FILOSOFII,
NO. 2 (1969), pp. 26–31.

ROSENKO, M. N. "SOVREMENNAIA EPOKHA I NEKOTORYE TEORII NATSII," VOPROSY ISTORII, NO. 7 (1968), pp. 85–100.

SADYKOV, M. "NARODNOST' I NATSIIA KAK SOTSIAL'NO-ETNICHESKIE FORMY OBSHCHNOSTI LIUDEI," KOMMUNIST TATARII, NO. 1 (1967), pp. 12–18.

SAVASTENKO, A. "ISTORICHESKIE FORMY OBSHCHNOSTI LIUDEI (V POMOSHCH' PROPAGANDISTAM I SLUSHATELIAM SHKOL OSNOV MARKSIZMA-LENINIZMA)," KOMMUNIST BELORUSSII, NO. 3 (1969), pp. 45–49.

STRELKOVA, N. K. "OBZOR NEOPUBLIKOVANNYKH MATERIALOV DISKUSSII O TEORII NATSII (V REDAKTSII ZHURNALA 'VOPROSY ISTORII')," VOPROSY ISTORII, NO. 6 (1968), pp. 95–116.

SUDNITSYN, IU. G. "OSNOVNYE VOPROSY TEORII NATSIONAL'NOGO SUVERENITETA," IZVESTIIA VYSSHIKH UCHEBNYKH ZAVEDENII. PRAVOVEDENIE, NO. 4 (1967), pp. 48–55.

TAVAKALIAN, N. A. "NEKOTORYE VOPROSY PONIATIIA 'NATSIIA'," VOPROSY ISTORII, NO. 2 (1967), pp. 115–23.

TSAMERIAN, I. P. "AKTUAL'NYE VOPROSY MARKSISTSKO-LENINSKOI TEORII NATSII," VOPROSY ISTORII, NO. 6 (1967), pp. 107–22.

V.3. Logic. Psychology.

VAKHIDOV, M. "K VOPROSU IZMENENIIA NATSIONAL'NOGO PSIKHOLOGICHESKOGO SKLADA NARODOV (NA PRIMERE UZB. NARODA)," NAUCHNYE TRUDY (TASHK. UN-T), VYP. 327 (1968), pp. 3–19.

VI. 2. Auxiliary historical disciplines. Archeology. Ethnography.

LASHUK, L. P. "O FORMAKH DONATSIONAL'NYKH ETNICHESKIKH SVIAZEI," VOPROSY ISTORII, NO. 4 (1967), pp. 77–92.

PIMENOV, V. V. "O NEKOTORYKH ZAKONOMERNOSTIAKH V RAZVITII NARODNOI KUL'TURY," SOVETSKAIA ETNOGRAFIIA, NO. 2 (1967), pp. 130–39.

VAFAEV, O. "RAZVITIE INTERNATSIONAL'NYKH CHERT BYTA SOVETSKIKH SOTSIALISTICHESKIKH NATSII," OBSHCHESTVENNYE NAUKI V UZBEKISTANE, NO. 2 (1967), pp. 19–24.

VI.4. History of the USSR.

ALADZHIKOV, V. B. "FORMIROVANIE NATSIONAL'NYKH OTRIADOV RABOCHEGO KLASSA I EGO ZNACHENIE DLIA STANOVLENIIA SOTSIAL'NOI ODNONARODNOSTI SOTSIALISTICHESKIKH NATSII V SSSR," SBORNIK TRUDOV VSESOIUZNOGO ZAOCHNOGO POLITEKHNICHESKOGO INSTITUTA, VYP. 42 (1967), pp. 191–208.

GALOIAN, G. A.   "NATSIONAL'NYI VOPROS V ZAKAVKAZ'E V PERIOD
IMPERIALISTCHESKOI VOINY (1914–1917, FEVRAL')," VESTNIK
EREVANSKOGO UN-TA, OBSHCHESTV. NAUKI, NO. 2 (1969), pp. 78–97.

IX.1. General questions about communist development in the USSR.

ALADZHIKOV, V. IA.   "O NEKOTORYKH OB"EKTIVNYKH OSNOVAKH
SBLIZHENIIA SOTSIALISTICHESKIKH NATSII V SSSR," SBORNIK TRUDOV
(VSESOIUZ. ZAOCH. POLITEKH. IN-T), VYP. 44 (1968), pp. 70–91.

ANTONIUK, D.   "POBEDA VELIKOI OKTIABR'SKOI SOTSIALISTICHESKOI
REVOLIUTSII I RAZRESHENIE NATSIONAL'NOGO VOPROSA V SSSR. V
POMOSHCH' PROPAGANDISTAM I SLUSHATELIAM SISTEMY PART.
OBRAZOVANIIA," KOMMUNIST MOLDAVII, NO. 4 (1967), pp. 47–54.

ASADOV, A.   "UZY DRUZHBY I BRATSKOI VZAIMOPOMOSHCHI (NARODOV
SSSR)," LITERATURNYI AZERBAIDZHAN, NO. 10 (1967), pp. 89–96.

BURANOV, K.   "FORMIROVANIE I RAZVITIE TRADITSII SOTSIALISTICHESKIKH
NATSII SSSR," KOMMUNIST UZBEKISTANA, NO. 9 (1967), pp. 13–21.

CHIGAREV, I. S.   "SOTSIAL'NOE, POLITICHESKOE I IDEINOE EDINSTVO
SOVETSKOGO NARODA," UCHENYE ZAPISKI MOSK. PED. IN-TA, NO. 306
(1968), pp. 3–17.

DROBIZHEVA, L. M.   "O SOTSIAL'NOI ODNORODNOSTI RESPUBLIK I RAZVITII
NATSIONAL'NYKH OTNOSHENII V SSSR. IZ MATERIALOV
PODGOTAVLIVAEMOGO K PECHATI XII TOMA (1959–1965 GG.) 'ISTORII
SSSR S DREVNEISHIKH VREMEN DO NASHIKH DNEI'," ISTORIIA SSSR,
NO. 1 (1967), pp. 67–82.

DZHUNUSOV, M. S.   "SOVETSKII OPYT RESHENIIA NATSIONAL'NOGO
VOPROSA I EGO MEZHDUNARODNOE ZNACHENIE," ISTORIIA SSSR, NO. 6
(1967), pp. 16–43.

ERALIEV, E. E.   "IZ ISTORII DRUZHBY NARODOV SSSR," SBORNIK STATEI
ASPIRANTOV KAFEDR OBSHCHESTV. NAUK (KIRG. UN-T), VYP. 2 (1967),
pp. 120–23.

GAFUROV, B.   "DRUZHNAIA SEM'IA NARODOV SSSR," KUL'TURA I ZHIZN',
NO. 8 (1967), pp. 18–19.

GAFUROV, B.   "DRUZHBA, POZHDENNAIA REVOLIUTSIEI. (O TORZHESTVE
LENINSKOI NATS. POLITIKI SSSR)," AZIIA I AFRIKA SEGODNIA, NO. 11
(1967), pp. 8–17.

GOROVSKII, F.   "LENINSKAIA DRUZHBA NARODOV—VELIKOE ZAVOEVANIE
SOTSIALIZMA," KOMMUNIST UKRAINY, NO. 2 (1968), pp. 34–44.

IGITKHANIAN, M.   "EDINSTVO OBSHCHESTVA, ROZHDENNOE
SOTSIALIZMOM," KOMMUNIST, NO. 3 (1968), pp. 55–66.

KARAKEEV, K. K.; V. P. SHERSTOBITOV.   "OKTIABR'SKAIA REVOLIUTSIIA I
RESHENIE NATSIONAL'NOGO VOPROSA V KIRGIZSTANE," IZVESTIIA AN
KIRG. SSSR, NO. 2 (1967), pp. 3–15.

KHANAZAROV, K. KH. "OB ODNOM ASPEKTE DAL'NEISHEGO SBLIZHENIIA NATSII V SSSR. (IZ OPYTA KONKRETNO-SOTSIOL. ISSLEDOVANIIA)," OBSHCHESTV. NAUKI V UZBEKISTANE, NO. 6 (1968), pp. 23–26.

KHARCHENKO, G. V. "OSUSHCHESTVLENIE LENINSKOI NATSIONAL'NOI POLITIKI V PERIOD KOMMUNISTICHESKOGO STROITEL'STVA," IZVESTIIA AN KIRG. SSSR, NO. 4 (1967), pp. 83–89.

KHASHIMOV, U. IU. "K VOPROSU UKREPLENIIA DRUZHBY I SOTRUDNICHESTVA SOVETSKIKH NARODOV V PERIOD STROITEL'STVA KOMMUNIZMA," NAUCH TRUDY (TASHK. UN-T), VYP. 333 (1968), pp. 310–19.

KHOLMOGOROV, A. "SBLIZHENIE I RASTSVET SOTSIALISTICHESKIKH NATSII," KOMMUNIST SOVETSKOI LATVII, NO. 9 (1969), pp. 21–27.

KOLUPAEV, D. P. "POBEDA SOTSIALIZMA V SSSR I NEKOTORYE ZAKONOMERNOSTI PROTSESSA DAL'NEISHEGO RASTSVETA SOTSIALISTICHESKIKH NATSII I IKH SBLIZHENIIA V PERIOD STROITEL'STVA KOMMUNIZMA," UCHENYE ZAPISKI (RYBIN. VECHERNII TEKHNOL. IN-T), VYP. 2 (1968), pp. 70–112.

KUNAEV, D. "SOTSIALISTICHESKOE BRATSTVO NARODOV SSSR," PARTIINAIA ZHIZN', NO. 21 (1967), pp. 25–31.

"LENINSKAIA DRUZHBA SOVETSKIKH NARODOV (PEREDOVAIA)," KOMMUNIST UKRAINY, NO. 5 (1967), pp. 2–11.

MAMYRBAEV, A. "NERUSHIMOE BRATSTVO NARODOV. (O PRINTSIPAKH EKON., POLIT., I KUL'TURNOGO SOTRUDNICHESTVA NATSII V SSSR)," PARTIINAIA ZHIZN' KAZAKHSTANA, NO. 4 (1967), pp. 50–53.

MATIUSHKIN, N. I. "RAZRESHENIE NATSIONAL'NOGO VOPROSA V SSSR," VOPROSY ISTORII, NO. 12 (1967), pp. 3–20.

METELITSA, L. V.; E. V. TADEVOSIAN. "LENINSKIE PRINTSIPY RESHENIIA NATSIONAL'NOGO VOPROSA I IKH OSUSHCHESTVLENIIA V SSSR," VOPROSY ISTORII KPSS, NO. 11 (1967), pp. 47–61.

"MNOGONATSIONAL'NYI SOVETSKII NAROD," KOMMUNIST TATARII, NO. 12 (1967), pp. 2–8.

MOROZOV, M. A. "O NEKOTORYKH VOPROSAKH RAZVITIIA SOVETSKIKH SOTSIALISTICHESKIKH NATSII," VOPROSY ISTORII KPSS, NO. 10 (1968), pp. 104–11.

"NAUCHNAIA KONFERENTSIIA PO PROBLEMAM RAZVITIIA I SBLIZHENIIA SOVETSKIKH NATSII I NARODNOSTEI," KOMMUNIST MOLDAVII, NO. 1 (1967), pp. 48–57.

NESTEROVICH, V. "SOTSIALISTICHESKOE BRATSTVO NARODOV (SSSR)," KOMMUNIST BELORUSSII, NO. 10 (1968), pp. 13–17.

NIIAZBEKOV, S. B. "OKTIABR'SKAIA REVOLIUTSIIA I TORZHESTVO LENINSKOI NATSIONAL'NOI POLITIKI V SSSR," VESTNIK AN KAZ. SSSR, NO. 11 (1967), pp. 8–21.

NUROVA, S. S. "OB OSOBENNOSTIAKH SBLIZHENIIA SOTSIALISTICHESKIKH

NARODNOSTEI S NATSIIAMI (V SSSR)," SBORNIK STATEI ASPIRANTOV
KAFEDR OBSHCHESTV. NAUK (KIRG. UN-T), VYP. 2 (1967), pp. 29–34.

OVEZOV, B. "MY—INTERNATSIONALISTY (O DRUZHBE NARODOV SSSR.
BESEDA S PERVYM SEKT. TSK KP TURKMENISTANA B. OVEZOVYM),"
OGONEK, NO. 29 (1968), pp. 6–7.

PALETSKIS, IU. I. "50 LET SOVETSKOGO MNOGONATSIONAL'NOGO
GOSUDARSTVA," SOVETSKOE GOSUDARSTVO I PRAVO, NO. 11 (1967),
pp. 13–21.

PALETSKIS, IU. "POD LENINSKIM ZNAMENEM DRUZHBY NARODOV,"
AGITATOR, NO. 21 (1967), pp. 19–23.

PALETSKIS, IU. "'VELIKII OKTIABR' V RASTSVET SOTSIALISTICHESKIKH
NATSII," KOMMUNIST, NO. 8 (1967), pp. 22–23.

PALETSKIS, IU. "RAVNOPRAVIE VSEKH NATSII. LENINSKIE OSNOVY NATS.
POLITIKI SSSR," NOVOE VREMIA, NO. 18 (1969), pp. 8–11.

PIALL', E. "O NEKOTORYKH VOPROSAKH RAZVITIIA NATSII I
NATSIONAL'NYKH IAZYKOV SOVETSKOGO SOIUZA," IZVESTIIA AN EST.
SSR, T. 17, OBSHCHESTV. NAUKI, NO. 4 (1968), pp. 386–403.

RUTGAIZER, V. "TORZHESTVO LENINSKOI NATSIONAL'NOI POLITIKI V
EKONOMICHESKOM STROITEL'STVE," KOMMUNIST, NO. 18 (1968),
pp. 24–35.

SALAVATOVA, Z. M. "UKREPLENIE DRUZHBY DAGESTANSKIKH NARODOV S
BRATSKIMI NARODAMI STRANY," TRUDY," DAGEST. S.-KH. IN-TA,
T. 18 (1968), pp. 3–8.

SHKLIAR, E. E. "BRATSKAIA VZAIMOPOMOSHCH' SOVETSKIKH
NARODOV—IARKOE PROIAVLENIE PROLETARSKOGO INTERNATSIONALIZMA,"
UCH. ZAPISKI (MOSK. PED. IN-T), NO. 276 (1967), pp. 177–225.

SHAGINIAN, A. "TORZHESTVO LENINSKOI NATSIONAL'NOI POLITIKI,"
LITERATURNAIA ARMENIIA, NO. 10–11 (1967), pp. 73–81.

SMIRNOV, A. "KLASSOVOE I NATSIONAL'NOE V SOVETSKOM NARODE,"
KOMMUNIST (VILNIUS), NO. 4 (1969), pp. 10–14.

STEPANOV, A. S. "OT NATSIONAL'NOGO UGNETENIIA NARODOV—K IKH
SVOBODE I RAVENSTVU, DRUZHBE I BRATSTVU (USPEKHI KOMMUNIST.
STROITEL'STVA V SOIUZNYKH RESPUBLIKAKH)," POLIT.
SAMOOBRAZOVANIE, NO. 6 (1967), pp. 29–32.

TSAMERIAN, I. "LENINSKAIA NATSIONAL'NAIA POLITIKA V DEISTVII,"
KOMMUNIST, NO. 9 (1968), pp. 18–28.

TURSUN-ZADE, M. "STRANA LENINA (O VOPLOSHCHENII LENINSKOI
NATSIONAL'NOI POLITIKI)," VOPROSY LITERATURY, NO. 8 (1968),
pp. 3–11.

VEDISHCHEV, A. "RASTSVET SOTSIALISTICHESKIKH NATSII," NOVOE
VREMIA, NO. 49 (1967), pp. 3–5.

VIAL', E. "VAZHNAIA ZAKONOMERNOST' (SBLIZHENIE I SODRUZHESTVO
NATSII V SSSR)," KOMMUNIST BELORUSSII, NO. 3 (1969), pp. 26–29.

VORONIN, P. "LENINSKOE EDINSTVO I DRUZHBA SOVETSKIKH NARODOV," KOMMUNIST MOLDAVII, NO. 5 (1969), pp. 37–44.

IX.3. Communist development and the economics of the union republics, oblasts, regions and cities.

DANIIALOV, A. "V BRATSKOI SEM'E SOVETSKIKH NARODOV (O RAZVITII EKONOMIKI I KUL'TURY DAGEST. ASSR)," KOMMUNIST, NO. 15 (1967), pp. 44–52.

DUBINA, K. K. "RASTSVET SOVETSKOI UKRAINY V BRATSKOI SEM'E NARODOV SSSR," VESTNIK OBSHCHESTV. NAUK, NO. 8 (1967), pp. 81–94.

DZHALILOV, SH. "IARKOE PROIAVLENIE SOTSIALISTICHESKOGO INTERNATSIONALIZMA (O POMOSHCHI SOIUZNYKH RESPUBLIK V LIKVIDATSII POSLEDSTVII ZEMLETRIASENIIA V TASHKENTE)," OBSHCHESTV. NAUKI V UZBEKISTANE, NO. 2 (1969), pp. 8–11.

KUNAEV, D. "TORZHESTVO LENINSKOI NATSIONAL'NOI POLITIKI. (O RAZVITII NAR. KHOZ-VA KAZ. SSR)," SEL'SKOE KHOZIAISTVO KAZAKHSTANA, NO. 11 (1967), pp. 4–7.

MURADOVA, G. O. "TORZHESTVO LENINSKOI NATSIONAL'NOI POLITIKI. (KHOZ.-EKON. I KUL'TURNYE PREOBRAZOVANIIA V TURKM. SSSR)," IZVESTIIA AN TURKM. SSSR, SERIIA OBSHCHESTV. NAUK, NO. 5 (1967), pp. 3–9.

NURIEV, Z. "POD ZNAMENEM LENINSKOI NATSIONAL'NOI POLITIKI (K 50-LETIIU BASHK. ASSR)," PARTIINAIA ZHIZN', NO. 6 (1969), pp. 12–18.

NUSUPBEKOV, A. "VELIKII OKTIABR' I KONSOLIDATSIIA KAZAKHSKOGO NARODA V SOTSIALISTICHESKUIU NATSIIU," IZVESTIIA AN KAZ. SSR, SERIIA OBSHCHESTV., NO. 5 (1967), pp. 16–24.

POLIAKOV, D. E. "TORZHESTVO LENINSKOI NATSIONAL'NOI POLITIKI V SREDNEM POVOLZH'E (NA PRIMERE UL'IANOVSKOI OBLASTI)," TRUDY UL'IAN. S.-KH. IN-TA, T.14, VYP. 2 (1968), pp. 84–93.

SINEGLAZOVA, M. A. "FORMIROVANIE SOTSIALISTICHESKIKH OBSHCHESTVENNYKH OTNOSHENII V PROTSESSE PREOBRAZOVANIIA KUL'TURY BYTA I SEM'I NARODOV SREDNEI AZII I KAZAKHSTANA," SBORNIK RABOT MOSK. LESOTEKHN. IN-TA, VYP. 26 (1969), pp. 195–213.

"TORZHESTVO LENINSKOI NATSIONAL'NOI POLITIKI (K 50-LETIIU OBRAZOVANIIA BASHK. ASSR)," VOPROSY ISTORII KPSS, NO. 4 (1969), pp. 83–96.

VIRNYK, D. "PO LENINSKOMU PUTI EDINSTVA I SOTSIALISTICHESKOI VZAIMOPOMOSHCHI. (EKON. RASTSVET SOVETSKOI UKRAINY)," KOMMUNIST UKRAINY, NO. 9 (1967), pp. 10–20.

ZALIALOV, A.; M. GALIMOV; Z. GIL'MANOV. "TORZHESTVO LENINSKOI NATSIONAL'NOI POLITIKI. (PO MATERIALAM RESP. NAUCH.-TEORET. KONFERENTSII NA TEMU 'TORZHESTVO LENINSKOI NATSIONAL'NOI

POLITIKI V TATARII', KAZAN. IIUN' 1967 G.)," KOMMUNIST TATARII,
NO. 9 (1967), pp. 21–29.

XII.2. Trade unions of the USSR.
GORDIENKO, A. A. "SAMOOPREDELENIE NARODOV I OBRAZOVANIE
SOVETSKOI NATSIONAL'NOI GOSUDARSTVENNOSTI V SREDNEI AZII,"
SOVETSKOE GOSUDARSTVO I PRAVO, NO. 5 (1967), pp. 76–84.

XIII.1. General questions about state and law. Theory and history of state and law.
BEGIIAN, A. Z. "SOOTNOSHENIE OBSHCHESOTSIAL'NOGO I NATSIONAL'NOGO
SOVETSKOGO GOSUDARSTVA I NATSIONAL'NOI GOSUDARSTVENNOSTI,"
VESTNIK OBSHCHESTVENNYKH NAUK, NO. 1 (1967), pp. 14–20.
KOPOLEV, A. I. "GOSUDARSTVO I NATSII (O FORMAKH NATS.
GOSUDARSTVENNOSTI PRI SOTSIALIZME)," VESTNIK LENINGR. UN-TA,
NO. 17, EKONOMIKA, FILOSOFIIA, PRAVO, VYP. 3 (1968), pp. 75–83.

XIII.2. State and law of the USSR. a. General questions; Soviet development; State and administrative law. b. Other branches of Soviet law. c. Court and prosecution; Work of the agencies of justice.
ARUTIUNIAN, N. "RAVNAIA SREDI RAVNYKH, (ARM. SSSR)," SOVETY
DEPUTATOV TRUDIASHCHIKHSIA, NO. 11 (1967), pp. 15–21.
GRISHIN, V. M.; M. I. KULICHENKO. "PROBLEMY NATSIONAL'NO-
GOSUDARSTVENNOGO STROITEL'STVA V PERVOI SOVETSKOI KONSTITUTSII,"
VOPROSY ISTORII KPSS, NO. 7 (1968), pp. 21–34.
LISITSYNA, L. N.; E. S. SHAGALOV. "KONFERENTSIIA PO VOPROSAM
NATSIONAL'NO-GOSUDARSTVENNOGO STROITEL'STVA (DUSHANBE MAI,
1968 G.)," ISTORIIA SSSR, NO. 6 (1968), pp. 215–18.
NURBEKOV, K. N. "K VOPROSU SOVETSKOI NATSIONAL'NOI
GOSUDARSTVENNOSTI NA SOVREMENNOM ETAPE," TRUDY KIRG. UN-T,
SERIIA IURID. NAUK, VYP. 5 (1967), pp. 3–19.
PALETSKIS, IU. "SILA MNOGONATSIONAL'NOI SOVETSKOI FEDERATSII,"
KOMMUNIST, NO. 1 (1968), pp. 2–9.
ZLATOPOL'SKII, D. L. "PROBLEMY RAZVITIIA ZAKONODATEL'STVA V
OBLASTI NATSIONAL'NO-GOSUDARSTVENNYKH OTNOSHENII," UCHENYE
ZAPISKI (VNII SOVETSKOGO ZAKONODATEL'STVA), VYP. 10 (1967), pp.
200–202.

A Selection of Soviet Books, 1967–1969, about Nationality Problems, taken from Knizhnaia letopis'

BURMISTROVA, T. IU. NATSIONAL'NYI VOPROS I RABOCHEE DVIZHENIE V ROSSII (LENINSKAIA POLITIKA PROLETARSKOGO INTERNATSIONALIZMA. 1907–1917 GG.) MOSCOW: "MYSL'," 1969.

BUTSKO, N. A.; O. A. BORODIN: V. IU. MALANCHUK, et al. DRUZHBA NARODOV SSSR—VELIKOE ZAVOEVANIE LENINSKOI NATSIONAL'NOE POLITIKI KPSS. KIEV: IZDATEL'STVO KIEVSKOGO UNIVERSITETA, 1969. (In Ukrainian)

DZHUNUSOV, M. S. AKTUAL'NYE VOPROSY TEORII I PRAKTIKI SOTSIALISTICHESKOGO INTERNATSIONALIZMA. DOKLAD NA NAUCH. KONFERENTSII PO TEORET. PROBLEMAM SOTS. INTERNATSIONALIZMA. MAI, 1968 G. MOSCOW: "ZNANIE," 1968.

————. TEORIIA I PRAKTIKA NATSIONAL'NYKH OTNOSHENII. ALMA ATA: "KAZAKHSTAN," 1969.

ERZHANOV, A. USPEKHI NATSIONAL'NOI POLITIKI KPSS V KAZAKHSTANE (1946–1958 GG.). ALMA ATA: "NAUKA," 1969.

FAZYLOV, M. S. RELIGIIA I NATSIONAL'NYE OTNOSHENIIA. ALMA ATA: "KAZAKHSTAN," 1969.

GADOEV, KH. LENINSKAIA NATSIONAL'NAIA POLITIKA V DEISTVII. DUSHANBE: "IRFON," 1969.

ISTORIIA NATSIONAL'NO-GOSUDARSTVENNOGO STROITEL'STVA V SSSR. T. 1, NATSIONAL'NO-GOSUDARSTVENNOE STROITEL'STVO V SSSR V PEREKHODNYI PERIOD OT KAPITALIZMA K SOTSIALIZMU (1917–1936 GG.). MOSCOW: "MYSL'," 1968.

LIUBIMOV, V.; B. IULDASHBAEV. LENIN I SAMOOPREDELENIE NATSII. (NA PRIMERE NARODOV SRED. POVOLZHIA I PRIURALIA). CHEBOKSARY: 1967.

LOPAEVA, D. T. NATSII I NASIONAL'NYE OTNOSHENII V PERIOD STROITEL'STVA SOTSIALIZMA I KOMMUNIZMA. KIEV: IZD. KIEVSKOGO UNIVERSITETA, 1967.

MAGOMEDOV, A. M., et al., EDS. TORZHESTVO LENINSKOI NATSIONAL'NOI POLITIKI KPSS. MATERIALY MEZHVUZOVSKOI NAUCH. KONFERENTSII 8–9 IIUNIA 1967 G. MAKHACHKALA: DAGKNIGOIZDAT, 1968.

MAKAROVA, G. P. OSUSHCHESTVLENIE LENINSKOI NATSIONAL'NOI POLITIKI V PERVYE GODY SOVETSKOI VLASTI (1917–1920 GG.).

NARYNBAEV, A. I.; IA. A. RISS. OPYT RAZRESHENIIA NATSIONAL'NOGO VOPROSA V SSSR I EGO ISTORICHESKOE ZNACHENIE. FRUNZE: "KYRGYZSTAN," 1967.

PALETSKIS, IU. I. LENINSKAIA NATSIONAL'NAIA POLITIKA. MOSCOW: "ZNANIE," 1969.

RASTSVET SOTSIALISTICHESKIKH NATSII I IKH SBLIZHENIE. MATERIALY

NAUCHNOI SESSII. 21–22 IIUNIA 1966 G. TASHKENT: IZDATEL'STVO "FAN" UZBEKSKOI SSR, 1967.

ROGACHEV, P. M.; M. A. SVERDLIN.   NATSII—NAROD—CHELOVECHESTVO. MOSCOW: POLITIZDAT, 1967.

ROSENKO, MARGARITA N.   STROITEL'STVO KOMMUNIZMA V SSSR I ZAKONOMERNOSTI RAZVITIIA SOTS. NATSII. LENINGRAD: IZD. LENINGR. UN-TA, 1968.

————; I. A. ROSENKO.   NATSIONAL'NYI VOPROS I SOVREMENNYE MEZHDUNARODNYE OTNOSHENIIA. LENINGRAD: (O-VO "ZNANIE" RSFSR LENING. ORGANIZATSIIA), 1967.

SSSR. RAZVITIE NATSIONAL'NYKH OKRAIN. MOSCOW: "NOVOSTI," 1969. (In English)

SAIADOV, S. A.   NATSIONAL'NAIA POLITIKA KPSS I DRUZHBA NARODOV SSSR. BAKU: AZERNASHR, 1969.

SHARAPOV, IA. SH.   NATSIONAL'NYE SEKTSII RKP (B). KAZAN: IZD. KAZAN. UN-TA, 1967.

STRUZHIKHIN, N. T.   UCHASTIE KAZAKHSTANA VO VNESHNEEKONOMICHESKIKH SVIAZIAKH SOVETSKOGO SOIUZA. ALMA ATA: (O-VO "ZNANIE" KAZ. SSR), 1968.

TUGANBAEV, A.   OKTIABR'SKAIA REVOLIUTSIIA I RAZVITIE KAZAKHSKOI SOVETSKOI NATSIONAL'NOI GOSUDARSTVENNOSTI. ALMA ATA: "KAZAKHSTAN," 1967.

TUZMUKHAMEDOV, R. A.   OTVET KLEVETNIKAM. SAMOOPREDELENIE NARODOV SREDNEI AZII I MEZHDUNARODNOE PRAVO. MOSCOW: IZDATEL'STVO "MEZHDUNARODNYE OTNOSHENIIA," 1969.

URAZAEV, SH. Z.   V. I. LENIN I STROITEL'STVO SOVETSKOI GOSUDARSTVENNOSTI V TURKESTANE. TASHKENT: "FAN," 1967.

VELIKII OKTIABR' I LENINSKAIA DRUZHBA NARODOV SSSR. TASHKENT: "UZBEKISTAN," 1969.

ZHUCHKOV, B.   LENIN O RESHENII NATSIONAL'NOGO VOPROSA. MOSCOW: IZD. AGENSTVA PECHATI "NOVOSTI," [1968].

3. SELECTED READINGS

These titles have been suggested by the authors of the book for readers who wish to pursue the different nationality problems dealt with here. Footnotes placed at the end of most essays provide further references.

Abetsedarskii, L. S., *et al.*, eds. *Istoriia Belorusskoi SSR v dvukh tomakh.* Second supplemented edition. Minsk: Izdatel'stvo Akademii Nauk Belorusskoi SSR, 1961.

Adelman, Fred. *Kalmyk Cultural Renewal.* Ann Arbor: University Microfilms, 1960.

Agaev, Akhed G. *K voprosu o teorii narodnosti; zakonomernosti sotsialisticheskogo razvitiia narodnostei v SSSR.* Makhachkala: Dagestanskoe Knizhnoe Izd-vo, 1965.

Aleksandrov, V. A. *et al.*, eds. *Narody evropeiskoi oblasti SSSR.* vol. I. Moscow: Izdatel'stvo Nauka, 1964.

Allworth, Edward, ed. *Central Asia: A Century of Russian Rule.* New York: Columbia University Press, 1967.

————. *Central Asian Publishing and the Rise of Nationalism. An Essay and a List of Publications in the New York Public Library.* New York: New York Public Library, 1965.

————. *Nationalities of the Soviet East. Publications and Writing Systems. A Bibliographical Directory and Transliteration Tables for Iranian- and Turkic-Language Publications, 1818–1945, located in U.S. Libraries.* New York and London: Columbia University Press, 1971.

————. "The 'Nationality' Idea in Czarist Central Asia," *Ethnic Minorities in the Soviet Union.* New York: Frederick A. Praeger, 1968, pp. 229–50.

————. *Uzbek Literary Politics.* New York: Humanities Press; London-The Hague: Mouton, 1964.

Aminov, R. Kh., *et al.*, eds. *Istoriia uzbekskoi SSR v chetyrekh tomakh.* Tashkent: Izdatel'stvo "Fan" Uzbekskoi SSR, 1967–1968.

Arakelian, V. N.; A. R. Ioannisian, eds. *Istoriia armianskogo naroda* Vol. I. Erevan: Aipetrat, 1951.

Armstrong, John A. *Ukrainian Nationalism.* New York: Columbia University Press, 1963, 2d edition.

Arsharuni, A. "Iz istorii natsional'noi politiki tsarizma," *Krasnyi arkhiv* Nos. 4, 5 (1929), pp. 61–83, 107–27.

Arutiunian, S. M. *Natsiia i ee psikhicheskii sklad.* Krasnodar: M-vo Prosveshcheniia RSFSR . . . , 1966.

Asfendiarov, S. "Problema natsii i novoe uchenie o iazyke," *Novyi Vostok* No. 22 (1928), pp. 169–83.

Bacon, Elizabeth. *Central Asians under Russian Rule.* Ithaca: Cornell University Press, 1966.

Bakhrushin, S. V.; V. Ia. Nepomnina; V. A. Shishkin, eds. *Istoriia narodov Uzbekistana* Vol. II. (*Ot obrazovaniia gosudarstva Sheinbanidov do velikoi oktiabr'skoi sotsialisticheskoi revoliutsii*). Tashkent: Izdatel'stvo AN UzSSR, 1947.

Barghoorn, Frederick C. *Soviet Russian Nationalism.* New York: Oxford University Press, 1956.

Bassor, A.; G. Naan, eds. *Istoriia Estonskoi SSR* vol. I (*S drevneishikh vremen do serediny XIX veka*). Tallin: Estonskoe Gosudarstvennoe Izdatel'stvo, 1961.

Bennigsen, Alexandre. "La Famille Musulmane en Union soviétique," *Cahiers du Monde russe et soviétique* 1 (May 1959), pp. 83–109.

Bennigsen, Alexandre; Chantal Lemercier Quelquejay. *The Evolution of Muslim Nationalities of the USSR and their Linguistic Problems.* London: Central Asian Research Centre, 1961.

————. *Islam in the Soviet Union.* London-New York: Pall-Mall-Praeger, 1967.

————. *Les Mouvements Nationaux chez les Musulmans de Russie—le Sultangalievisme au Tatarstan.* Paris-The Hague: Mouton, 1960.

————. *La Presse et le Mouvement national chez les Musulmans de Russie avant 1920.* Paris-The Hague: Mouton, 1964.

Berdzenishvili, N.; G. Khachpuridze, eds. *Istoriia Gruzii,* vol. I (*S drevneishikh vremen do 60 kh godov XIX veka*). Tbilisi: "Tsodna," 1962.

Bilinsky, Yaroslav. *The Second Soviet Republic: The Ukraine After World War II.* New Brunswick: Rutgers University Press, 1964.

Bloom, Solomon F. *The World of Nations. A Study of the National Implications in the Work of Karl Marx.* New York: Columbia University Press, 1941.

Breton, Raymond. "Institutional Completeness of Ethnic Communities and the Personal Relations of Immigrants," *American Journal of Sociology* No. 70 (1964), pp. 193–205.

Brumberg, A., ed. *Russia under Krushchev. An Anthology from Problems of Communism.* New York: Frederick A. Praeger, 1962.

Brzezinski, Zbigniew, ed. *Dilemmas of Change in Soviet Politics.* New York: Columbia University Press, 1969.

————. *Ideology and Power in Soviet Politics.* New York: Frederick A. Praeger, 1967 rev. ed.

Campbell, Donald T.; Robert A. LeVine. "A Proposal for Cooperative Cross-Cultural Research on Ethnocentrism," *Journal of Conflict Resolution* V, No. 1 (1961), pp. 82–108.

Carr, E. H. *German-Soviet Relations Between the Two World Wars, 1919–1939.* New York: Macmillan, 1952.

————. *The October Revolution. Before and After.* New York: Alfred A. Knopf, 1969.

Carrere d'Encausse, Héléne. *Reforme et Revolution chez les Musulmans de l'Empire Russe: Bukhara 1867–1924.* Paris: Armand Colin, 1966.

Chekalin, M. *The National Question in the Soviet Union.* New York: Workers Library Publishers, 1941.

Cherepnin, L. V., *et al.*, eds, *Istoriia Moldavskoi SSR*, vol. I (*S drevnei-shikh vremen do velikoi oktiabr'skoi sotsialisticheskoi revoliutsii*). Kishinev: Izdatel'stvo "Kartia Moldaveniaske," 1965.

Chkhikvadze, Victor M., ed. *The Soviet State and Law.* Moscow: Progress Publishers, 1969.

Conquest, Robert. *Russia after Khrushchev.* New York: Frederick A. Praeger, 1965.

————. *The Soviet Deportation of Nationalities.* London: Macmillan; New York: St. Martin's Press, 1960.

————, ed. *Soviet Nationalities Policy in Practice.* London: The Bodley Head, 1967.

Denisov, Andrei I.; M. Kirichenko. *Soviet State Law.* Moscow: Foreign Languages Publishing House, 1960.

Deutsch, Karl W. *Nationalism and Social Communication. An Inquiry Into the Foundation of Nationality.* Cambridge: MIT Press, 1953.

————; W. J. Holtz, eds. *Nation Building.* New York: Atherton, 1963.

Deutscher, Isaac. *Russia in Transition.* New York: Frederick A. Praeger, 1960, rev. ed.

————. *The Unfinished Revolution 1917–1967.* New York: Oxford University Press, 1967.

Dunn, Stephen; Ethel Dunn. "Soviet Regime and Native Culture in Central Asia and Kazakhstan: The Major Peoples," *Current Anthropology*, No. 8 (1967), pp. 147–208.

Dzhunusov, M. *Vsestoronee razvitie i tesnoe sblizhenie sovetskikh natsii v period razvernutogo stroitel'stvo kommunizma.* Frunze: Kirgizgosizdat, 1962.

Erygin, Stepan Karpovich; F. D. Ryzhenko. *Leninskaia programma po natsional'nomu voprosu. Materialy k lektsiam po kursu "Istoriia KPSS".* Moscow: "Sovetskaia Nauka" Gosudarstvennoe Izdatel'stvo, 1959.

Fainsod, Merle. *How Russia is Ruled.* Cambridge: Harvard University Press, 1963, 2d ed.

————. "Roads to the Future," *Problems of Communism,* vol. XVI, No. 4 (July/August 1967), pp. 21–24.

Gafurov, B. G. *Istoriia tadzhikskogo naroda v kratkom izlozhenii,* vol. I. (*S drevneishikh vremen do velikoi oktiabr'skoi sotsialisticheskoi revoliutsii 1917 g.*). Third revised and supplemented edition. Moscow: Gosudarstvennoe Izdatel'stvo Politicheskoi Literatury, 1955.

Gafurov, Babadzhan G. *Nekotorye voprosy natsional'noi politiki KPSS.* Moscow: Gos. Izd-vo Polit-Literatury, 1959.

Gardanov, V. K.; B. O. Dolgikh; T. A. Zhdanko. "Osnovnye napravleniia etnicheskikh protsessov u narodov SSSR," *Sovetskaia etnografiia,* No. 4 (1961), pp. 9–29. Translation in *Soviet Anthropology and Archeology,* No. 1 (Summer 1962), pp. 3–18.

Goldhagen, Erich, ed. *Ethnic Minorities in the Soviet Union.* New York: Frederick A. Praeger, 1968.

Grzybowski, Kazimierz. *Soviet Legal Institutions: Doctrines and Social Functions.* Ann Arbor: University of Michigan Press, 1962.

Guseinov, I. A., *et al.,* eds. *Istoriia Azerbaidzhana v trekh tomakh.* Baku: Izdatel'stvo Akademii Nauk Azerbaidzhanskoi SSR, 1958–1963.

Harris, Chauncy D. *Cities of the Soviet Union.* Chicago: Rand McNally and Co., 1970.

———. "Ethnic Groups in the Cities of the Soviet Union," *Geographical Review,* No. 3 (July 1945), pp. 466–73.

Hayit, Baymirza. *Sowjetrussische Orientpolitik am Beispiel Turkestan.* Berlin-Cologne: Kiepenhauer Wirt, 1962.

———. *Turkestan im XX. Jahrhundert.* Darmstadt: Leske Verlag, 1956.

Hazard, John N. *The Soviet System of Government.* Chicago: University of Chicago Press, 1968, 4th ed.

———; Isaac Shapiro; Peter B. Maggs. *The Soviet Legal System: Contemporary Documentation and Historical Commentary.* Dobbs Ferry: Oceana Publications, Inc., 1969, 2d ed.

Hostler, Charles Warren. *Turkism and the Soviets. The Turks of the World and Their Political Objectives.* London: George Allen and Unwin Ltd., 1957.

The Impact of the Russian Revolution 1917–1967. The influence of Bolshevism on the World outside Russia. New York: Oxford University Press, 1967.

Inkeles, Alex. *Social Change in Soviet Russia.* Cambridge: Harvard University Press, 1968.

Ioannisiana, Ashota, ed. *Armiano-Russkie otnosheniia v pervoi treti XVIII veka. Sbornik dokumentov.* vol. II, parts 1, 2. Erevan: Izdatel'stvo Akademii Nauk Armianskoi SSR, 1964–1967.

Istoriia Buriat-Mongol'skoi ASSR. vol. I, second revised and supplemented edition. Ulan Ude: Buriat-Mongol'skoe Knizhnoe Izdatel'stvo, 1954.

Istoriia Dagestana. vol. III. Moscow: Izdatel'stvo "Nauka," Glavanaia Redaktsiia Vostochnoi Literatury, 1968.

Istoriia Iakutskoi ASSR. 3 vols. Moscow-Leningrad: Izdatel'stvo Akademii Nauk SSSR, 1955–1963.

Istoriia Kazakhskoi SSR. 2 vols. Alma Ata: Izdatel'stvo Akademii Nauk Kazakhskoi SSR, 1957–1959.

Istoriia Kirgizii vol. I. Frunze: Kirgizskoe Gosudarstvennoe Izdatel'stvo, 1963.

Istoriia sovetskoi konstitutsii (v dokumentakh) 1917–1956. Moscow: Gosudarstvennoe Izdatel'stvo Iuridicheskoi Literatury, 1957.

Istoriia Tadzhikskogo naroda 3 vols. Moscow: Izdatel'stvo Vostochnoi Literatury "Nauka," 1963–1965.

Istoriia Tatarskoi ASSR 2 vols. Kazan: Tatknigaizdat. Redaktsiia Politicheskoi i Istoricheskoi Literatury. Tatarskoe Knizhnoe Izdatel'stvo, 1955–1960.

Istoriia Uzbekskoi SSR vol. I (kniga pervaia i vtoraia). Tashkent: Izdatel'stvo Akademii Nauk Uzbekskoi SSR, 1955–1956.

Ivanov, P. P. *Ocherki po istorii Srednei Azii (XVI-seredina XIX v.)*. Moscow: Izdatel'stvo Vostochnoi Literatury, 1958.

Janowsky, Oscar I. *Nationalities and National Minorities (With Special Reference to East-Central Europe)*. New York: Macmillan Company, 1945.

Johelson, Waldemar. *Peoples of Asiatic Russia*. New York: American Museum of Natural History, 1928.

Juviler, Peter H., H. W. Morton, eds. *Soviet Policy-Making. Studies of Communism in Transition*. New York: Frederick A. Praeger, 1967.

Kabardino-russkie otnosheniia v XVI–XVIII vv. Dokumenty i materialy v 2-kh tomakh. Moscow: Izdatel'stvo Akademii Nauk SSSR, 1957.

Kafadarian, K. G.; A. R. Nersisian, eds. *Istoriia armianskogo naroda* vol. I (*S drevneishikh vremen do kontsa XVIII veka*). Erevan: Izdatel'stvo Akademii Nauk Armianskoi SSR, 1944.

Kaikhanidi, A. E. *Leninskaia teoriia i programma po natsional'nomu voprosu*. Minsk: Gosudarstvennoe Izdatel'stvo BSSR, 1962.

Kaltakhchian, S. T. *Istoricheskie formy obshchnosti liudei*. Moscow. Izdatel'stvo Politicheskoi Literatury, 1966.

Kammari, M. D. *K polnomu edinstvu. O rastsvete i sblizhenii natsii SSSR na putiakh k kommunizmu*. Moscow: "Znanie," 1962.

Kargal'tseva, E. S. *Natsional'nyi vopros v programme KPSS*. Moscow: (O-vo po Rasprostraneniiu Polit. i Nauch. Znanii RSFSR), 1961.

Karryev, A.; O. K. Kuliev; M. E. Masson, *et al.*, eds. *Istoriia Turkmenskoi SSR* vols. I, II. Ashkhabad: Izdatel'stvo Akademii Nauk Turkmenskoi SSR, 1957.

Kasimenko, A. K., *et al. Istoriia ukrains'koi SSR* vol. I. Kiev: Izdatel'stvo Akademii Nauk Ukrains'koi SSR, 1953.

Kennan, George F. *Russia and the West under Lenin and Stalin*. New York: New American Library, 1962.

Khanazarov, K. Kh. *Sblizhenie natsii i natsional'nye iazyki v SSSR*. Tashkent: Izdatel'stvo Akademii Nauk UzSSR, 1963.

Kirimal, Edige. *Der nationale Kampf der Krim Türken*. Emsdetten: Leske Verlag, 1952.

Kohn, Hans. *Nationalism in the Soviet Union.* New York: Columbia University Press, 1933. (Reprinted by AMS Press, 1966).

————. "The Nationality Policy of the Soviet Union," Samuel N. Harper, ed. *The Soviet Union and World Problems.* Chicago: University of Chicago Press, 1935, pp. 85–121.

Kolarz, Walter. *Russia and Her Colonies.* New York: Frederick A. Praeger, 1952.

Kosven, M. O., ed. *Narody Kavkaza.* Vols. I, II. Moscow: Izdatel'stvo Akademii Nauk SSSR, 1960–1962.

Krader, Lawrence. *Peoples of Central Asia.* Bloomington: Indiana University Publications; Uralic and Altaic Series Vol. 26, 1966, 2d ed.

Kravtsev, I. E. *Sblizhenie sotsialisticheskikh natsii v protsesse perekhoda k kommunizmu.* Kiev: (O-vo po Rasprostraneniiu Polit. i Nauch. Znanii SSSR), 1960.

Lamont, Corliss. *The Peoples of the Soviet Union.* New York: Harcourt, Brace and Co., 1946.

Lamser, Václav. *Problémy sovětských národností v městských a venkovských oblastech. Sborník Čs. společnosti zemepisné.* Prague: ČSAV, 1960.

Lewis, Robert A.; Richard H. Rowland. "Urbanization in Russia and the USSR: 1897–1966," *Annals of the Association of American Geographers* No. 4 (Dec. 1969), pp. 776–96.

Libby, Dorothy. "Three Hundred Years of Chuckchi Ethnic Identity," A. F. C. Wallace, ed. *Man and Culture.* Philadelphia: University of Pennsylvania Press, 1960, pp. 298–304.

Lorimer, Frank. *The Population of the Soviet Union: History and Prospects.* Geneva: League of Nations, 1946.

Low, Alfred D. *Lenin on the Question of Nationality.* New York: Bookman Associates, 1958.

M. "M. N. Pokrovskii i natsional'nyi vopros," *Revoliutsionnyi Vostok* No. 3/4 (1932), pp. 115–25.

Makarov, P. I. *Lektsiia "Leninskaia programma po natsional'nomu voprosu."* Moscow: (M-vo Vyssh. i Sred. Spets. Obrazovaniia RSFSR . . .), 1960.

Martovych, Oleh R. *National Problems in the U.S.S.R.* Edinburgh: Foreign Affairs Information Service (No. 8) Scottish League for European Freedom, 1953.

Massell, Gregory J. "Law as an Instrument of Revolutionary Change in a Traditional Milieu: the Case of Soviet Central Asia," *Law and Society Review* vol. II, No. 2 (1968), pp. 179–228.

Medlin, William K.; F. Carpenter; W. Cave. *Education and Social Change: A Study of the Role of the School in a Technically Developing Society in Central Asia.* Ann Arbor: University of Michigan Press, 1965.

Meisel, James H.; Edward S. Kozera. *Materials for the Study of the*

Soviet System: State and Party Constitutions, Laws, Decrees, Decisions, and Official Statements of the Leaders, in Translation. Ann Arbor: George Wahr Publishing Co., 1953, 2d. ed.

Metelitsa, Lev Vladimirovich. *Torzhestvo leninskoi natsional'noi politiki v SSSR.* Moscow: Vysshaia Shkola, 1962.

Meyer, Alfred G. *The Soviet Political System. An Interpretation.* New York: Random House, 1965.

Naana, G. I., ed. *Istoriia estonskoi SSR (S drevneishikh vremen do nashikh dnei).* Tallin: Estonskoe Gosudarstvennoe Izdatel'stvo, 1958.

Narody Sibiri. Moscow-Leningrad: Izdatel'stvo Akademii Nauk SSSR, 1956.

Narody Srednei Azii i Kazakhstana vol. I. Moscow: Izdatel'stvo Akademii Nauk SSSR, 1962.

Natsiia i natsional'nye otnosheniia. Frunze: "Ishim," 1966.

Ocherki istorii Karelii 2 vols. Petrozavodsk: Gosudarstvennoe Isdatel'stvo Karel'skoi ASSR, 1957–1964.

Ocherki po istorii Bashkirskoi ASSR vol. I, parts 1, 2. Ufa: Bashkirskoe Knizhnoe Izdatel'stvo, 1956–1959.

Ocherki po istorii Komi ASSR 2 vols. Syktyvkar: Knizhnoe Izdatel'stvo, 1955–1962.

Park, Alexander G. *Bolshevism in Turkestan 1917–1927.* New York: Columbia University Press, 1957.

Pavlovskii, E. N.; O. A. Konstantinov, eds. *Geografiia naseleniia v SSSR. Osnovnye problemy.* Moscow: Izdatel'stvo "Nauka," 1964.

Perchik, Lev Medelevich. *How the Soviet Government Solves the National Question.* Moscow: Cooperative Publishing Society of Foreign Workers in the USSR, 1932.

Pertsev, V. N.; K. I. Shabuni; L. S. Abetsedarskii, eds. *Istoriia belorusskoi SSR* 2 vols. Minsk: Izdatel'stvo Akademii Nauk Belorusskoi SSR, 1954–1958.

Petrukhin, A. A. *Teoriia i programma kommunisticheskoi partii po natsional'nomu voprosu.* Moscow: Izdat. "Sovetskaia Nauka," 1955.

Pierce, Richard A. *Russian Central Asia 1867–1917.* Berkeley: University of California Press, 1957.

Pipes, Richard. *The Formation of the Soviet Union: Communism and Nationalism, 1917–1923.* Cambridge: Harvard University Press, 1964, 2d ed.

———. "Muslims of Soviet Central Asia: Trends and Prospects," *Middle East Journal* IX (1955), pp. 147–62.

Pod"iachikh, P. G. *Naselenie SSSR.* Moscow: Gosudarstvennoe Izdatel'-stvo Politicheskoi Literatury, 1961.

Polenina, S. V. *Osnovy grazhdanskogo zakonodatel'stva i grazhdanskii kodeks.* Moscow: Iuridicheskaia Literatura, 1968.

Price, C. A. "Immigration and group Settlement," W. D. Boorie, ed., *The*

Cultural Integration of Immigrants. Paris: UNESCO, 1959, pp. 267–88.

Problems of Communism vol. XVI, No. 5 (*Special Issue: Nationalities and Nationalism in the USSR*) (Sept.–Oct. 1967).

Problemy sblizheniia sotsialisticheskikh natsii v period stroitel'stva kommunizma. Frunze: "Mektep," 1966.

Raeff, Marc. *Siberia and the Reforms of 1822.* Seattle: University of Washington Press, 1956.

Redfield, Robert; Milton Singer. "The Cultural Role of Cities," *Economic Development and Culture Change.* Chicago: University of Chicago Press, 1954, pp. 53–73.

Reshetar, J. S., Jr. "National Deviation in the Soviet Union," *The American Slavic and East European Review* XII (April 1953), pp. 162–74.

Robinson, Geroid Tanquary. "American Thought and the Communist Challenge," Edward Mead Earle, ed., *Nationalism and Internationalism.* New York: Columbia University Press, 1950, pp. 336–51.

Rubel, Paula G. *The Kalmyk Mongols: A Study in Continuity and Change.* Bloomington: Indiana University Press, 1967.

Rysakoff, A. *The National Policy of the Soviet Union.* New York: International Publishers, 1933.

Rywkin, Michael. *Russia in Central Asia.* New York: Collier Books, 1963.

Schapiro, Leonard. *The Government and Politics of the Soviet Union.* New York: Random House, 1965.

———, ed. *The USSR and the Future. An Analysis of the New Program of the CPSU.* New York: Frederick A. Praeger, 1962.

Schwarz, Solomon M. "The Soviet Concept and Conquest of National Cultures," *Problems of Communism* No. 6, vol. 2 (1953), pp. 41–46.

Simmons, Ernest J., ed. *Continuity and Change in Russian and Soviet Thought.* Cambridge: Harvard University Press, 1955.

Smal-Stocki, Roman. *The Nationality Problem of the Soviet Union and Russian Communist Imperialism.* Milwaukee: Bruce Publishing Co., 1952.

Snyder, L. L., ed. *The Dynamics of Nationalism: Readings in Its Meaning and Development.* Princeton: Van Nostrand, 1964.

Stalin, Joseph. *Marxism and Linguistics.* New York: International Publishers, 1951.

Strazdin, K. Ia., *et al.,* eds. *Istoriia Latviiskoi SSR* 3 vols. Riga: Izdatel'stvo Akademii Nauk Latviiskoi SSR, 1952.

Sugar, Peter F.; Ivo J. Lederer, eds. *Nationalism in Eastern Europe.* Seattle: University of Washington Press, 1969.

Tillett, Lowell. *The Great Friendship. Soviet Historians on the Non-Russian Nationalities.* Chapel Hill: The University of North Carolina Press, 1969.

Tokarev, S. A. "Problema tipov etnicheskikh obshchnostei (k metodologicheskim problemam etnografii)," *Voprosy filosofii* No. 11 (1964), pp. 43–53.

Torzhestvo leninskoi natsional'noi politiki. Moscow: Izd-vo VPSh i AON pri TsK KPSS, 1963.

Towster, Julian. *Political Power in the U.S.S.R. 1917–1947.* New York: Oxford University Press, 1948, 5th printing, 1955.

Treadgold, D. W., ed. *The Development of the USSR. An Exchange of Views.* Seattle and London: University of Washington Press, 1964.

Triska, J. F. *Soviet Communism: Program and Rules.* San Francisco: Chandler, 1962.

Tsamerian, I. *Novyi etap v razvitii natsional'nykh otnoshenii v SSSR.* Moscow: "Moskov. Rabochii," 1962.

Tuzmukhamedov, R. A. *Natsional'nyi suvernitet.* Moscow: Izdatel'stvo Instituta Mezhdunarodnykh Otnoshenii, 1963.

Ulam, Adam B. *The New Face of Soviet Totalitarianism.* New York: Frederick A. Praeger, 1965.

Von Harpe, Werner. *Die Sowiet Union. Finnland und Skandinavien, 1945–1955.* Tübingen: (Arbeitsgemeinschaft für Osteuropaforschung, No. 12, ed. by Werner Markert), 1956.

Von Laue, Theodore. *Why Lenin? Why Stalin? A reappraisal of the Russian Revolution, 1900–1930.* Philadelphia: Lippincott, 1964.

Von Mende, Gerhard. *Der nationale Kampf der Russlandtürken.* Berlin: Weidmannsche Buchhandlung, 1936.

Vyshinsky, Andrei Y. *The Law of the Soviet State.* Trans. Hugh W. Babb. New York: Macmillan Co., 1948.

Weinstock, S. A. "Some Factors that Retard or Accelerate the Rate of Acculturation, with Specific Reference to Hungarian Immigrants," *Human Relations* No. 17 (1964), pp. 321–40.

Wheeler, Geoffrey E. *The Peoples of Soviet Central Asia.* London: The Bodley Head, 1966.

———. *Racial Problems in Soviet Muslim Asia.* London: Oxford University Press, 1960.

Wurm, Stephan. *Turkic Peoples of the USSR.* London: Central Asian Research Centre, 1954.

Yarmolinsky, Avrahm. *The Jews and Other Minor Nationalities under the Soviets.* New York: Vanguard Press, 1928.

Zhuchkov, B. *Lenin: Ways of Settling the Nationality Problem.* Moscow: Novosti Press Agency Publishing House, 1966.

APPENDIX: THE POPULATION OF SOVIET NATIONALITIES, 1970

The following statistics were not released in time for use by the authors of this study.

Extract from Preliminary Report, Soviet Census, January 1970

["Naselenie nashei strany. Soobshchenie Tsentral'nogo Statisticheskogo Upravleniia pri Sovete Ministrov SSSR. O vozrastnoi strukture, urovne obrazovaniia, natsional'nom sostave, iazykakh i istochnikakh sredstv sushchestvovaniia naseleniia SSSR po dannym vsesoiuznoi perepisi naseleniia na 15 ianvaria 1970 goda," *Pravda* (April 17, 1971), pp. 1–3.]

Nationality in USSR as a whole (thousands)		*Nationality: number in* *titular administrative unit* (thousands)	
Ukrainian	40,753	UkSSR	35,284
Uzbek	9,195	UzSSR	7,734
Belorussian	9,052	BSSR	7,290
*Tatar	5,931		
Kazakh	5,299	KazSSR	4,161
Azerbaijan	4,380	AzSSR	3,777
Armenian	3,559	ArmSSR	2,208
Georgian	3,245	GSSR	3,131
Moldavian	2,698	MSSR	2,304
Lithuanian	2,665	LitSSR	2,507
Jewish	2,151		
Tajik	2,136	TajSSR	1,630
German	1,846		
Chuvash	1,694		
Turkmen	1,525	TurSSR	1,417
Kirgiz	1,452	KirSSR	1,285
Latvian	1,430	LatSSR	1,342
Dagestan	1,365		
Mordvin	1,263		
Bashkir	1,240		
Polish	1,167		
Estonian	1,007	EstSSR	925
(Russians	129,015)	(RSFSR	107,748)

* Data concerning the nationality composition of titular administrative units below the union-republic level are not yet available.

Nationality in USSR as a whole

(thousands)		(thousands)		(thousands)	
Udmurt	704	Ingush	158	Khakass	67
Chechen	613	Gagauz	157	Balkar	60
Mari	599	Nationalities of		Altay	56
Ossetic	488	the North,		Cherkess	40
Komi	322	Siberia, and		Dungan	39
Komi-Permyak	153	the Far East	151	Iranian (Persian)	28
Koryak	357	Karelian	146	Abazin	25
Bulgarian	351	Tuvin	139	Assyrian	24
Greek	337	Kalmyk	137	Czech	21
Buryat	315	Rumanian	119	Tat	17
Yakut	296	Karachay	113	Shor	16
Kabardin	280	Adyge	100	Slovak	12
Karakalpak	236	Kurd	89	Other national-	
Gypsy	175	Finnish	85	ities	138
Uyghur	173	Abkhaz	83		
Hungarian	166	Turk	79		

TOTAL NATIONALITIES   112,717

Preliminary reports based upon the Soviet census taken in 1970 and printed in *Pravda,* April 17, 1971, pp. 1–3, are reproduced on the following pages. Data reproduced on the end sheets of this volume appeared in *Pravda,* April 19, 1970, pp. 1–2.

Сообщение Центрального статистического

О возрастной структуре, уровне образования,
средств существования населения СССР по данным

В апреле 1970 года в печати были опубликованы краткие предварительные итоги переписи населения. В настоящее время ЦСУ СССР закончило разработку первой очереди основных итогов переписи, характеризующих состав населения по полу, возрасту, состоянию в браке, образованию, национальности, языку и источнику средств существования.

Ниже приводятся данные переписи 1970 года в сравнении с данными предыдущих переписей.

1. Общая численность наличного населения Советского Союза на 15 января 1970 года по уточненным данным составила 241 720 134 человека, в том числе 111 399 377 мужчин и 130 320 757 женщин; численность городского населения составила 135 991 514 человек, сельского — 105 728 620 человек.

Изменение численности городского и сельского населения страны в современных границах характеризуется следующими данными:

	Все население (млн. человек)	В том числе		В процентах ко всему населению	
		город-ское	сель-ское	город-ское	сель-ское
1913 г.	159,2	28,5	130,7	18	82
1939 г.	190,7	60,4	130,3	32	68
1959 г.	208,8	100,0	108,8	48	52
1970 г.	241,7	136,0	105,7	56	44

Увеличение городского населения за период с 1959 по 1969 год на 36 миллионов произошло за счет естественного прироста в городах, составившего за одиннадцать лет 14.6 миллиона, за счет преобразования сельских пунктов с населением 5 миллионов в городские и за счет перехода из села в город более 16 миллионов сельских жителей. Переход сельского населения в города связан со значительным ростом промышленного производства и стал возможным благодаря возрос-

шему уровню механизации и повышению производительности труда в социалистическом сельском хозяйстве.

Естественный прирост населения в сельских местностях за этот период составил более 18 миллионов, однако численность сельского населения по указанным выше причинам не увеличилась, а сократилась на 3 миллиона человек.

2. Численность населения союзных республик и отдельных экономических районов за период между последними переписями изменилась так:

	Численность населения (тыс. человек)		1970 г. в процентах к 1959 г.
	на 15 января 1959 г	на 15 января 1970 г	
СССР	208 827	241 720	116
РСФСР	117 534	130 079	111
Украинская ССР	41 869	47 126	113

Белорусская ССР
Узбекская ССР
Казахская ССР
Грузинская ССР
Азербайджанская ССР
Литовская ССР
Молдавская ССР
Латвийская ССР
Киргизская ССР
Таджикская ССР
Армянская ССР
Туркменская ССР
Эстонская ССР

Экономические районы РС
  Северо-Западный
  Центральный
  Волго-Вятский
  Центрально-Черноземный
  Поволжский
  Северо-Кавказский
  Уральский
  Западно-Сибирский
  Восточно-Сибирский
  Дальневосточный
  Калининградская область
Экономические районы УС
  Донецко-Приднепровский
  Юго-Западный
  Южный

3. Изменение возрастной структуры населения СССР

	Тысяч чел	
	1939 г.	1959
Все население	190 678	208 8
в том числе:		
0— 4 лет	23 716	24 3
5— 9 »	19 760	22 0
10—15 »	28 366	17 1
16—19 »	13 029	14 6
20—24 »	15 786	20 3
25—29 »	18 520	18 1
30—34 »	15 598	18 9
35—39 »	12 958	11 5
40—44 »	9 603	10 4
45—49 »	7 776	12 2
50—54 »	6 636	10 4
55—59 »	5 897	8 6

...ациональном составе, языках и источниках

...союзной переписи населения на 15 января 1970 года

8 056	9 002	112
8 261	11 960	145
9 153	12 849	140
4 044	4 686	116
3 698	5 117	138
2 711	3 128	115
2 883	3 569	124
2 093	2 364	113
2 066	2 933	142
1 981	2 900	146
1 763	2 492	141
1 516	2 159	142
1 197	1 356	113
0 865	12 157	112
5 718	27 652	108
3 252	8 348	101
7 769	7 998	103
9 675	18 374	115
601	14 281	123
4 184	15 185	107
252	12 109	108
473	7 463	115
4 834	5 780	120
611	732	120
766	20 057	113
028	20 689	109
075	6 380	126

...теризуется следующими ...ми:

	В процентах ко всему населению		
...г.	1939 г	1959 г.	1970 г.
20	100,0	100,0	100,0
10	12,4	11,7	8,5
76	10,4	10,5	10,1
24	14,9	8,2	12,3
263	6,8	7,0	7,1
05	8,3	9,7	7,1
70	9,7	8,7	5,7
45	8,2	9,1	8,7
94	6,8	5,6	6,9
03	5,0	5,0	7,9
56	4,1	5,9	5,1
78	3,5	5,0	3,8
13	3,1	4,2	5,0

60—69 ›	8 535	11 736	17 595	4,5	5,6	7,3
70 лет и старше	4 462	7 972	10 919	2,3	3,8	4,5
Из общей численности населения находилось в трудоспособном возрасте (мужчин 16—59 лет, женщин 16—54 лет)	102 241	119 822	130 487	53,6	57,4	54,0

В связи с некоторым снижением рождаемости в последние годы уменьшился процент детей младших возрастов.

В связи с увеличением средней продолжительности предстоящей жизни, составляющей сейчас 70 лет, значительно возрос процент лиц старших возрастов.

4. Ниже приводятся данные о численности мужчин и женщин по отдельным возрастным группам:

	Численность на 15 января 1970 г. (тысяч)		На 1 000 женщин данного возраста приходится мужчин		
	мужчин	женщин	1939 г.	1959 г.	1970 г.
Все население в том числе:	111 399	130 321	921	819	855
0—4 лет	10 435	10 075	1 020	1 040	1 036
5—9 ›	12 475	12 001	997	1 035	1 039
10—15 ›	15 145	14 579	1 006	1 037	1 039
16—19 ›	8 810	8 453	955	1 002	1 042
20—24 ›	8 627	8 478	937	978	1 018
25—29 ›	6 813	6 957	953	962	979
30—34 ›	10 408	10 737	988	829	969
35—39 ›	8 140	8 454	875	641	963
40—44 ›	8 759	10 244	867	624	855
45—49 ›	4 744	7 512	833	623	631
50—54 ›	3 430	5 648	828	623	607
55—59 ›	4 273	7 740	656	502	552
60—69 ›	5 922	11 673	688	537	507
70 лет и старше	3 288	7 631	595	468	431
Из общей численности в возрасте:					
0—43 лет	88 243	88 075	968	932	1 002
44 лет и старше	23 026	42 107	733	558	547

В 1970 году процент мужчин во всем населении составил 46,1, женщин — 53,9, в городе — соответственно 46,3 и 53,7, в селе — 45,8 и 54,2. Такое соотношение между чис-

(Окончание на 3-й стр.)

НАСЕЛЕНИЕ Н

(Окончание.
Начало на 1-й стр.)

ленностью мужчин и женщин сложилось за счет старших возрастов и вызвано, главным образом, последствиями войн.

Разрыв в численности мужчин и женщин постепенно сокращается: во всем населении в 1959 году женщин было больше, чем мужчин, на 20,7 млн., а в 1970 году — на 18,9 млн.; в возрасте до 43 лет включительно женщин было больше, чем мужчин, на 5,5 миллиона, а сейчас число мужчин и женщин в этих возрастах стало одинаковым.

5. Число лиц, состоящих в браке, изменилось по сравнению с 1939 и 1959 годами так:

	На 1 000 лиц данного пола и возраста состояло в браке					
	мужчин			женщин		
	1939	1959	1970	1939	1959	1970
Всего в возрасте 16 лет и старше	690	695	722	605	522	579
в том числе в возрасте:						
16—19 лет	27	26	21	140	112	105
20—24 »	336	274	289	614	501	559
25—29 »	738	800	772	787	759	827
30—34 »	891	922	887	818	776	853
35—39 »	929	953	933	800	725	839
40—44 »	940	962	946	759	623	790
45—49 »	935	963	952	688	549	719
50—54 »	921	956	952	593	485	603
55—59 »	900	943	948	497	433	501
60—69 »	823	908	920	363	361	371
70 лет и старше	611	739	758	168	169	196

В 1970 году в СССР состояли в браке 107,2 миллиона мужчин и женщин против 86,5 миллиона в 1959 году и 76,6 миллиона в 1939 году. Число состоящих в браке увеличилось по сравнению с 1959 годом на 23,8 проц., при этом число женщин, состоящих в браке, увеличилось за этот период во всех возрастных группах, начиная с 19 лет.

Из каждой тысячи мужчин в 1970 году в браке состояли 722 человека, а из тысячи женщин 579 человек. Меньшая доля женщин, состоящих в браке, по сравнению с мужчинами объясняется превышением численности женщин над численностью мужчин (как сказано выше, при переписи учтено 111,4 миллиона мужчин и 130,3 миллиона женщин).

6. Изменение уровня грамотности населения в 1970 году по сравнению с предыдущими переписями видно из следующих данных:

	Процент грамотных в возрасте 9—49 лет		
	оба пола	мужчины	женщины
Городское и сельское население			
1897 г.	28,4	40,3	16,6
1926 г.	56,6	71,5	42,7
1939 г.	87,4	93,5	81,6
1959 г.	98,5	99,3	97,8
1970 г.	99,7	99,8	99,7
Городское население			
1897 г.	57,0	66,1	45,7
1926 г.	80,9	88,0	73,9
1939 г.	93,8	97,1	90,7
1959 г.	98,7	99,5	98,1
1970 г.	99,8	99,9	99,8
Сельское население			
1897 г.	23,8	35,5	12,5
1926 г.	50,6	67,3	35,4
1939 г.	84,0	91,6	76,8
1959 г.	98,2	99,1	97,5
1970 г.	99,5	99,6	99,4

В дореволюционной России почти три четверти населения было неграмотным. Народы Крайнего Севера, Средней Азии и других окраин страны были почти сплошь неграмотными. Грамотность сельского населения, численность которого составляла более 80 проц. населения страны, была

родского и сельского населения. В 1970 г. было учтено всего лишь 170 тыс. неграмотных мужчин и 209 тыс. женщин в этом возрасте, преимущественно из числа лиц, не имеющих возможности посещать школу по причине физических недостатков или хронической болезни. Неграмот-

10. Доля лиц, имеющих высшее и среднее образование, у мужчин и женщин сближается, а у работающих мужчин и женщин она стала практически одинаковой:

	На 1000 человек соответствующего пола приходится лиц с образованием					
	высшим и средним (полным и неполным)		в том числе			
			высшим		средним	
	мужчины	женщины	мужчины	женщины	мужчины	женщины
Все население в возрасте 10 лет и старше:						
1939 г.	127	90	11	5	116	85
1959 г.	392	338	27	20	365	318
1970 г.	522	452	48	37	474	415
Лица, имеющие занятия:						
1939 г.	136	104	16	9	120	95
1959 г.	434	431	34	32	400	399
1970 г.	654	651	68	62	586	589

11. Соотношение доли лиц, имеющих высшее и среднее образование, в городе и селе изменилось так:

	На 1000 человек населения приходится лиц с образованием					
	высшим и средним (полным и неполным)		в том числе			
			высшим		средним	
	город	село	город	село	город	село
Все население в возрасте 10 лет и старше:						
1939 г.	218	52	19	2	199	50
1959 г.	469	256	40	7	429	249
1970 г.	592	332	62	14	530	318
Лица, имеющие занятия:						
1939 г.	242	63	32	3	210	60
1959 г.	564	316	59	11	505	305
1970 г.	748	499	90	25	658	474

К концу 1970 года доля лиц со средним (полным и неполным) и высшим образованием составила в городах более трех четвертей, а в селах более половины занятого населения.

12. По союзным республикам уровень образования населения изменился следующим образом:

	На 1000 человек населения в возрасте 10 лет и старше приходится лиц с высшим и средним (полным и неполным) образованием			На 1000 занятых имеют высшее и среднее (полное и неполное) образование		
	1939	1959	1970	1939	1959	1970
СССР	108	361	483	123	433	653
РСФСР	109	361	489	124	440	656
Украинская ССР	120	373	494	139	438	668
Белорусская ССР	92	304	440	113	331	594
Узбекская ССР	55	352	456	61	447	647
Казахская ССР	83	348	470	99	447	655
Грузинская ССР	165	448	554	163	492	711
Азербайджанская ССР	113	400	471	112	423	674
Литовская ССР	81	232	382	св. нет	250	616
Молдавская ССР	57	264	397	св. нет	280	508
Латвийская ССР	176	431	517	св. нет	502	661
Киргизская ССР	46	342	452	56	429	643
Таджикская ССР	40	325	420	45	407	608
Армянская ССР	128	445	516	135	527	697
Туркменская ССР	65	387	475	78	497	682
Эстонская ССР	161	386	506	св. нет	448	660

13. По автономным республикам изменение уровня образования характеризуется следующими данными:

...мы	6,7	8,8	99,4	99,4	39,8	9,6
...ва	1 285	1 263	78,1	77,8	65,7	8,1
...иры	989	1 240	61,9	66,2	53,3	2,6
...ки	1 380	1 167	45,2	32,5	37,0	12,7
...щы	989	1 007	95,2	95,5	29,0	2,0
...рты	625	704	89,1	82,6	63,3	6,9
...ицы	419	613	98,8	98,7	66,7	1,0
...йцы	504	599	95,1	91,2	62,4	6,2
...ины	413	488	89,1	88,6	58,6	10,7
...и коми-...ки	431	475	88,7	83,7	64,8	5,2

з них:

...и	287	322	89,3	82,7	63,1	5,4
...и-пермяки	144	153	87,6	85,8	68,5	4,6
...цы	314	357	79,3	68,6	50,3	1,7
...ры	324	351	79,4	73,1	58,8	7,9
...ы	309	337	41,5	39,3	35,4	14,5
...ы	253	315	94,9	92,6	66,7	2,7
...и	233	296	97,6	96,3	41,7	1,1
...одинцы	204	280	97,9	98,0	71,4	0,8
...калпаки	173	236	95,0	96,6	10,4	3,6
...не	132	175	59,3	70,8	53,0	16,4
...ры	95	173	85,0	88,5	35,6	9,5
...ы	155	166	97,2	96,6	25,8	0,9
...ши	106	158	97,9	97,4	71,2	0,9
...зы	124	157	94,0	93,6	63,3	8,6

...ности Севера,
...бири и Дальне-
...Востока

	130	151	75,9	67,4	52,5	7,1

з них:

...цы	23	29	84,7	83,4	55,1	3,3
...нки	25	25	55,9	51,3	54,9	7,5
...ты	19	21	77,0	68,9	48,1	7,3
...ны	12	14	93,9	82,6	58,7	4,8
...ы	9,1	12	81,4	56,0	46,4	17,6
...айцы	8,0	10	86,3	69,1	58,0	9,4
...си	6,45	7,7	59,2	52,4	38,6	5,4
...яки	6,3	7,5	90,5	81,1	64,3	5,5
...ганы	3,9	4,9	93,9	89,8	61,9	3,2
...хи	3,7	4,4	76,3	49,5	43,8	6,6
...купы	3,8	4,3	50,6	51,1	40,8	8,6
...чи	2,1	2,4	84,9	60,8	56,8	7,0
...мы	1,8	1,9	69,9	56,2	52,9	9,3
...гейцы	1,4	1,5	73,7	55,1	46,0	10,1
...льмены	1,1	1,3	36,0	35,7	32,5	4,3
...и	1,0	1,2	77,1	74,9	59,1	2,0
...чи	0,8	1,1	68,4	48,6	44,4	6,6
...насаны	0,75	1,0	93,4	75,4	40,0	15,7
...агиры	0,4	0,6	52,5	46,8	29,1	32,8
...цы	167	146	71,3	63,0	59,1	15,1
...ыки	100	139	99,1	98,7	38,9	0,4
...ны	106	137	91,0	91,7	81,1	1,5
...ны	106	119	83,3	63,9	28,5	16,3
...чаевцы	81	113	96,8	98,1	67,6	1,2
...ейцы	80	100	96,8	96,5	67,9	1,4
...цы	59	89	89,9	87,6	19,9	36,2
...зы	93	85	59,5	51,0	47,0	8,5
...зы	65	83	95,0	95,9	59,2	2,8
...ы	35	79	82,2	92,3	22,4	31,2
...сы	57	67	86,0	83,7	65,5	3,4
...арцы	42	60	97,0	97,2	71,5	2,5
...йцы	45	56	88,5	87,2	54,9	3,2
...есы	30	40	89,7	92,0	70,0	2,5
...ане	22	39	95,1	94,3	48,0	5,7
...цы (персы)	21	28	44,7	36,9	33,3	12,7
...ины	20	25	94,8	96,1	69,5	6,1
...зы	22	24	64,3	64,5	46,2	14,7
...йцы	25	21	49,0	42,9	35,6	21,4
...	11	17	70,9	72,5	57,5	15,3
...ы	15	16	83,7	73,5	59,8	5,9
...ки	15	12	61,2	52,0	39,3	31,3
...е национальности	108	126	61,6	69,4	38,4	12,8

...он переписи национальность и языки записывались на осно-
...обственных заявлений переписываемых. Национальность де-
...записывалась по заявлениям родителей.

...го при переписи указали ...ловек назвали русский язык в
...естве родного языка рус- качестве второго языка, кото-
...язык 141,8 миллиона че- рым свободно владеют.
...(при переписи 1959 го-
...124,1 миллиона чело- 15. Изменение численности
...из них 128,8 миллиона населения отдельных нацио-
...их и 13 миллионов чело- нальностей по союзным рес-
...других национальностей. публикам характеризуется
...е того, 41,9 миллиона че- следующими данными:

евреи	95	103	1,2	0,9
туркмены	55	71	0,7	0,6
другие национальности	288	365	3,5	3,0
Казахская ССР — всего	9 153	12 849	100,0	100,0
в том числе:				
казахи	2 723	4 161	29,8	32,4
русские	3 950	5 500	43,2	42,8
украинцы	756	930	8,3	7,2
татары	189	284	2,1	2,2
узбеки	130	208	1,4	1,6
белорусы	106	198	1,2	1,5
уйгуры	60	121	0,7	0,9
корейцы	71	78	0,8	0,6
дунгане	10	17	0,1	0,1
другие национальности	1 158	1 352	12,4	10,7
Грузинская ССР — всего	4 044	4 686	100,0	100,0
в том числе:				
грузины	2 601	3 131	64,3	66,8
осетины	141	150	3,5	3,2
абхазы	63	79	1,6	1,7
армяне	443	452	11,0	9,7
русские	408	397	10,1	8,5
азербайджанцы	154	218	3,8	4,6
греки	73	89	1,8	1,9
евреи	52	55	1,3	1,2
украинцы	52	50	1,3	1,1
курды	16	21	0,4	0,4
другие национальности	41	44	0,9	0,9
Азербайджанская ССР — всего	3 698	5 117	100,0	100,0
в том числе:				
азербайджанцы	2 494	3 777	67,5	73,8
русские	501	510	13,6	10,0
армяне	442	484	12,0	9,4
лезгины	98	137	2,7	2,7
другие национальности	163	209	4,2	4,1
Литовская ССР — всего	2 711	3 128	100,0	100,0
в том числе:				
литовцы	2 151	2 507	79,3	80,1
русские	231	268	8,5	8,6
поляки	230	240	8,5	7,7
белорусы	30	45	1,1	1,5
украинцы	18	25	0,7	0,8
евреи	25	24	0,9	0,8
другие национальности	26	19	1,0	0,5
Молдавская ССР — всего	2 885	3 569	100,0	100,0
в том числе:				
молдаване	1 887	2 304	65,4	64,6
украинцы	421	507	14,6	14,2
русские	293	414	10,2	11,6
гагаузы	96	125	3,3	3,5
евреи	95	98	3,3	2,7
болгары	62	74	2,1	2,1
другие национальности	31	47	1,1	1,3
Латвийская ССР—всего	2 093	2 364	100,0	100,0
в том числе:				
латыши	1 298	1 342	62,0	56,8
русские	556	705	26,6	29,8
белорусы	62	95	2,9	4,0
поляки	60	63	2,9	2,7
украинцы	29	53	1,4	2,3
литовцы	32	41	1,5	1,7
евреи	37	37	1,7	1,6
другие национальности	19	28	1,0	1,1
Киргизская ССР — всего	2 066	2 933	100,0	100,0
в том числе:				
киргизы	837	1 285	40,5	43,8
русские	624	856	30,2	29,2
узбеки	219	333	10,6	11,3
украинцы	137	120	6,6	4,1
татары	56	69	2,7	2,4
уйгуры	14	25	0,7	0,8
казахи	20	22	1,0	0,8
таджики	15	22	0,7	0,7
другие национальности	144	201	7,0	6,9
Таджикская ССР — всего	1 981	2 900	100,0	100,0
в том числе:				
таджики	1 051	1 630	53,1	56,2
узбеки	455	666	23,0	23,0
русские	263	344	13,3	11,9
татары	57	71	2,9	2,4
киргизы	26	35		

В дореволюционной России почти три четверти населения *было неграмотным. Народы Крайнего Севера, Средней Азии и других окраин страны* были почти сплошь неграмотными. Грамотность сельского населения, численность которого составляла более 80 проц. населения страны, была значительно ниже грамотности городского населения. Уровень грамотности среди мужчин на селе был почти вдвое, а у женщин в 3,7 раза ниже, чем в городе.

В результате осуществления мероприятий по ликвидации неграмотности в первые годы Советской власти процент грамотного населения уже к концу 1926 г. увеличился почти вдвое. При переписи 1959 г. 98,7 проц. городского населения и 98,2 проц. сельского населения в возрасте 9—49 лет были грамотными, т. е. уже тогда были почти полностью ликвидированы различия в грамотности городского и сельского населения. В 1970 г. было учтено всего лишь 170 тыс. неграмотных мужчин в 269 тыс. женщин в этом возрасте, преимущественно из числа лиц, не имеющих возможности посещать школу по причине физических недостатков или хронической болезни. Неграмотность ликвидирована во всех союзных республиках.

Ликвидация неграмотности в стране сопровождалась значительным ростом числа лиц, имеющих высшее и среднее образование. При этом более высокими темпами рос уровень образования населения Таджикской, Киргизской, Узбекской, Туркменской, Молдавской, Казахской ССР и народов Крайнего Севера.

7. Уровень образования населения СССР непрерывно повышается.

Ниже приводятся данные об изменении численности лиц, имеющих высшее и среднее образование:

	Тысяч человек		1970 г. в проц. к 1959 г.	На 1 000 человек населения в возрасте 10 лет и старше	
	1959 г.	1970 г.		1959 г	1970 г
Всего лиц, имеющих высшее и среднее (полное и неполное) образование	58 708	95 046	162	361	483
в том числе					
высшее законченное	3 778	8 262	219	23	42
высшее незаконченное	1 738	2 605	150	11	13
среднее специальное	7 870	13 420	171	48	68
среднее общее	9 936	23 391	235	61	119
неполное среднее	35 386	47 368	134	218	241

8. Еще более увеличилась доля лиц с высшим и средним образованием среди работающего населения:

	Тысяч человек		1970 г. в проц. к 1959 г.	На 1000 занятых	
	1959 г.	1970 г.		1959 г.	1970 г.
Из общей численности лиц, имеющих занятия, имеют высшее и среднее (полное и неполное) образование	42 932	75 447	176	433	653
в том числе:					
высшее законченное	3 306	7 544	228	33	65
высшее незаконченное	942	1 457	155	9	13
среднее специальное	6 605	12 123	184	67	105
среднее общее	6 347	18 347	289	64	159
неполное среднее	25 732	35 976	140	260	311

В то же время доля лиц с начальным и незаконченным семилетним и восьмилетним образованием среди работающего населения уменьшилась с 33 проц. в 1959 году до 25 проц. в 1970 году и доля лиц с образованием ниже начального — с 24 проц. до 10 проц.

9. Изменение доли лиц, имеющих высшее и среднее образование, за период между переписями 1939, 1959 и 1970 годов характеризуется следующим:

	На 1 000 человек населения приходится лиц с образованием		
	высшим и средним (полным и неполным)	в том числе	
		высшим	средним
Все население в возрасте 10 лет и старше:			
1939 г.	108	8	100
1959 г.	361	23	348
1970 г.	483	42	441
Лица, имеющие занятия:			
1939 г.	123	13	110
1959 г.	433	33	400
1970 г.	653	65	588

Грузинская ССР	165	448	554	163	492	711
Азербайджанская ССР	113	400	471	122	473	674
Литовская ССР	81	232	382	св. нет	250	496
Молдавская ССР	57	264	397	св. нет	280	508
Латвийская ССР	176	431	517	св. нет	502	661
Киргизская ССР	46	342	452	56	429	643
Таджикская ССР	40	325	420	45	407	602
Армянская ССР	128	445	516	135	527	697
Туркменская ССР	65	387	475	78	497	682
Эстонская ССР	161	386	506	св. нет	448	660

13. По автономным республикам изменение уровня образования населения характеризуется следующими данными:

	На 1000 человек населения в возрасте 10 лет и старше приходится лиц с высшим и средним (полным и неполным) образованием			На 1000 заняты средним и высшим (полное и неполное) образование		
	1939	1959	1970	1939	1959	1970
Башкирская АССР	67	332	441	75	419	635
Бурятская АССР	86	310	448	108	385	604
Дагестанская АССР	63	281	358	72	322	503
Кабардино-Балкарская АССР	86	352	469	97	440	657
Калмыцкая АССР	51	244	381	73	304	521
Карельская АССР	132	361	493	155	427	638
Коми АССР	96	417	540	99	467	686
Марийская АССР	73	317	438	71	382	615
Мордовская АССР	68	292	421	70	364	595
Северо-Осетинская АССР	150	430	519	191	520	694
Татарская АССР	89	359	468	100	456	664
Тувинская АССР	св. нет	246	414	св. нет	291	586
Удмуртская АССР	82	318	456	88	393	636
Чечено-Ингушская АССР	71	299	361	87	386	516
Чувашская АССР	99	365	467	94	441	665
Якутская АССР	89	349	501	104	415	653
Каракалпакская АССР	28	272	406	37	358	611
Абхазская АССР	127	417	523	134	459	687
Аджарская АССР	165	420	541	177	475	708
Нахичеванская АССР	74	383	446	78	442	667

14. Распределение населения СССР по национальностям и родному языку изменилось так (национальности расположены в убывающем порядке по их численности в 1970 году):

	Число лиц данной национальности (тысяч)		Из них считают родным языком этой же национальности (в процентах)		Кроме того, свободно владеют вторым языком народов СССР (в процентах)	
	1959	1970	1959	1970	русским	другим
Все население СССР	208 827	241 720	94,3	93,9	17,3	3,0
Русские	114 114	129 015	99,8	99,8	0,1	3,0
Украинцы	37 253	40 753	87,7	85,7	36,3	6,0
Узбеки	6 015	9 195	98,4	98,6	14,5	3,2
Белорусы	7 913	9 052	84,2	80,6	49,0	7,1
Татары	4 968	5 931	92,1	89,2	62,5	5,4
Казахи	3 622	5 299	98,4	98,0	41,8	1,8
Азербайджанцы	2 940	4 380	97,6	98,2	16,6	2,2
Армяне	2 787	3 559	89,9	91,4	30,1	6,6
Грузины	2 692	3 245	98,6	98,4	21,3	1,5
Молдаване	2 214	2 698	95,2	95,0	36,1	3,0
Литовцы	2 326	2 665	97,8	97,9	35,9	1,5
Евреи	2 268	2 151	21,5	17,7	16,3	28,8
Таджики	1 397	2 136	98,1	98,5	15,4	12,0
Немцы	1 620	1 846	75,0	66,8	59,6	1,2
Чуваши	1 470	1 694	90,8	86,9	58,4	5,4
Туркмены	1 002	1 525	98,9	98,9	15,4	1,7
Киргизы	969	1 452	98,7	98,8	19,1	3,5
Латыши	1 400	1 430	95,1	95,2	45,2	2,3
Народности Дагестана	945	1 365	96,2	96,5	41,7	8,6
из них:						
аварцы	270	396	97,2	97,2	37,8	5,5
лезгины	223	324	92,7	93,9	31,6	22,0
даргинцы	158	231	98,6	98,4	43,0	2,4
кумыки	135	189	98,0	98,4	57,4	1,7
лакцы	64	86	95,8	95,6	56,0	3,3
табасараны	35	55	99,2	98,9	31,9	10,0
ногайцы	39	52	90,0	89,8	68,5	1,4
рутульцы	6,7	12	99,9	98,9	30,7	18,2
цахуры	7,3	11	99,2	96,5	12,2	43,5

Ниже приводятся данные об изменении численности лиц, имеющих высшее и среднее образование среди работающего населения:

Центральное стат*

* При переписи национальность и языки записывались на осно-
ве собственных заявлений переписываемых. Национальность детей записывалась по заявлениям родителей.

Всего при переписи указали человек назвали русский язык в
качестве родного языка рус- качестве второго языка, кото-
ский язык 141,8 миллиона чело- рым свободно владеют.
век (при переписи 1959 го-
да — 124,1 миллиона чело- **15. Изменение численности**
век), из них 128,8 миллиона населения отдельных нацио-
русских и 13 миллионов чело- нальностей по союзным рес-
век других национальностей. публикам характеризуется
Кроме того, 41,9 миллиона че- следующими данными:

	Численность (тысяч)		В процентах к итогу	
	1959 г.	1970 г.	1959 г.	1970 г.
РСФСР — всего	117 534	130 079	100,0	100,0
в том числе:				
русские	97 864	107 748	83,3	82,8
татары	4 075	4 758	3,5	3,7
украинцы	3 359	3 346	2,9	2,6
чуваши	1 436	1 637	1,2	1,3
башкиры	954	1 181	0,8	0,9
мордва	1 211	1 177	1,0	0,9
народности Дагестана	797	1 152	0,7	0,9
белорусы	844	964	0,7	0,7
евреи	875	808	0,7	0,6
удмурты	616	678	0,5	0,5
марийцы	498	581	0,4	0,4
чеченцы	261	572	0,2	0,4
казахи	382	478	0,3	0,4
коми и коми-пермяки	426	466	0,4	0,4
из них:				
коми	283	316	0,3	0,3
коми-пермяки	143	150	0,1	0,1
осетины	248	313	0,2	0,2
буряты	252	313	0,2	0,2
армяне	256	299	0,2	0,2
якуты	232	295	0,2	0,2
кабардинцы	201	277	0,2	0,2
народности Севера, Сибири и Дальнего Востока	128	149	0,1	0,1
карелы	164	141	0,1	0,1
тувинцы	100	139	0,1	0,1
ингуши	56	137	0,05	0,1
калмыки	101	131	0,1	0,1
карачаевцы	71	107	0,1	0,1
адыгейцы	79	98	0,1	0,1
азербайджанцы	71	96	0,1	0,1
молдаване	62	88	0,05	0,1
грузины	58	69	0,05	0,1
хакасы	56	65	0,05	0,05
алтайцы	45	55	0,04	0,04
балкарцы	35	53	0,03	0,04
черкесы	29	38	0,02	0,03
другие национальности	1 692	1 670	1,4	1,3
Украинская ССР — всего	41 869	47 126	100,0	100,0
в том числе:				
украинцы	32 158	35 284	76,8	74,9
русские	7 091	9 126	16,9	19,4
евреи	840	777	2,0	1,6
белорусы	291	386	0,7	0,8
поляки	363	295	0,9	0,6
молдаване	242	266	0,6	0,6
болгары	219	234	0,5	0,5
другие национальности	665	758	1,6	1,6
Белорусская ССР — всего	8 056	9 002	100,0	100,0
в том числе:				
белорусы	6 532	7 290	81,1	81,0
русские	660	938	8,2	10,4
поляки	539	383	6,7	4,3
украинцы	133	191	1,7	2,1
евреи	150	148	1,9	1,6
другие национальности	42	52	0,4	0,6
Узбекская ССР — всего	8 261	11 960	100,0	100,0
в том числе:				
узбеки	5 044	7 734	61,1	64,7
каракалпаки	168	230	2,0	1,9
русские	1 114	1 496	13,5	12,5
татары	448	578	5,4	4,8
казахи	407	549	4,9	4,6
таджики	314	457	3,8	3,8
корейцы	142	151	1,7	1,3
евреи	93	115	1,1	1,0
киргизы	93	111	1,1	0,9

украинцы	137	120	6,6	4,1
татары	56	69	2,7	2,4
уйгуры	14	25	0,7	0,8
казахи	20	22	1,0	0,7
таджики	15	22	0,7	0,7
другие национальности	144	201	7,0	6,9
Таджикская ССР — всего	1 981	2 900	100,0	100,0
в том числе:				
таджики	1 051	1 630	53,1	56,2
узбеки	455	666	23,0	23,0
русские	263	344	13,3	11,9
татары	57	71	2,9	2,4
киргизы	26	35	1,3	1,2
украинцы	27	32	1,4	1,1
казахи	13	8,3	0,6	0,3
другие национальности	89	114	4,4	3,9
Армянская ССР — всего	1 763	2 492	100,0	100,0
в том числе:				
армяне	1 552	2 208	88,0	88,6
азербайджанцы	108	148	6,1	5,9
русские	56	66	3,2	2,7
курды	26	37	1,5	1,5
другие национальности	21	33	1,2	1,3
Туркменская ССР — всего	1 516	2 159	100,0	100,0
в том числе:				
туркмены	924	1 417	60,9	65,6
русские	263	313	17,3	14,5
узбеки	125	179	8,3	8,3
казахи	70	69	4,6	3,2
татары	30	36	2,0	1,7
украинцы	21	35	1,4	1,6
армяне	20	23	1,3	1,1
другие национальности	63	87	4,2	4,0
Эстонская ССР — всего	1 197	1 356	100,0	100,0
в том числе:				
эстонцы	893	925	74,6	68,2
русские	240	335	20,1	24,7
украинцы	16	28	1,3	2,1
финны	17	19	1,4	1,4
белорусы	11	19	0,9	1,4
евреи	5,4	5,3	0,5	0,4
другие национальности	15	25	1,2	1,8

**16. Распределение населе- ществования в 1970 году ха-
ния по источникам средств су- рактеризуется следующим:**

	Численность (тысяч)	В процентах к итогу
Все население	241 720	100,0
Лица, имеющие занятия (кроме занятых только в личном подсобном сельском хозяйстве)	115 493	47,8
Пенсионеры и другие лица, находящиеся на обеспечении государства *	33 107	13,7
Стипендиаты	3 547	1,5
Иждивенцы отдельных лиц (дети, пожилые и другие лица, занятые только домашним хозяйством и воспитанием детей), а также члены семей колхозников, рабочих и служащих, занятые в личном подсобном сельском хозяйстве	89 108	36,8
Имеющие другие источники средств существования и не указавшие источник	465	0,2

* Общая численность пенсионеров на начало 1970 года составляла 40,1 млн человек. При переписи к группе пенсионеров от-
несли себя лишь те лица, для которых главным источником
средств существования является пенсия. Пенсионеры, находив-
шиеся на постоянной работе, учтены в числе лиц, имеющих
занятия.

Численность лиц, занятых в сти населения происходило в
народном хозяйстве (то есть основном за счет вовлечения в
не считая занятых в домаш- общественное производство
нем хозяйстве и в личном под- лиц в трудоспособном возра-
собном сельском хозяйстве), сте, занятых в домашнем и
составила при переписи 115 личном подсобном сельском
миллионов человек, или 47,8 хозяйстве; численность этих
проц. всего населения. Из них лиц, не считая учащихся,
в трудоспособном возрасте уменьшилась с 17,9 миллио-
(мужчины 16—59 лет, женщи- на человек в 1959 году до 5,9
ны 16—54 лет) учтено 111 миллиона человек в 1970 году.
млн. человек, или 84,8 проц. Более подробные данные о
населения в трудоспособном распределении населения по
возрасте. источникам средств существо-
Из 130,5 млн. человек в вания, отраслям, отдельным
трудоспособном возрасте, за- занятиям, видам производств и
нятые в народном хозяйстве, а общественным группам, а так-
также учащиеся составили же данные о числе и составе
120,6 млн. человек, или 92,4 семей и миграция населения
проц. этого населения против будут опубликованы после
82 проц. в 1959 году. разработки второй очереди ос-
Увеличение уровня занято- новных итогов переписи.

ническое управление при Совете Министров СССР

INDEX

This Index gives the number of each page in the book upon which reference is made to a particular "Soviet nationality" (by definition excluding Russians), and to each non-Russian ethnic or tribal group, language family, nationality or other administrative unit, official economic region, and conventional or geographic designation such as Turkistan or Siberia.